Carolyn Barraclough   or

Activate!

B1

Students' Book

PEARSON
Longman

This year we want you to meet some amazing people:

Some of them are real …

… and a few of them are not!

Hi! I'm Sam!

Hello! I'm Lizzy!

Some of them are famous …

… but most of them are teenagers just like you. Skim through your book now to answer these questions:

MAD!
What's different about Aaron's room?
See page 33.

BAD?
Guess what kind of clothes Becci wears.
See page 58.

HATE IT?
Which TV show did these teenagers take part in?
See page 19.

RATE IT!
Which places did these teenagers travel to?
See page 106.

Music and sport, TV and computer games, real-life stories and fascinating facts: it's all here! And don't forget … your opinion counts too!

Look out for these features in every unit:

Get ideas:
to start you thinking about the topic

Wordzones:
to explain how English words work

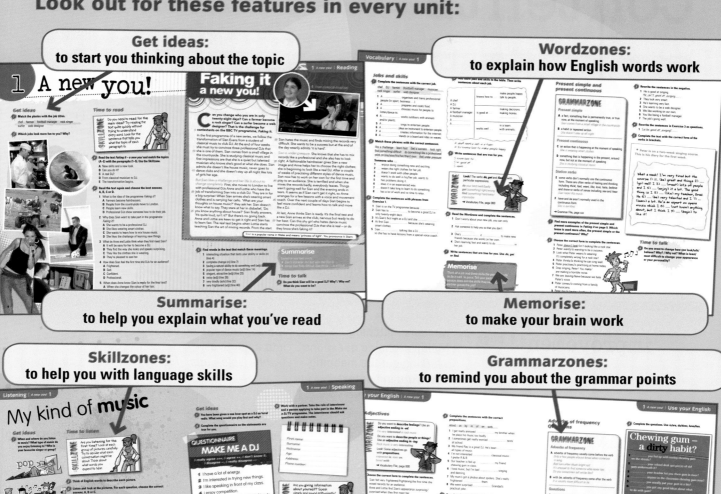

Summarise:
to help you explain what you've read

Memorise:
to make your brain work

Skillzones:
to help you with language skills

Grammarzones:
to remind you about the grammar points

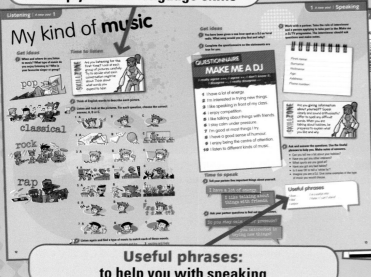

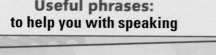

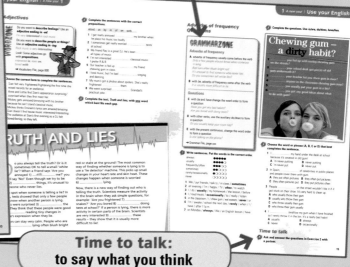

Useful phrases:
to help you with speaking

Time to talk:
to say what you think

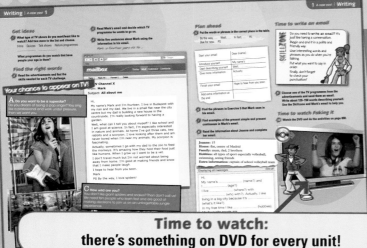

Time to watch:
there's something on DVD for every unit!

Hi! Look out for us in the Skillzones and the Wordzones. We're here to help!

We're on the DVD, too! See you soon!

Contents

Listening	Speaking	Use your English	Writing / DVD
My kind of music Multiple-choice questions	**Giving personal information** Completing a questionnaire Role play	**Vocabulary** Adjectives (*-ed /-ing*) Adjective + preposition **Grammar** Adverbs of frequency; Questions	**An email** **DVD** *Faking it*
It's a teen's life Listening for specific information True/False Intonation	**Apologising and making excuses** Conversation practice Sentence stress	**Vocabulary** Verbs and phrases v. phrasal verbs **Grammar** Relative clauses	**A story** **DVD** *Rule the school*
Spend! Spend! Spend! Listening for specific information Multiple-choice questions	**Giving advice and making suggestions** Role play Intonation	**Vocabulary** Word building: making adjectives negative (*un-, im-, in-*) **Grammar** Certainty, probability and possibility (modal verbs)	**A formal letter** **DVD** *Teens know how*
Making music Predicting True/False	**Giving explanations and reasons** Asking and answering questions	**Vocabulary** Adverbs **Grammar** Word order: direct and indirect objects	**An article** **DVD** *Scotland's fire festival*
Body art Multiple matching Matching speakers with statements	**Giving opinions, agreeing and disagreeing** Conversation practice Sentence stress	**Vocabulary** Verbs with prepositions **Grammar** *so, such a, too, not … enough*	**A letter of advice** **DVD** *Solving a problem*
'Why don't we … ?' Multiple-choice questions Answer questions about situations, attitudes, opinions	**Expressing preferences** Asking and answering questions **Saying what you have done recently**	**Vocabulary** Order of adjectives **Grammar** Countable and uncountable nouns; Quantifiers	**A review** **DVD** *Computer games*

Listening	Speaking	Use your English	Writing DVD
Messages from the past Multiple-choice questions Making notes	**Describing and comparing photos**	**Vocabulary** Expressions using time **Grammar** Ability (modal verbs)	**An article** **DVD** *Pirate legends*
Write? Text? Phone? Multiple-choice questions Choosing the correct picture	**Describing a picture or an object** Asking and answering questions	**Vocabulary** Phrasal verbs **Grammar** Question tags	**A letter of complaint** **DVD** *Robot challenges*
'I can't stand ...' Multiple matching Matching speakers with statements	**Giving opinions and expressing strong feelings** Role play	**Vocabulary** *a/an, the* or zero article **Grammar** *-ing* form and *to*-infinitive	**A description** **DVD** *Friends united*
Eat me! Multiple matching Deciding who says something	**Asking for and giving information** Role play Asking and answering questions	**Vocabulary** *-less, -free, re-* **Grammar** *have/get something done*	**A report** **DVD** *Serious Amazon*
Have a go! Completing notes	**Showing interest, reacting to somebody else's opinion** Asking and answering questions Conversation practice Keeping the conversation going	**Vocabulary** *do, play, go* **Grammar** *could/ must/should* + *have* + past participle	**An essay** **DVD** *Tough triathlon*
Fear or fun? Multiple matching Matching feelings to speakers	**Expressing preferences** **Comparing** Conversation practice	**Vocabulary** Strong adjectives and descriptive verbs **Grammar** Future continuous and future perfect	**A story** **DVD** *Europa-Park*

1 A new you!

Get ideas

1 Match the photos with the job titles.

chef   farmer   football manager   rock singer
surfer   web designer

2 Which jobs look more fun to you? Why?

Time to read

SKILL ZONE
Do you need to **read** for the main idea? Try reading the text quite quickly without trying to understand every word. Look for the sentence that tells you what the topic of each paragraph is.

3 Read the article on page 9 and match the topics (A–E) with the paragraphs (1–5). Use the Skillzone.

A New skills and a new look.
B Can you do it?
C A real DJ?
D From classical musician to DJ.
E The transformation begins.

4 Read the text again and choose the best answer, A, B, C or D.

1 What is the idea of the programme *Faking it*?
   A Farmers become hairdressers.
   B People from the countryside move to London.
   C People learn new skills.
   D Professional DJs show someone how to do their job.

2 Why does Sian want to take part in the programme *Faking it*?
   A She wants to be a professional DJ.
   B She likes wearing smart clothes.
   C She wants to learn how to mix house music.
   D She likes the challenge of learning new things.

3 What do Anne and Lottie think when they first meet Sian?
   A It will be easy for her to become a DJ.
   B They find the way she looks and speaks surprising.
   C They like the clothes she is wearing.
   D They're pleased to see her.

4 How does Sian feel the first time she DJs for an audience?
   A Frightened.
   B Sad.
   C Confident.
   D Professional.

5 When does Anne know Sian is ready for the final test?
   A When she changes the colour of her hair.
   B When she starts mixing records well.
   C When she finally looks and acts like a DJ.
   D When she gets some new clothes.

Faking it
a new you!

1 From classical musician ...

2 ... to DJ

1 **C**an you change who you are in only twenty-eight days? Can a farmer become a rock singer? Can a surfer become a web designer? That is the challenge for
5 contestants on the Channel 4 programme, *Faking it.*

2 In the first programme of a new series, we follow the transformation of Sian Evans from a student of classical music to club DJ. At the end of four weeks she must try to convince three professional DJs that
10 she is one of them. Sian comes from a small village in the countryside. She is studying classical music and first impressions are that she is a quiet but talented musician who knows she's good at what she does. Sian admits she doesn't like dance music, never goes to
15 dance clubs and she doesn't stay up all night like lots of girls her age.

3 But Sian likes a challenge and her life is about to change completely. First, she moves to London to live with professional DJs Anne and Lottie who have the
20 job of transforming Sian into a club DJ. They are in for a big surprise! When Sian arrives she's wearing smart clothes and is carrying her cello. 'What are your thoughts on house music?' they ask her. Sian doesn't know what to say. They stare at her in disbelief, 'Do
25 you know anything about house?' Sian finally answers, 'It's quite loud, isn't it?' But there's no going back. Anne and Lottie are keen to get it right and Sian has to learn fast. The real test begins when Lottie starts teaching Sian the art of mixing records. From the start

30 Sian hates the music and finds mixing the records very difficult. She wants to be a success but at the end of the day wearily admits 'it is hard'.

4 Sian is under pressure. She knows that she has to mix records like a professional and she also has to look
35 right. A fashionable hairdresser gives Sian a new image and Anne helps her to choose the right clothes; she is beginning to look like a real DJ. After a couple of weeks of practising different styles of dance music, Sian now has to work on her own for the first time and
40 play to an audience. She is terrified and when she mixes the records badly, everybody leaves. Things aren't going well for Sian and the evening ends in tears. It seems as if Sian can't get it right, so Anne arranges for a few lessons with a voice and movement
45 coach. Over the next couple of days Sian begins to feel more confident and learns how to talk and move like a DJ.

5 At last, Anne thinks Sian is ready. It's the final test and a new Sian arrives at the club, nervous but ready
50 to do her best. Can this shy girl who hates dance music convince the professional DJs that she is real – or do they know she's faking it?

> **Sian** is a popular name in Wales and means 'princess of light'. You pronounce it *Sharn*.

5 **Find words in the text that match these meanings.**

1 interesting situation that tests your ability or skills (n) (line 4)
2 complete change (n) (line 7)
3 having the natural ability to do something well (adj) (line 12)
4 popular type of dance music (adj) (line 14)
5 elegant, attractive (adj) (line 21)
6 noisy (adj) (line 26)
7 very tiredly (adv) (line 32)
8 very frightened (adj) (line 40)

Summarise

Explain in your own words:
- Sian's character *The text says that Sian is ...*
- things Sian finds difficult *Sian thinks ... is difficult.*

Time to talk

6 **Do you think Sian will be a good DJ? Why/Why not? What do you want to be?**

Coming up ... *Faking it* on DVD. See page 17.

Jobs and skills

1 Complete the sentences with the correct job.

chef   DJ   farmer   (football) manager   musician
rock singer   surfer   web designer

1 A .... organises and trains professional people (in sport, business ...).
2 A .... prepares and cooks food.
3 A .... chooses music for people to listen/dance to.
4 A .... works outdoors with animals and/or plants.
5 A .... sings to entertain people.
6 A .... plays an instrument to entertain people.
7 A .... creates information for the internet.
8 A .... stands on a board and rides on waves.

2 Match these phrases with the correct sentences.

like a challenge   learn fast   (be) a success   look right
find (something) difficult   do (something) like a professional
work on (my/your/his/her/their) own   (be) under pressure

Someone who ...
1 ... enjoys doing something new and exciting.
2 ... wears the right clothes for her job.
3 ... doesn't work with other people.
4 ... wants to do well in his/her job, wants to ... .
5 ... has problems doing it.
6 ... does it in an experienced way.
7 ... doesn't take long to learn to do something.
8 ... has a lot of work and no time to relax.

3 Complete the sentences with phrases from Exercise 2.

1 Sian is on the TV programme because she ....
2 Sian has to .... to become a good DJ in only twenty-eight days.
3 It's Sian's first night as a DJ and she ....
4 At first Sian .... because she's wearing smart clothes.
5 Sian .... talking like a DJ .... , so she has to have lessons from a special voice coach.

4 Add more jobs and skills to the table. Then write sentences about each job.

A chef A DJ A farmer A football manager A musician A .... A	knows how to ...	make people happy. talk to people. ....
	is good at ...	making decisions. making money. ....
	works well ...	in a team. with animals. ....

A chef works well in a team.
A DJ knows how to make people happy.

5 Write sentences that describe your skills.

I know how to ...
I'm good at ...
I work ...

> **WORDZONE**
>
> **Look!** The verbs **do**, **get** and **find** go with particular expressions.
>
> **do** your best/well/badly
> **get** (something) right/wrong
> **find** (something) hard/easy/impossible
>
> → Vocabulary File, page 152

6 Complete the sentences with phrases from the Wordzone.

1 Don't worry about your new job, you can only ....
2 Ask someone to help you so that you don't ....
3 She .... it .... to make new friends because she works on her own.
4 She's learning fast and wants to do .... in her job.

7 Write sentences that are true for you. Use **do, **get** or **find**.

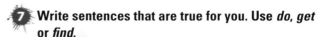

Memorise

Think of a job and three skills the person needs to do it well. In pairs: Tell your partner what the person does and the skills they need. Can your partner guess the job?

Present simple and present continuous

GRAMMARZONE

Present simple

A a fact or situation that is permanently true or true at the moment of speaking
Sian comes from a small village in the countryside.

B a habit or repeated action
She doesn't stay up all night.

Present continuous

C an action that is happening at the moment of speaking
Look! She is wearing smart clothes.

D a situation that is true for a limited period, at present (temporary)
She is studying classical music this year.

State verbs

E not used in the continuous form: e.g. *think, feel, want, like, love, hate, believe, know, see, hear,*
Sian hates the music.

F *have* and *be* aren't normally used in the continuous form
She is terrified.

→ Grammar File, page 164

1 Find more examples of the present simple and present continuous in the article on page 9. Which tense is used more often, the present simple or the present continuous? Why?

2 Choose the correct form to complete the sentences.
1 Peter *doesn't look*/*isn't looking* like a rock star.
2 Peter *wants*/*is wanting* to be a success.
3 Look what Peter *wears*/*is wearing*. It's completely wrong for a rock star!
4 Peter *thinks*/*is thinking* he can sing well.
5 Peter *practises*/*is practising* at home today.
6 Stop singing, Peter! You *make*/*are making* a horrible noise.
7 We *are leaving*/*leave* because we hate Peter's voice.
8 Peter *comes*/*is coming* from a family of musicians.
9 Peter *has*/*is having* a brother who is a famous rock star.

3 Rewrite the sentences in the negative.
1 He is good at singing.
   He isn't good at singing .
2 They look very smart.
3 He's learning very fast.
4 She wants to be a web designer.
5 We like working on our own.
6 You like being a football manager.
7 The job's going well.

4 Rewrite the sentences in Exercise 3 as questions.
1 Is he good at singing?

5 Complete the text with the correct form of the verbs in brackets.

● Peter is on a two-week singing course. This is his diary for the first week.

What a week! I'm very tired but the course 1) .is. (be) great and things 2) ..... (go) well! I 3) ..... (meet) lots of people and I 4) ..... (enjoy) it a lot. The good thing is I 5) ..... (like) my teacher, Brad. He 6) ..... (be) very talented and I 7) .... (learn) a lot. He's an expert on opera music which I 8) ..... (not know) anything about, but I think I 9) ..... (begin) to like it!

Time to talk

6 Do you want to change how you look/talk/behave? Why/Why not? What is least/most difficult to change: your appearance or your personality?

My kind of music

Get ideas

1 When and where do you listen to music? What type of music do you enjoy listening to? Who is your favourite singer or group?

pop

classical

rock

rap

Time to listen

2 Think of English words to describe each picture in Exercise 3.

1.2 **3** Listen and look at the pictures. For each question, choose the correct answer, A, B or C.

1 A   B   C

2 A   B   C

3 A   B   C

4 A   B   C

5 A   B   C

6 A   B   C

7 A   B   C

SKILL ZONE

Are you going to listen only once? Look at each group of pictures carefully. Try to decide what each conversation might be about. Think about what words you expect to hear.

1.3 **4** Listen again and find a type of music to match each of these moods.

1 calm and serious   **2** relaxing and fun   **3** exciting and lively

Get ideas

1 Imagine you are the DJ for an hour on the local radio. What song would you play first and why?

2 Complete the questionnaire for yourself. Find out if you would make a good DJ.

QUESTIONNAIRE
MAKE ME A DJ

I really agree +++, I agree ++, I don't know 0,
I disagree --, I really disagree ---

1 I have a lot of energy.

2 I'm interested in trying new things.

3 I like speaking in front of my class.

4 I enjoy competition.

5 I like talking about things with friends.

6 I stay calm under pressure.

7 I'm good at most things I try.

8 I have a good sense of humour.

9 I enjoy being the centre of attention.

10 I listen to different kinds of music.

Time to speak

3 Tell your partner five important things about yourself.

> I have a lot of energy.

> I like talking about things with friends.

4 Ask your partner questions to find out more answers.

> Do you stay calm under pressure?

> Are you interested in trying new things?

5 Work with a partner. You are the interviewer and your partner is applying to take part in the *Make me a DJ* TV programme. Ask questions and make notes.

First name:

Surname:

Nickname:

Age:

Address:

Phone number:

SKILLZONE

Are you giving information about yourself? Speak clearly and sound enthusiastic! Offer to spell any difficult words. When you are talking about hobbies, be prepared to explain what you like and why.

6 Work with a partner. Ask and answer the questions. Use the Useful phrases to help you.

- Can you tell me a bit about your hobbies?
- Have you got any other interests?
- What sports are you good at?
- Have you got any bad habits?
- Is it ever OK to tell a 'white lie'?
- Imagine you are a DJ. Give some examples of the type of music you would choose.

Useful phrases

I love …   I'm (really) into …
I like …   I hate / I can't stand …
I enjoy …

13

Adjectives

Do you want to **describe feelings**? Use an **adjective ending in -ed**.
*I'm very **interested** in rock music.*

Do you want to **describe people or things**? Use an **adjective ending in -ing**.
*Rock music is very **interesting**.*

Look! Some adjectives go with **prepositions**.
*interested **in**, keen **on**, bored **with***

➔ Vocabulary File, page 152

1 **Choose the correct form to complete the sentences.**

1 Sian felt very *frightened*/*frightening* the first time she mixed records for an audience.
2 Anne and Lottie find Sian's appearance *surprising/surprised* when they first meet her.
3 Mickey gets *annoyed/annoying* with his brother because he can't stand classical music.
4 Mickey thinks Eminem's lyrics are *amazed/amazing*.
5 Sian doesn't find house music *interested/interesting*.
6 The audience at Sian's first evening as a DJ felt *bored/boring*, so they left.

2 **Complete the sentences with the correct prepositions.**

about   at   by   in   of   on   with

1 I get really annoyed ....**with**.......... my brother when he plays his music too loudly.
2 I sometimes get really worried .... tests at school.
3 My friend Ray is a great DJ. He's keen .... all types of music.
4 I'm not interested .... classical music. I prefer R & B.
5 Our teacher is fed up .... my friend chewing gum in class.
6 I love music, but I'm bad .... singing and dancing.
7 My mum's got a phobia about spiders. She's really frightened .... them.
8 We were surprised .... Grandad's practical joke.

3 **Complete the article with one word which best fits each gap.**

TRUTH AND LIES

Do you always tell the truth? Or is it sometimes OK to tell a small 'white lie'? When a friend says 'Are you annoyed 1) ....**with**.......... me?' you may well say 'No!' Even though we try to be honest 2) .... things, it's unusual to find someone who never lies.

Can you spot when someone is telling a lie? In the USA, tests showed that only a few people always know when another person is lying. Scientists were surprised 3) .... the results. They think that these people were good 4) .... reading tiny changes in someone's expression when they lie.

Good liars can stay very calm. People who are bad 5) .... lying often blush bright red or stare at the ground! The most common way of finding whether someone is lying is to use a 'lie detector' machine. This picks up small changes in your heart rate and skin heat. These changes happen when someone is worried 6) .... lying.

Now, there is a new way of finding out who is telling the truth. Scientists measure the activity in the brain when they ask simple questions, for example: 'Are you frightened 7) .... snakes?' 'Are you bored 8) .... doing tests at school?' If a person is lying, there is more activity in certain parts of the brain. Scientists are very interested 9) .... these results – they show that it is usually more difficult to lie!

Adverbs of frequency
Questions

GRAMMARZONE

Adverbs of frequency

A adverbs of frequency say how often something happens; they usually come before the verb
Bad liars often blush bright red.
It's unusual to find someone who never lies.
Do you sometimes tell white lies?

B adverbs of frequency come after the verb *be*
It is usually more difficult to lie.

Questions

C with *be* and *have* change the word order
Have you got any bad habits?
Are you bored with doing tests?

D with other verbs, use the auxiliary *do/does*
Do you usually keep your room tidy?

E with the present continuous, change the word order
Is she talking on the phone?

→ Grammar File, page 164

1 **Write sentences. Put the words in the correct order.**

always	●●●●●
usually	●●●●○
frequently/often	●●●○○
sometimes	●●○○○
rarely/occasionally	●○○○○
never	○○○○○

1 We / our friends / talk to / in class. / **sometimes**
2 all evening. / I'm / happy / TV / **often** / to watch
3 I / do / **usually** / my homework / the lesson. / before
4 I / loud music. / **occasionally** / to / really / listen
5 in the classroom. / I / chew gum / eat sweets / **never** / or
6 I'm / awake / school the next day. / **rarely** / when / I / have / after 11p.m.
7 on Monday. / **always** / We / an English lesson / have

2 **Complete the questions. Use *is/are, do/does, have/has*.**

Chewing gum – a dirty habit?

1 .... you fed up with seeing chewing gum on the streets?
2 .... your school desk got pieces of old gum underneath it?
3 .... your teacher let you chew gum in class?
4 .... anyone in the classroom chewing gum now?
5 .... you usually put your gum in a bin?
6 .... you got any good ideas about what to do with gum?

3 **Choose the word or phrase (A, B, C or D) that best completes the sentence.**

1 I .... my hand under the desk at school because it's covered in old gum!
A 'm never putting **B** never putting
C 'm never put **D** never put

2 In Spain, ... of celebrities in public places and people cover them with gum.
A they put often pictures **B** they often put pictures
C they often pictures put **D** they put pictures often

3 People .... on the street wouldn't like it if it got stuck on their shoe. It's very hard to clean up.
A who usually throw their gum
B usually who throw their gum
C who throw usually their gum
D who throw their gum usually

4 I .... swallow my gum when I have finished so I rarely throw it in the bin. It's a really bad habit!
A usually **B** always
C never **D** occasionally

Time to talk

4 **Ask and answer the questions in Exercise 2 with a partner.**

Get ideas

1 What type of TV shows do you most/least like to watch? Add two more to the list and choose.

Films   Quizzes   Talk shows   Nature programmes

....

What programmes do you watch that are about people of your age?

Find the right words

2 Read the advertisements and find what skills you need for each TV challenge.

3 Read Mark's email and decide which TV programme he wants to go on.

4 Write five sentences about Mark using the information in his email.

Mark is fourteen years old. He ...

Your chance to appear on TV!

A Do you want to be a superstar?
Do you dream of being a pop singer? You sing like a professional and work under pressure, then we want you.

B Sporting challenge
You're good at sport, you like working in a team, and you're looking for a challenge. What are you waiting for?

mailbox   Today | Mail | Calendar | Contacts

Reply | Reply All | Forward | Delete

V Channel X
From: **Mark**
Subject: **All about me**

Hi,

My name's Mark and I'm fourteen. I live in Budapest with my nan and my dad. We live in a small flat near the city centre but my dad is building a new house in the countryside. I'm really looking forward to having a garden.

Well, what can I tell you about myself? I like school and I am good at science. In fact, I'm especially interested in nature and animals. At home I've got three cats, two rabbits and a scorpion. I love looking after them and am never bored when I'm near my animals. My scorpion is fascinating.

Actually, sometimes I go with my dad to the zoo to feed the monkeys. It's amazing how they hold their food just like humans. When I grow up I want to be a vet.

I don't travel much but I'm not worried about being away from home. I'm good at making friends and know that I make people laugh.

I hope to hear from you soon.

Mark

PS By the way, I love spiders!

C How wild are you?
You don't like giant spiders and snakes? Then don't call us! We need ten people who learn fast and are good at making decisions to join us on an unforgettable jungle experience.

Plan ahead

5 Put the words or phrases in the correct place in the table.

By the way, …   Well, …   In fact, …   Hi,
Bye for now.   PS

Start your email	Dear (name) ....
Introduce yourself	My name's ...
Start describing yourself	Well, ...
Give more information	Actually ....
Finish your email	Hope to hear from you soon. ....
Add extra information at the end	....

6 Find the phrases in Exercise 5 that Mark uses in his email.

7 Find examples of the present simple and present continuous in Mark's email.

8 Read the information about Joanne and complete her email.

Joanne: 15
Home: flat, centre of Madrid
Family: mum, dad, 2 brothers
Hobbies: all types of sport especially volleyball, swimming, seeing friends
Extra information: captain of school volleyball team

▼ Messages
Displaying all messages   See all

Hi,
My name's .... (name?) and
I .... (age?)
I live .... (where?) with
.... (who with?). Actually, I like
living in a big city because it's ....
(what's it like?).
In my free time I like .... (hobbies).
My favourite sports are ....
I'm good at working in a team and in fact,
.... (extra information).
I love meeting people and want to be on this
TV programme.
I hope to hear from you soon.
Joanne

Time to write *an email*

SKILL ZONE
Do you need to **write an email**? Begin and end it in a polite and friendly way.
Use interesting words and phrases as you do when you're talking.
Put what you want to say in order.
Finally, don't forget to check your punctuation!

9 Choose one of the advertisements on page 16 and send them an email describing yourself. Write about 120–150 words. Use the Skillzone and Mark's email to help you.

Time to watch *Faking it*

10 Watch the DVD and do the activities on page 152.

Get ideas

1 Do you learn these things at school?

Science

football

text-messaging

break dancing

2 **Who knows more about these subjects, you or your teachers?**

computer gaming   History   languages   popstars

Time to read

3 **Look at the title and the photos on page 19 and discuss with your partner.**

1 Who is teaching?
2 What do you think he/she is teaching?

4 **Read quickly and check your answers.**

SKILL ZONE

Do you need to understand **details in a text?** Slow down and read it carefully! If you need to, read parts of the text more than once.

5 **Read the article on page 19 and choose the best answer, A, B, C or D.**

1 The students in the classrooms were . . .
   A actors.   B teenagers.
   C real teachers.   D children.

2 The subjects taught were . . .
   A unusual.   B boring.
   C ridiculous.   D unpopular.

3 When they saw their school uniform, the adults . . .
   A were pleased.   B were fashionable.
   C loved it.   D didn't want to wear it.

4 The punishment of listening to teenage music . . .
   A didn't work.   B was silly.
   C was enjoyable.   D worked very well.

5 By the end of the programme, the real teachers were . . .
   A feeling fed up.   B working harder.
   C getting lazy.   D behaving badly.

6 In the exams, the adults . . .
   A did quite well.   B failed.
   C got mixed results.   D got top marks.

6 **Find words in the text that match these meanings.**

1 an unexpected direction (line 7)
2 tried to solve a problem (line 27)
3 laughed quickly (in a high voice) (line 30)
4 invent (line 34)
5 adults (line 43)

Summarise

Explain in your own words:
• what was unusual *One unusual thing is that . . .*
• what surprised you *It was surprising that . . .*

Time to talk

7 **Who do you think enjoyed their week more? Why? What would you like to teach your teachers?**

Who **rules** the school?

Are kids good at teaching? Six teenagers from Scotland found out … They became teachers for an unusual TV programme!

Could *you* teach your teachers? Thirteen-year-old Laura did exactly that when she became a head teacher! So how did this happen? Laura was studying at secondary school when she answered an advert for a TV programme called *Rule*
5 *the school*. She and five other young 'teachers' chose the subjects they wanted to teach. However, there was another twist to the programme – the students in this school were adults … and they were real-life teachers. The aim of the lessons was to get these teachers to be more 'cool' in one
10 week.

The curriculum was very different from a normal school. Laura taught text-messaging, Beth taught break dancing and Fraser taught computer gaming. The other subjects included popstar skills and 'funky football' and a project to
15 make their clothes more fashionable. All the real teachers took part in every lesson. They couldn't make excuses! Of course, they had homework and examinations in every subject at the end. They were also surprised by the school uniform: three-quarter-length shorts, a sports top and
20 trainers! 'These clothes are ridiculous,' they complained.

On the first morning, the new 'teachers' felt quite nervous. Some unusual 'students' were waiting in the classrooms, and a few of them weren't behaving very well. Some of the adults were chewing gum. Others had their feet on
25 the desks. They were all chatting to their friends when their new teacher came in. These actions surprised the teenagers, but they dealt with bad behaviour quickly. In the school assembly, the adult students were laughing. One teacher immediately shouted, 'You're just making fools
30 of yourselves.' His audience giggled even more, but he carried on. 'This isn't cool, this is immature!'

'You're just making fools of yourselves!'

What did the 'teachers' do to punish bad behaviour? They didn't give detentions or extra homework. Instead, they used their imagination to make up better punishments.
35 For example, the adults who misbehaved in assembly had to wear headphones and listen to 'techno' music for half an hour. Towards the end, they were begging the teacher to turn off the music. After that, they promised to be good! Gradually, there were improvements as the
40 adults concentrated on their lessons. They finished their fashion projects and learned some cool dance moves. They didn't write any essays, though! Finally, the grown-ups revised for their exams. Most of them got good results, but some people were disappointed
45 because they didn't pass. However, they all agreed that the week was a very educational experience!

Coming up … *Rule the school* on DVD. See page 27.

Education

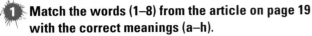

1 **Match the words (1–8) from the article on page 19 with the correct meanings (a–h).**

1 project
2 uniform
3 assembly
4 curriculum
5 detention
6 essay
7 revise
8 skill

a a regular meeting of all the students and teachers
b a punishment in which you have to stay behind after school
c (all) the subjects you learn at school
d to prepare for a test by studying
e a piece of writing about a subject
f an ability to do something well
g school work you have to collect information for
h clothes that all students wear at school

2 **Put the words and phrases in the correct column. Add two more words to each list.**

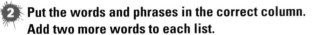

assembly hall   canteen   cleaner   corridors   dance
film club   library   orchestra   school secretary
Science lab   staff room   teacher

People	Places	After-school activities
caretaker	head teacher's office	football

3 **Complete each sentence with a word or phrase from Exercise 2.**

1 At break time, the teachers all have coffee in the ....
2 The .... will need to clear up all this messy paint after school.
3 Walk sensibly in the .... when you go to your next lesson.
4 If you're working in the .... , you must be very quiet.
5 When you are ill, your parents should phone the ....
6 I don't like having lunch in the .... because it's so noisy!

WORDZONE

Do you want to make a **verb into a noun**? Then add a new ending: *-ment*, *-(at)ion*.

*entertain (v) – entertain**ment** (n)*
*educate (v) – educat**ion** (n)*

→ Vocabulary File, page 153

4 **Complete the table with the correct verb or noun.**

	Verb	Noun
1	....	advertisement
2	explain	....
3	discuss	....
4	....	embarrassment
5	organise	....

5 **Change the verbs in capitals into nouns. Be careful, there is one irregular form!**

1 I don't think that ..punishment.. was very fair!   PUNISH
2 Before an exam, I always do lots of ....   REVISE
3 He writes great stories because he has a very strong ....   IMAGINE
4 To do well at computer games, you need good ....   CONCENTRATE
5 The pupils are usually good, but sometimes their .... is poor!   BEHAVE
6 Luke's exam results were a .... to his parents.   DISAPPOINT
7 My sister's studying for her university entrance ....   EXAMINE
8 There has been a huge .... in your English this year.   IMPROVE

Memorise

1 Choose three verbs from Exercises 4 and 5. Ask your partner to spell the nouns.
2 How many people, places and after-school activities can you remember? Write a list and compare with your partner.

Past simple and past continuous

GRAMMARZONE

Past simple

A a completed past action
Laura taught text-messaging.

B one completed past action after another
The audience giggled ... , but he carried on.

C a past habit or regular past event
Teachers took part in every lesson.

Past continuous

D an action in progress in the past
Laura was studying at secondary school ...

E two actions in progress at the same past time
Some unusual 'students' were waiting ... and a few of them weren't behaving ...

Past simple and past continuous

F a short action (past simple) interrupts an action in progress (past continuous) in the past
They were chatting when the teacher came in.

➔ Grammar File, page 165

1 Find one more example of the past simple and past continuous in the article on page 19. Match them with one of the uses in the Grammarzone.

2 Match the school facts (1–4) with the uses (A–F) in the Grammarzone.

British schools 150 years ago:

1 As a punishment, teachers put naughty children in a big basket and then hung the basket high up in the classroom.

2 Pupils left school when they were twelve years old.

Roman schools about 2,000 years ago:

3 While boys were learning their lessons at school, girls were usually cleaning their homes.

4 Children went to school every day of the week. There was no break for the weekend!

3 Complete the web article with the correct form of the verbs in brackets. Use past simple or past continuous.

Time to talk

4 How many hours did you spend on homework last week? Was that too much/about right/not enough?

A private school in Yorkshire, England, recently (1) .... (make) an unusual school rule: no more homework! The pupils were amazed when they (2) .... (hear) about the new rule. The head teacher explained: 'I (3) .... (sit) in my office at the end of a long school day when I heard some pupils outside talking about all their homework. They (4) .... (not / want) to study all evening! That's when I decided to abolish homework.'

What about exam results? After the new rule, (5) .... (they/ change)? Actually, the pupils got good results, so parents were happy.

Several years ago, Dr Susan Hallam (6) .... (study) at the University of London when she wrote a report about homework. She (7) .... (say) that too much homework made students bored or anxious. Her conclusion (8) .... (be) that: 'Homework ... should help students to understand their lessons.'

It's a **teen's** life

Get ideas

1 Do you have any free time? Is it enough? Why/Why not? Which of these activities do you do?

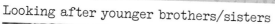

Looking after younger brothers/sisters

Washing up

Cooking

Playing football

Chatting on the phone

Time to listen

1.4 **2** Sophie is on a local radio show, talking about her school life. Listen and find the activities in Exercise 1 she mentions.

SOPHIE'S HOUR
it's a teen's Life!

SKILL ZONE
Are you listening for specific information? Try reading the statements carefully and deciding what information you are listening for.

1.5 **3** Listen again and decide whether the statements are true (T) or false (F).

1 The History teacher is popular with students.
2 The Maths exam is on Thursday.
3 Sophie talked to Tanya instead of doing her homework.
4 Sophie wanted to work on her Art project.
5 The computer wasn't working when she got home.
6 Sophie is captain of the football team.
7 Laura is Sophie's older sister.
8 Laura isn't interested in watching football.
9 Sophie spoke to her friends after football practice.
10 Sophie wants to have some fun.

1.6 **4** You can sound more interesting by using the correct intonation. Listen to Sophie, then repeat.

1 I just couldn't concentrate on anything.
2 How cool is that?
3 It was so embarrassing.
4 It's just not fair!
5 I just want to have some fun.

Get ideas

1 Read the excuses teenagers give for not doing homework. Can you add three more?

The 5 Favourite Excuses

According to a survey, students who don't do their homework are using some old excuses and inventing some imaginative new ones.

❶ Homework's in the dog
❷ Not enough time
❸ Couldn't be bothered
❹ Lost my coursebook
❺ Felt ill

2 Have you ever used any of these excuses? What for?

3 Complete the conversation with these phrases. Then listen and check.

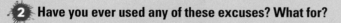

you see   Sorry about that,   I'm very sorry, Sir,
I couldn't do my homework last night because

Teacher: Amy, you're late again!
Amy: 1) .... Sir, but I missed the bus.
Teacher: And what about your homework?
Amy: 2) I'm really sorry Sir, but .... it was so hot.
Teacher: Everybody was hot, Amy. That's no excuse!
Amy: 3) .... but I fell asleep on the balcony. It was lovely and cool.
Teacher: But Amy, you didn't sleep all evening!
Amy: No Sir, 4) .... when I woke up the balcony door was shut. I couldn't get back into the house. I had to wait until Mum came home and then it was too late!

Time to speak

4 Practise the conversation in Exercise 3 with your partner.

5 Look at the photos and make excuses. Explain to your teacher why you didn't revise for your exam.

Useful phrases

I'm really sorry I didn't do my homework but …
Sorry I'm late but …
I wasn't able to do my homework last night because …
I'm very sorry, but you see …

felt ill

lost my schoolbooks

looked after my brother

went shopping

Verbs and phrases v. phrasal verbs

WORDZONE

Look! Some phrases go with particular verbs.

take part in, *make* friends with, *keep* an eye on, *put* pressure on

A **phrasal verb** is a verb + one or more prepositions and/or adverbs. The meaning may be different from the meaning of the verb and the preposition/adverb separately.

take off (clothes) = remove
make for = move towards
keep on = continue
put on (clothes) = get dressed

→ Vocabulary File, page 153

1 Choose the phrasal verb in each pair.

1 take up	take care of
2 make sure	make up
3 keep up with	keep a record of
4 put up with	put your heart into

2 Complete the sentences with the correct form of the verbs from the Wordzone or Exercise 1.

1 The teacher asked us to ....take off.... our coats in the classroom.
2 My English teacher is really good at .... funny stories.
3 Our head teacher doesn't .... graffiti. He makes us clean the walls and desks.
4 The school secretary .... everybody's phone number in case of an emergency.
5 It's important to .... your appearance because it makes a good impression.
6 Our teacher always .... that we understand the homework before we leave.

3 Complete the sentences in your own words.

1 I take ....
2 The teacher puts ....
3 My mum keeps ....
4 It's difficult to make ....

4 Complete the article with the correct form of the verbs *take, make, keep* or *put*.

More school, more fun?

In Denmark some pupils stay at school from 8a.m. to 6p.m. In the afternoon they can 1) ......take............ part in indoor and outdoor activities from rollerblading and uni-cycling to film and circus skills. It's a system that busy parents and their children use and appreciate. Parents who work long hours know that professionals are 2) .... care of their children. Meanwhile, the children 3) .... friends with other pupils and enjoy activities which are varied and fun. The older pupils 4) .... an eye on the younger ones and the younger pupils learn from the older children's experience.

After-school clubs, which are separate from the main school building, are not homework clubs. Nobody is there to take an exam or 5) .... up with their homework. The idea is that children 6) .... up new interests and activities that aren't on their school timetable. The atmosphere is relaxed and friendly and pupils only do homework if they want to.

The number of schools which offer these clubs 7) .... on growing. According to Danish professionals: 'After school clubs don't 8) .... pressure on the pupils to study. They offer the choice and the freedom to do what they want in their free time.'

Relative clauses

GRAMMARZONE

Defining relative clauses

A *which/that* refers to things and animals
The children enjoy activities which/that are varied and fun.

B *who/that* refers to people
Parents who/that work long hours know that ...

C when *that*, *which* or *who* is the object of the relative clause, you can leave it out
It's a system (that) busy parents use and appreciate.

Non-defining relative clauses

D to add information which is not necessary; use commas before *who/which*; don't use *that*
After-school clubs, which are often separate from the main school building, are not homework clubs.

➔ Grammar File, page 165

1 Choose the correct relative pronoun to complete the sentences.

1 The clubs, *who/which* are very popular, start at 4p.m.
2 I don't know anyone *which/who* can breakdance.
3 The subject *who/that* everybody loves is text-messaging.
4 The new school uniform, *which/that* everybody hates, is very old-fashioned.
5 Are there any school rules *which/who* could be abolished?
6 My friend, *which/who* speaks five languages, is Dutch.
7 The new school is great for children *which/who* like sport.

2 Find the sentences in Exercise 1 where you can omit the relative pronoun.

3 Complete the sentences with the correct relative pronouns. Use a relative pronoun where necessary.

1 She didn't do the homework .... you gave her.
2 That's the boy........................ came on the school trip with us.
3 The school, ... is one of the best in the country, teaches breakdancing.
4 Can I have a look at the CD .... you bought on Saturday?
5 I thought the boy .... taught computer gaming was very funny.
6 I want to go to a school .... offers lots of after-school activities.

4 Rewrite the two sentences as one. Use a relative pronoun and add commas where necessary.

1 The film is about a boy. He runs away from home.
The film is about a boy who runs away from home.
2 He had a detention. It lasted for two hours.
3 I see my friend Joe every day. He lives in the same village.
4 The pupils did well in their exams. They left early.
5 Our school basketball team is really good. It will win the league.
6 Where are the books? They belong to my teacher.
7 We did our homework together. It was about the weather.
8 I didn't study for the test. I got a bad mark for it.
9 I've got a cousin in Poland. I see him every summer.
10 Did you see that boy? He had purple hair!
11 That's Julia. I met her at the party.

5 Complete the second sentence so that it has a similar meaning to the first sentence using the word given. Add commas where necessary.

1 Mr Sampson teaches Chemistry and Biology.
Mr Sampson, *who teaches Chemistry,* also teaches Biology. WHO
2 We watched a fantastic video in Religion.
The video .... was fantastic. THAT
3 Everybody failed the Maths test because it was too difficult.
Everybody failed the Maths test .... too difficult. WHICH
4 Joe's wearing some really cool jeans.
The jeans .... really cool. THAT
5 If you arrive late the teacher gives you detention.
Students .... get detention. WHO
6 The pupils painted the new gym and it looks great.
The new gym, ... painted, looks great. WHICH

Time to talk

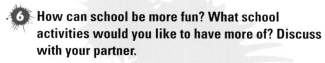

6 How can school be more fun? What school activities would you like to have more of? Discuss with your partner.

Get ideas

1 What makes you laugh in class? Choose two of these situations and add one of your own.

> Somebody opens their bag and everything falls out.

> Somebody falls asleep.

> Somebody's tummy starts rumbling.

2 Read the stories and choose A, B or C to show how embarrassing each situation is.

Find the right words

3 Match the underlined linking words with their correct function.

1 extra information *and*
2 reason for something
3 time when something happened *when*

4 Complete the sentences with suitable linking words.

1 I didn't do well in the Science test or the Maths test, ... I got top marks in English!
2 We played football .... it got dark, ... we went home.
3 Max wanted to watch his favourite programme at 8p.m., ... he decided to do his homework .... watching TV.
4 Alexia plays basketball .... volleyball .... she enjoys team games.
5 Great, it's lunch time! .... lunch we've got Art, ... it's ICT.

RED WITH EMBARRASSMENT!

1 It wasn't my fault!

I was walking down the corridor <u>after</u> my Maths lesson <u>when</u> an older boy pushed me very hard. I bumped into the head teacher who shouted at me. <u>Then</u> I dropped my books on his foot! I tried to explain that it was an accident, <u>but</u> I was too nervous. Luckily, I didn't get a detention!

Paul, 13

2 Shocking shorts

A really embarrassing thing happened to me last week. I was getting ready for our PE lesson when I realised I didn't have any shorts. The teacher gave me a spare pair to put on but they were really big. <u>As</u> I was running across the playing field I saw friends laughing at me <u>because</u> the shorts were falling down and my pants were showing!

Daniel, 14

3 See the sign

One day I needed the loo at the end of lunch break. The bell was ringing <u>so</u> I rushed to the toilet. I didn't see a sign on the door <u>and</u> when I tried to get out the lock was stuck! I waited for an hour <u>until</u> the caretaker came. He took off the door <u>then</u> he showed me the sign that said 'Out of order!'

Joanna, 12

Blush-o-meter

A blush!

B bright red with embarrassment!

C leave the country now!

Plan ahead

5 **Read Emily's story to *Activate!* magazine and answer the questions.**

1 Why did Emily write the story?
2 Is it a funny story? Why/Why not?
3 Is the language formal or informal? Find examples.

This week's prize-winning entry: Emily Walters from Devon!

When I was 13 I started a new school. I was very nervous of course, so I was pleased when a group of girls came to meet me. They took me around the school and showed me the classrooms, the gym and then the library.

As we were chatting, a man, who looked really mad, walked past us. He was wearing scruffy clothes and had a very long, grey beard.

I burst out laughing because he looked so funny. But guess what? My new friends weren't laughing and the man was staring at me.

I didn't understand what was happening until one of my friends told me that he was our teacher. I nearly died.

When I went into class I was really embarrassed but he's a fantastic teacher with a great sense of humour!

6 **Find examples of the past simple and past continuous in Emily's story.**

7 **Find the linking words in Emily's story.**

8 **Put the questions in the order the information appears in Emily's story.**

a **Where** did it happen?
b **Who** was Emily with?
c **When** did it happen?
d **What** happened in the end?
e **What** was she doing before the main action?
f **What** was the main action?

9 **Write answers to the questions in Exercise 8 in your own words.**

Time to write *a story*

SKILL ZONE Are you writing a narrative? Plan your ideas first and use questions (*who? what? where?* etc.) to help you order them. Use mainly the past simple and past continuous. Use linking words to make your sentences more interesting.

10 **Write your entry for *Activate!* magazine for the funniest school story of the month. Write about 120–150 words.**

Time to watch *Rule the school*

11 **Watch the DVD and do the activities on page 153.**

Time to revise 1 | Units 1–2

Vocabulary

1 Complete the sentences with these phrases.

be a success   get it right   is learning fast   is under pressure   likes a challenge   look right   working on your own

1 John ..is under pressure.. at the moment because he is studying for his exams.
2 She's doing a two-day course in web design and the teacher says that she ....
3 Naomi's new course is difficult and stressful but she ....
4 He's training very hard as a singer because he wants to .... in the future.
5 You have to be happy .... if you want to be a farmer.
6 I'm not keen on wearing smart clothes but I know it's important to .... in the job.
7 I like learning languages but I have problems with the grammar and never seem to ....

2 Choose the correct adjective to complete the sentences.

1 Singing in public for the first time is terrified/terrifying.
2 I am amazed/amazing that so many people are here for the meeting.
3 The teachers are always annoyed/annoying when students forget to do their homework.
4 It's really relaxed/relaxing listening to music when you're doing homework.
5 His parents are worried/worrying because they don't know where he is.
6 There aren't enough after-school clubs and it's not surprising/surprised that teenagers are boring/bored.

3 Choose the correct preposition to complete the sentences.

1 I'm not very good with/at dancing but I like watching other people.
2 She's really keen of/on house music but her friends hate it.
3 Joe's fed up with/at his new MP3 because it doesn't work properly.
4 It's hard speaking another language when you're frightened of/at making mistakes!
5 When you are annoyed with/about your friends it's best to talk about it.
6 He's worried about/by the exam next week but he always does well.
7 Melissa is interested in/at training as a farmer because she's keen on/of animals.

4 Complete the sentences with the names of places or people in a school.

1 Moving from one class to another is really difficult because there are so many students in the ..corridors. .
2 The .... usually starts work when the students have gone home.
3 If you need some books go to the ....
4 The .... is in her office if you need to get a form.
5 The .... fixed the lock on the toilet door.
6 We enjoy lessons in the .... because we do experiments.
7 Bye! See you later in the .... for lunch.
8 The teachers relax in the ....

5 Complete the text with the correct form of the words in brackets.

Last week my Maths results were a big 1) .disappointment. (DISAPPOINT). The teacher gave me back my paper with the comment, 'Room for 2) .... (IMPROVE) John!' Normally, I'm really good at Maths and I don't have to do much 3) .... (REVISE). But, the night before the 4) .... (EXAMINE) there was a match between Barcelona and Milan and I stayed up really late. During the exam I couldn't concentrate. The teacher didn't like my 5) .... (EXPLAIN). 'That's no excuse!' he said.

6 Complete the sentences with the correct phrases.

a record of   an eye on   care of   friends with   pressure on

1 Teachers don't put ..pressure on. students to do well.
2 In my school diary I keep .... all of my marks.
3 After-school activities are a great way to make .... other students.
4 During the exam, the teacher kept .... the students to make sure they weren't cheating.
5 It's important for older students to take .... the younger ones when they start secondary school.

7 Complete the sentences with the correct form of these phrasal verbs. Use the meanings in brackets to help you.

keep on   keep up with   make for   make up   put up with   take off   take up

1 Alan was ..making for.. the goal but Peter tackled him and got the ball. (moving towards)
2 The teachers didn't .... bad behaviour, they punished us immediately. (accept without complaining)
3 John .... the cello last year, and he plays really well now. (started to do)
4 She .... practising and now she mixes records really well. (continued)
5 We .... some new excuses, but the teacher didn't believe them. (invented)
6 I was hot so I .... my coat. (removed)
7 I can't .... my homework, I've got too much to do. (manage to do)

28

Grammar

8 Complete the sentences with the correct form (present simple or present continuous) of the verbs in brackets.

1 She ...wants to.... (want) to train as a hairdresser.
2 He .... (try) hard in every lesson.
3 What .... they .... (study) this year?
4 She .... (not like) going to concerts and she .... (hate) listening to classical music.
5 The caretaker........................ (not understand) why students write on the walls.
6 .... Jack .... (have) football training every Friday?
7 Lucy .... (run) down the corridor because she .... (be) late for her class.
8 Football .... (be) a popular sport.
9 We .... (have) a lesson in the Science lab now.

9 Make sentences or negative statements. Use *do/ does, don't/doesn't, is/are,* or *isn't/aren't* and the correct form of the verb.

1 They / not / play / football / today.
   They aren't playing football today.
2 / Daniel / go / skateboarding every day?
3 What / a DJ / do?
4 What / you / think / about?
5 / you / like / house music?
6 She / not / use the computer now.
7 How many / people / you / know?
8 He / not / want / go to school today.

10 Put the adverb in the correct place in the sentence.

1 She gets up at seven o'clock. (usually)
   She usually gets up at seven o'clock.
2 The teacher gives us too much homework. (always)
3 I wanted to be a pop star. (never)
4 Do you go to the beach with your friends? (often)
5 We are in the same place at the same time. (rarely)
6 I am late. (never)

11 Complete the sentences with the correct relative pronouns. Use the relative pronoun where necessary.

that   when   where   which   who

1 I've got a pen friend in Poland ....who.......... writes perfect English.
2 Do you remember the day .... we had to leave school early because of the snow?
3 My best friend, ... loves animals, wants to be a farmer.
4 Simon, ... you saw me with yesterday, has got the same bike as you.
5 The trainers, ... I bought last month, are really uncomfortable.
6 The new internet café is the place .... everybody meets at the weekend.

7 The books .... you need are in the library.

12 Complete the story with the correct form of the verbs in brackets.

A very long day!

This morning I 1) was .... (dream) about a lovely, sunny beach when the alarm 2) .... (go off). I 3) .... (get up) immediately, 4) .... (eat breakfast) quickly and 5) .... (leave) the house. It 6) .... (rain) heavily.

As I 7) .... (walk) to the bus stop a car 8) .... (drive) past and 9) .... (soak) me. Then the bus 10) .... (arrive) half an hour late.

When we finally 11) .... (arrive) at school the heating 12) .... (not work) so I spent the day feeling wet and cold. Finally, the bell 13) .... (ring) and I 14) .... (run) to the bus stop but the bus 15) .... (not wait) in its usual place.

16) '........................ you .... (not see) the notice?' said the Head Teacher as he 17) .... (come) down the school steps. 'The bus 18) .... (break down) this morning. You'll have to walk home today!'

Did you remember all the vocabulary and grammar points?

→ Vocabulary File, pages 152 and 153
→ Grammar File, pages 164 and 165

3 Room for improvement!

Get ideas

1 Do you have any of these in your room? If not, which would you like to have? Why/Why not?

Time to read

2 Which of these statements do you agree/disagree with most? Discuss with a partner.

1 Your bedroom is an expression of your identity.
2 Your room is the place where you can be on your own.
3 It doesn't matter what your room looks like, it's a place to keep things.
4 A bedroom is where you can do your homework and go to bed.

3 Match the emails (A–D) with the statements (1–4) in Exercise 2.

4 Read emails A and B and choose the best answer, A, B, C or D.

1 What does Adam do at the weekends?
   A He plays a lot of sport.
   B He talks to his mother.
   C He has a job to earn money.
   D He stays in his room.

2 What does Michael do in his room?
   A He sleeps and studies.
   B He plays basketball.
   C He plays computer games.
   D He listens to music on his iPod.

3 What is Michael worried about?
   A He thinks Adam will lose contact with family and friends.
   B He thinks Adam doesn't have much money.
   C He's afraid Adam will die soon.
   D He thinks Adam stays in bed too late.

A **From:** Adam **To:** Michael
Subject: This weekend

Hi Michael,

Great to hear you're going to get an iPod, I'll give you some tunes for it. I listen to mine all the time. What are you doing at the weekend? What's your room like? Tell me what cool gadgets you've got. I spend a lot of time in my room because it's so comfortable. With all the gadgets I've got, my room is really interesting and I like to be on my own. On Saturday I'm going to chat to friends on the internet. I'll find out what new games they've got. My grandparents are giving me some money for my birthday, and I'm going to spend it on games. New games cost a lot, but second-hand ones are a good price.
On Sunday I'm going to watch TV because there's a great programme on. My cousin Jack's coming round later and we'll probably spend a few hours playing on the computer.

Adam

> **DID YOU KNOW?**
>
> ### In the average American home:
> > Kids spend 6.5 hours a day using computers.
> > There are 3.6 CD players, 3.5 TVs, 2.5 radios, and at least one DVD player, games console, computer.

B *mailbox* Contacts

Reply | Reply All | Forward | Delete

To: Adam   **From: Michael**
Subject: The weekend

Dear Adam,
How can you spend so much time in your room and waste so much money on computer games? You'll end up sleeping all day and playing electronic games all night. You won't make friends because you're always in your bedroom. That's scary! You won't find me in my room when I'm not studying or sleeping – it's my bedroom, not my whole world. I'm going to listen to my iPod on my way to the sports centre, not in my room. On Saturday, I'm playing basketball – why don't you try it? Get out of your room and get a life before it's too late!
Your friend,
Michael

From: Lucy   To: Jessica
Subject: Re: A new friend

Hi Jessica,
Thanks for your email. Next time, tell me what your room is like. Mine's messy, but I don't mind. My favourite soft toys are on my bed. My wardrobe is full, so there are clothes on the chair, too. One day, I'm going to sort them out and sell things I don't wear now. I'll make a lot of money! My mum nags me and says she's going to throw out all my old things! I'm watching TV now, but – I'll clear up my room tomorrow … really I will!
Write soon,
Lucy

« Back to Inbox

Re: A New friend
Inbox

To: **Lucy** From: **Jessica**   More options

Hi!
Your room sounds really gross! How can you stand it? No wonder your mum nags you. When are you going to tidy up? Your bedroom says a lot about you – why don't you think about it?
I keep my room tidy and I often spend my pocket money on things for it. I'm going to buy some funky floor cushions because my friends are coming round. I want my room to be comfortable so we can chill out.
Why don't you stop watching TV and do something useful?

Jessica

PS Look at this:

'Stop watching TV for a year and I'll write you a cheque for $5,000!' says Dad.

Mr Rundle offered his sons a reward for a year without TV. Daniel found it impossible, but Cory took up the challenge. Instead of watching TV he learned to play the guitar, and his dad paid him. Cory's going to save the money … and he's not going to watch TV any more.

Quick Reply

---

5 **Read emails C and D and choose the best answer, A, B, C or D.**

1 What does Lucy say about her room?
   A She needs a new place to put her clothes.
   B She often buys new toys to put in her room.
   C Her mother tidies her room.
   D There are too many things in the room.

2 Which is the best statement of Jessica's opinion?
   A She enjoys cleaning.
   B She is very careful about the way her room looks.
   C Her friends won't come round if her room's a mess.
   D She spends too much money on things for her room.

3 What did Mr Rundle want his sons to do?
   A Learn to play the guitar.
   B Write a cheque for $5000.
   C Stop watching TV.
   D Save $5000 in a year.

 **SKILL ZONE** Do you need to work out the meaning of a word? Look at other words around it. Are they synonyms (similar meaning) or opposites?

6 **Match the words with the most suitable meaning, A or B.**

1 gadget
   A electronic equipment   B toy for children
2 average
   A typical   B modern
3 gross
   A big   B nasty
4 nag
   A ask once or twice   B ask again and again
5 reward
   A a prize or present for good behaviour   B pocket money
6 challenge
   A an easy job   B a difficult task

Summarise

Choose *either* the boys *or* the girls and explain:
• their opinions on bedrooms and money
  (Michael) believes that …
• the advice they give
  Michael/Jessica advises …

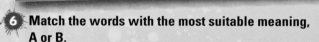 Coming up … *Teens know how*. See page 39.

31

Money and shopping

1 Match the words (1–7) with the meanings (a–g).

1 cheque (UK) / check (US)
2 spend
3 save / save up
4 price
5 cost
6 waste
7 pay (paid)

a to use your money to buy something (v)
b to keep your money so you can use it in the future (v)
c to give someone money, e.g. for an item you're buying or for a job they've done (v)
d the amount of money you have to pay for something in a shop (n)
e a printed piece of paper that you sign and use to pay for things (n)
f to spend money or time in a way that is not useful (v)
g to have a particular price (v)

2 Match the words with the pictures (A–D).

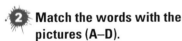

cash   change   credit card
pocket money

3 Choose the correct word to complete the sentence.

1 My parents will write a *cheque/cash* for my music lessons.
2 This shirt looks good. Can you see the *money/price* on it?
3 I want a CD, but I'm not going to *cost/spend* more than £10.
4 I think the shopkeeper gave me the wrong *pocket money/change*.
5 You can't have a *credit card/price* until you're eighteen.

4 Complete the sentences with the correct form of these verbs.

afford   cost   earn   lend   owe   save   spend   waste

1 My mum told me not to ......*waste*...... my money on silly things.
2 My older sister often .... money by babysitting for friends.
3 I'm .... my pocket money to buy a CD player next month.
4 Jack .... me £10 because I bought a CD for him yesterday.
5 Can you .... me five euros, please? I need to buy some lunch.
6 I want to buy a mobile phone but they .... a lot of money.
7 I can't .... to buy those jeans – they're too expensive.
8 Ella doesn't .... much money because she hates shopping!

WORDZONE

Do you want to make a **noun or a verb** into an **adjective**?
Add a new ending: *-able*, *-ible*, *-ous*, *-ful*, *-y*.

enjoy (v)   – *enjoy**able*** (adj)
terror (n)   – *terr**ible*** (adj)
fame (n)   – *fam**ous*** (adj)
hope (n/v)   – *hope**ful*** (adj)
sleep (n/v) – *sleep**y*** (adj)

→ Vocabulary File, page 154

5 Complete the sentences with the correct adjective. Use the words in capitals.

1 Be ......*careful*...... ! Don't scratch the DVD!   CARE
2 There's a pen mark on this cushion, but it's not very ....   NOTICE
3 He tried to paint his bedroom but he wasn't very ....   SUCCESS
4 Thomas is very .... – he usually saves his pocket money.   SENSE
5 Never use electronic gadgets near water – it's really .... DANGER
6 Sam's room is .... ! It's a real mess.   HORROR
7 When I'm tired I sometimes feel cross and ....   MOOD
8 I think watching too much TV can be .... for young children. HARM
9 I'll buy a cheap second-hand computer game. They're really .... AFFORD
10 I never watch thrillers late at night because they're too .... ! SCARE

Memorise

Work in groups. Choose a verb from Exercise 4 and ask another group to write a **correct sentence** using the verb. The group with the most correct sentences is the winner.

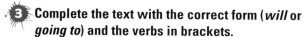

The future

GRAMMARZONE

will

A to make a prediction
I'll make a lot of money!

B to make a promise or an offer
I'll give you some tunes for it.

C to make an unplanned decision
I'll buy it!

going to

D to make a prediction
Great to hear you're going to get an iPod …

E to talk about intentions and plans
She's going to throw out my old things.

Present continuous for future use

F to talk about a fixed arrangement
On Saturday, I'm playing basketball.

shall

G to make suggestions and offers
Shall we walk into town?

➔ Grammar File, page 166

1 Find other examples of *will/going to* in the emails. Match them to the uses in the Grammarzone.

2 Choose the correct form to complete the conversation.

Anna: Look at this horrible mess! 1) *I'm going to/I'll start* clearing up.

Ben: It 2) *shall/will* take you hours! 3) *Shall/Will* I give you a hand?

Anna: Yes please. Right, 4) *shall/will* we throw all the rubbish in this bag?

Ben: OK. Oh, can I borrow this CD? 5) *I'm going to/I'll* give it back tomorrow, honestly.

Anna: All right. Now, move out of the way, 6) *I'm going to/I'll* clean the carpet. Mum 7) *is going to/will* be really surprised when she sees this room! What 8) *are you going to/will you* do with all those cups, Ben? Be careful!

Ben: 9) *I'm going to/I'll* take them to the kitchen, of course. It's OK, I promise 10) *I'm not going to/I won't* drop them … Oh!

CRASH!

3 Complete the text with the correct form (*will* or *going to*) and the verbs in brackets.

Aaron Evans

Do you have any plans for the weekend? 1) ..Are..you..going..out.. (you/go/out) with your friends? Aaron Evans, twelve, from Wales knows what will happen because he does the same thing every Saturday evening. His friends 2) .... (come) back to his room, but they 3) .... (not/watch) TV or play computer games. They'll listen to music and dance. Aaron saved up cash from his part-time job to equip his bedroom as a fully-functioning discotheque with lights and a smoke machine! He has other plans, too – he 4) .... (paint) the walls black!

Aaron 5) .... (be) a DJ when he's older. He'd like to be really good, then he 6) .... (earn) lots of money! 'Practising now 7) .... (help) me make it to the top,' he explains.

Meanwhile Aaron's mother, who is worried about the disco smoke coming out of his window, makes a prediction: 'I expect the fire brigade 8) .... (turn up) one day!'

4 Write sentences that are true for you.

1 The next thing you plan to spend money on:
The next thing I'm going to buy is …

2 A fixed arrangement you have made for this week.

3 One thing you intend to do after school today.

4 A promise you have made to your mum, dad or teacher!

Time to talk

5 What are your plans for the weekend? Are you going to spend a lot of time in your room? Why/ Why not?

Spend! Spend! **Spend!**

1.8 4 **Listen to Lucy's phone conversation and answer the questions.**

1 What are Lucy's two problems?
2 What did she buy?
3 Which two phrases from Exercise 3 does she use?

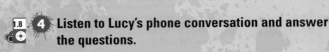

Do you need to listen for specific information? It's a good idea to read all the questions before you start listening. Then you know what information you need to listen for.

Get ideas

1 When you have some money, do you save it or spend it? Do you ever buy things on 'special offer'?

2 Look at the photos on pages 34 and 35. Would you buy any of these things for your bedroom? Why/ Why not?

Time to listen

3 Look at these offers. Which one is the best? Are any of them the same?

1.9 5 **Listen again and choose the correct answer, A, B or C.**

1 Why does Lucy's mother refuse to clean her room?
 A It's too dirty.
 B It's too untidy.
 C It's too big.

2 Why does Lucy spend so much money?
 A She has a lot of pocket money.
 B Her friends persuade her to buy things.
 C She is attracted to things which are in a sale.

3 What sort of people is the new TV series going to help?
 A Teenagers who need to sort out their things.
 B Teenagers who have problems saving their money.
 C Teenagers who annoy their parents.

4 What is the main idea of the TV series?
 A People have to throw away all their possessions.
 B People have to sell most of their possessions to raise money.
 C People have to decide what to keep and what to throw away.

5 What else will the TV team do?
 A Improve the bedroom.
 B Organise other rooms in the house.
 C Buy some special gifts for the bedroom.

6 How does Lucy feel about telling her mother?
 A Nervous.
 B Confident.
 C Unhappy.

Everything half price.

Sale! 25% discount.

Great bargains: 75% off!

Special offer: buy one, get one free.

Special offer: buy one, get one half price.

Get ideas

1 Read the suggestions below. Which do you think is the best/worst advice? Would you choose them to make suggestions to your friend?

... stay at home on Saturdays?

... skateboarding/swimming/cycling every weekend.

... go to the cinema/café instead?

... come round to my house for a change?

... saving your money for something special?

... get a part-time job/ask for some more pocket money.

Time to speak

2 Work with a partner. Choose from the ideas in Exercise 1 and make suggestions to each other. Use the Useful phrases to help you.

Useful phrases

Why don't you/we … ?	That's a great/good idea!
Shall we … ?	Mm, I'm not sure …
Do you want to … ?	I don't think so.
Let's …	OK, why not?
You/We could …	Yes, maybe I/we could do that.
What about … -ing?	I'd rather not.

SKILL ZONE

Are you giving advice or making suggestions? Make sure you use the correct intonation, and stress the main idea.

Questions have rising intonation. Suggestions have falling intonation.

Why don't we go shopping? ↗

Let's stay at home this weekend. ↘

3 Work with a partner.
Student A: You can't decide what to buy as a birthday present for your cousin. Ask Student B for advice.
Student B: Give some advice to Student A.

A I need to buy something for my cousin's birthday

B Well, there's lots of stuff here …

CD rack

Funky light

Clock

Floor cushion

Word building

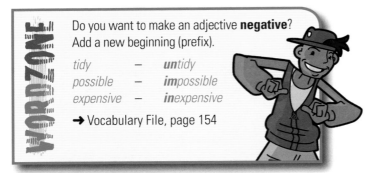

 Do you want to make an adjective **negative**? Add a new beginning (prefix).

tidy   –   **un**tidy
possible   –   **im**possible
expensive   –   **in**expensive

→ Vocabulary File, page 154

1 Choose the correct negative prefix for each group of adjectives.

un-   im-   in-

1 dependent   formal   visible
2 comfortable fit   usual
3 mature   practical

 2 Choose the correct form to complete the sentences for you.

1 I'm usually *able/unable* to go to sleep before midnight.
2 I think it is *acceptable/unacceptable* to stay up late on school nights.
3 In my opinion, it is *appropriate/inappropriate* to have a TV in your room.
4 My teacher would say I'm *reliable/unreliable*.
5 Normally I'm a very *patient/impatient* person.
6 I find it *possible/impossible* to get up very early if I need to.

 3 Complete the text with the correct form of the word in brackets.

BRIGHTSTUFF

Late nights
and
laziness

*I*s waking up in the morning a 1) ..horrible.. (horror) experience? Many teens have the energy to play computer games until late at night, but can't get out of bed in time for school. Their parents may find it almost 2) .... (possible) to wake them. However, this might be more than just laziness or 3) .... (reliable) behaviour.

It's possible that changes in teenagers' hormones could make them tired in the morning. Melatonin is a special hormone which makes people feel 4) .... (sleep). Most adults produce melatonin at about 10p.m., so this should be similar for teenagers. However, many teenagers are 5) .... (able) to produce this 'sleepy' hormone before 1a.m.

One reason for this difference might be playing computer games or watching television late at night. This is 6) .... (appropriate) behaviour because these activities make the brain work harder. On the other hand, the causes may be a natural part of growing up. Whatever the reason, many teenagers are suffering from lack of sleep. This may make them feel moody and 7) .... (patient).

In the USA some schools have delayed the start of their classes to give their teenagers extra time in bed. Many students found that school was more 8) .... (enjoy). Also, they were more 9) .... (success) in their tests. □

Certainty, probability and possibility (modal verbs)

GRAMMARZONE

Certainty

A *must/can't* + verb to express certainty in the future
There must be a reason why teenagers feel sleepy in the morning. (= I'm almost sure there is a reason ...)
He can't be at school yet because he's only just left home. (= I'm almost sure he isn't at school.)

Probability

B *should/ought to* + verb to express probability in the present or future
This should be similar for teenagers.
She's studied hard, so she ought to pass the exam.

Possibility

C *may/might/could* + verb to express possibility in the present or future
Changes in teenagers' hormones could be what makes them feel tired in the morning.
One reason for this difference might be playing computer games late at night.

→ Grammar File, page 166

1 Choose the correct meaning for each sentence.

1 It's 4p.m. so Jessica ought to be at home now.
  A She's probably at home.
  B She's not at home.

2 Olivia might have a DVD player.
  A It is possible that she has one.
  B She definitely has one.

3 Dan can't be asleep yet! It's too early.
  A He isn't able to sleep.
  B I'm sure he isn't asleep.

4 The film starts in an hour. We should get to the cinema in time.
  A I think we'll get there in time.
  B I don't think we'll get there in time.

5 My brother stayed up until 5a.m. He must be asleep now!
  A I'm certain that he's asleep.
  B I'm worried that he's asleep.

6 Tim isn't answering his phone. It could be switched off.
  A I'm quite sure his phone is switched off.
  B I'm guessing his phone is switched off.

2 Choose the correct answers to complete the text.

Message Madness

Beep! Beep! It's after midnight so most people 1) *ought to/could* be asleep but Paul Smith's mobile is beeping. It 2) *must/can't* be another text message. Paul is fourteen and often texts friends late at night.

The next day Paul feels sleepy. He is not unusual. Research shows that up to one in five teenagers said their friends 3) *should/might* wake them by texting late at night. One researcher studied how gadgets in the bedroom affect sleep patterns. He realised that television 4) *can't/could* be the only problem. Although some children 5) *may/must* sleep later at the weekend to catch up on their sleep, others never catch up. The researcher decided this 6) *should/could* be because, like Paul, these children are kept awake by their mobile phones. Although a TV or computer in your room 7) *ought to/might* make you stay up late, a mobile phone in your room is worse. '... mobile telephones 8) *can't/must* have a major impact on the quality of sleep of many teenagers.' What's the solution to Paul's problem? Simple! Switch off your mobile when you switch off the light. ◻

3 Complete the second sentence so that it has a similar meaning to the first sentence using the word given.

1 I'm sure she's in bed now.   MUST
  She ....

2 They'll probably arrive at 10p.m.   SHOULD
  They .... at 10p.m.

3 It's impossible that he'll forget your birthday.   CAN'T
  He .... your birthday.

4 He studied hard so he should do well in the test.   OUGHT
  He studied hard so .... in the test.

5 Perhaps I'll watch TV in my room.   MIGHT
  I .... in my room.

4 Write sentences that are true for you.

1 One thing you may **possibly** do this evening.
2 One school subject that you will **probably** do well in this year.
3 A fact about a friend which you are fairly **sure** is true.

Time to talk

5 Do you feel more awake in the mornings or evenings? Do you ever stay up late? When and why?

Get ideas

1 Imagine you are having a bedroom makeover! What would you do?

Buy (a) new ...
Clean ...
Paint ...
Move ...
Throw away ...
Tidy ...

2 Read the letter and underline the phrases that answer the questions.

1 Who is writing?
2 Who is he writing to?
3 Why is he writing?

8 Newbury Road
London
9th November

Dear Lucy,

Let me introduce myself. I am the producer for the new TV show, *Clear out the clutter*! We have read your application form and my assistant and I are very interested in visiting you to see your room, as we think it may be suitable for this programme. As you know, if your application is successful, we will help you to de-clutter your room. After that, we will also organise a makeover.

In order to arrange our visit, we'll need some more information. I'd like to know what days (Monday–Friday) your parents are available at the end of this month and what time would be convenient for you all. Also, could you tell me the best way to get to your house? Please let me know if you have any questions. My assistant will contact you to make the arrangements.

I look forward to hearing from you soon.
Yours sincerely,

Harry Roberts

Find the right words

3 Find in Harry's letters the three sentences where he asks Lucy:

1 What days/times Lucy and her parents are available.
2 The best way to get to Lucy's house.
3 If Lucy has any questions.

4 Look at Lucy's questions and rewrite them so that they are more polite. Use the sentences in Exercise 3 to help you.

1 How long will the meeting take?
  Could ....
2 What should I do with my room?
  Please let ....
3 When will you decide if my room is suitable?
  I'd ....

Plan ahead

5 Look at Lucy's family calendar and complete the sentences below.

November

MON	TUE	WED	THU	FRI	SAT	SUN
17	18	19	20	21	22	23
		← Dad – Sales conference →				
24 Mum Work	25 Harry Roberts 5p.m.	26 Mum Work	27 Harry Roberts 5p.m.	28 Lucy school trip	29	30

1 ✗ Dad isn't going to be available ....
2 ✗ Mum ....
3 ✗ I ....
4 The best dates for the meeting are .... or ....

ROYA

POSTAG

6 Look at the London–Oxford timetables and complete the sentences below.

Coach**Line** Timetable

Depart London	Arrive Oxford
15.10	16.30
17.10	18.30

Return fare: £20 per person
10% discount Monday–Thursday

RailOne >>>>>>>>>>>>

Depart London	Arrive Oxford
14.50	16.00
15.40	16.50

Return fare: £30 per person
Special offer: buy one ticket, get one free!

Taxi
Return fare: £50
Journey time: one hour twenty minutes

1 The fastest way to travel is …
2 The cheapest way for two people to travel is …
3 To arrive at the best time, you should …
4 The most comfortable way …

7 Complete Lucy's notes. Use these phrases and the information from Exercise 6 to help you.

The first/second	option
The next/Another	choice
The final/last	possibility

1 The first choice is to
....

2 The next possibility is to
....

3 The last
....

Time to write *a formal letter*

8 Write Lucy's reply to Harry Roberts. Use the plan to help you. Write about 120–150 words.

Plan
Starting:
Dear …
Thank the person for his/her letter.
Say why you are writing – give the most important information here (e.g. date and time for meeting).

Main points:
Write topic sentences to organise your main paragraphs.
(Use phrases from Exercise 7 to give information about transport).
Use full forms – they sound more formal.

Ending:
Ask any other questions you may have (choose one from Exercise 3).
Say you'll look forward to hearing from him/her.
Use *Yours sincerely* for formal and semi-formal letters.

SKILLZONE
Are you writing a letter?
Summarise the key information for your reader.
Don't explain all the details, because you will write too many words.
Organise the information clearly. Use these expressions: *The first choice …*, *The second option …*, *Finally,*

Time to watch *Teens know how*

9 Watch the DVD and do the activities on page 154.

4 Festival fever

Get ideas

1 What festivals do you have where you live? What other festivals do you know?

Time to read

2 Read the festival reports (A–D) and match the photos (1–4) with the correct festival.

A

Glastonbury Festival, England

I can't hear you, I'm at Glastonbury!

I've put up my tent, along with thousands of others. People have come from all over the world. Although there are thousands of people here, and queues for everything, the atmosphere is friendly and laid-back,
5 because everyone's in a good mood. Backstage crews have been working for days to get things ready, and musicians have been tuning up for what seems like hours.

Glastonbury is England's biggest music festival. It's been running for over thirty years, and it's been getting
10 bigger and more popular all the time. Every year, the organisers have not only booked famous bands to attract the crowds but also introduced new bands. I've always made sure I watch bands I've never heard of before and sometimes they've become my favourites.

15 Music isn't the only entertainment here. I've been watching some fantastic circus acts, and there are plays, body painting, craft workshops, and lots more.

B

The Night of Fire, Soller, Mallorca

I'm in the main square, Soller, Mallorca. It's nearly midnight and the tension has been building up here for over an hour. People, young and old, locals and visitors, have been gathering in the square since eight
5 o'clock. I've been talking to José and Martina, who live here. They've been looking forward to this evening all summer. Tonight, they've put on their oldest clothes and splashed themselves with water from the fountain. They're ready, but what is everyone waiting for?

A hot night is about to get hotter.

10 It's the annual Night of Fire festival and the final event, the race of fire, is about to begin. A hot night is about to get even hotter. The festival runners have just appeared; they're wearing animal skins, and carrying fireworks. They've started spraying the crowd with a
15 shower of fire. People are screaming and laughing at the same time. My new friends, José and Martina, have set off to race with the fire, but I'm happy just to watch.

C

West Coast Chocolate Festival, Canada

Have you ever been to a chocolate party?

No? Then make this the year that you come to the Canadian West Coast Chocolate Festival. It's the biggest chocolate party in the world! There has never been so much chocolate in one place before. The smell from over a hundred stalls is amazing and the taste is even better. Whatever type of chocolate you like: dark, milk or white, you haven't had the true chocolate experience until you've dipped fruit in the huge chocolate fountain! When you've eaten enough, relax with a chocolate massage or join a chocolate factory tour.

"It's the biggest chocolate party in the world!"

The festival is about more than just chocolate. For the past three years, young performers have been raising money for youth arts programmes. They have turned the event into a carnival! So come to the carnival! You won't leave without a smile on your face – and probably a bit of chocolate, too!

D

International Dance Festival, Ladek, Poland

Put on your dancing shoes and join in the fun at the International Dance Festival in Ladek!

'One of the best things at the festival is the dance parade through the streets of Ladek Zdroj,' says Eva, a ballet fan who has been coming to Ladek since the festival started eight years ago. 'My friends and I have spent weeks making our colourful costumes, so don't miss it!'

"We've spent weeks making our costumes."

Ivan hasn't been to the festival before and he's interested in a very different style of dance. 'I've decided to try a breakdancing workshop,' he says. 'It's something I've always wanted to do.'

The festival ends with a fantastic live performance in the Ladek Amphitheatre. The professional dancers invite people who have done well in the workshops to perform with them. So get practising – next year it could be you on stage!

SKILLZONE

Do you need to match facts or information with texts? First read the statements and underline the key words. Then read the texts quickly. Don't worry about words you don't know, just look for words and phrases that match.

3 Match the statements (1–6) with the festivals (A–D).
This festival
1 … is for people of all ages
2 … is international
3 … requires special clothes
4 … offers the chance to learn something
5 … offers a big choice of activities
6 … offers an unusual form of relaxation

4 Find words in the texts that match these meanings.
1 made of cloth and ropes and used for camping (Text A line 1)
2 lines of people waiting for something (Text A line 3)
3 films and TV shows intended to amuse or interest people (Text A line 15)
4 made wet (Text B line 8)
5 a celebration or party arranged for a particular date or time (Text B line 10)
6 pressing someone's body in order to help them relax (Text C line 11)
7 a meeting where you learn about something and do practical exercises (Text D line 10)
8 happening at the same time as you are watching it (Text D line 12)

Summarise

In your own words, describe:
• the entertainment at each festival
  At Glastonbury, there's …
• the best thing about each festival
  I think the best thing about the … is …

Time to talk

5 Which festival would you prefer to go to? Why? What do you think makes a good festival?

Coming up … *Scotland's fire festival* on DVD. See page 49.

Outdoor entertainment

1 Complete the sentences with these words.

carnival   costumes   crowd   fireworks   parade
perform   raise money   stage   stalls

1 When the band came on .... everybody started clapping.
2 The .... were so beautiful. Somebody must have spent a long time making them.
3 The .... in Brazil is the biggest in the world.
4 You should have seen the .... They lit up the whole sky!
5 Festivals are a great opportunity to .... for special causes.
6 I love looking at the .... and always find something unusual to buy.
7 The .... took hours to pass through the town and the .... started to get a bit bored.
8 Lots of musicians, dancers and acrobats .... at summer festivals.

2 Find the odd word out. Explain why.

1 entertainer, performer, actor, organiser
2 event, stage, show, festival
3 audience, spectators, participants, crowd
4 cabaret show, circus act, religious tradition, play
5 costumes, hats, T-shirts, tents
6 band, musician, acrobat, artist

3 Replace the underlined words or phrases with these words. There's one extra word!

an acrobat   amazing   atmosphere   audience
carnival   costume   theme parks

1 The band tried to get the people who were watching them to join in the singing.
2 I've never tasted such fantastic food. There were samples from all over the world.
3 Apparently it's one of the biggest outdoor entertainment areas in the world with the highest water slide.
4 I'd love to wear a traditional dress and hat for the local festival.
5 Physical fitness is really important if you want to become a performer in a circus.
6 The festival was a disaster. It rained all day and there just wasn't a nice feeling about the place.

4 Match the beginnings (1–5) with the endings (a–e).

1 The band played so badly ...
2 They were in the middle of the performance ...
3 I enjoyed the concert so much ...
4 The crowd in the street cheered ...
5 When the main singer came on stage ...

a ... that I clapped until my hands were red.
b ... the girls in the audience started to scream.
c ... as the parade passed by.
d ... when the lights went off.
e ... that the crowd started to boo.

WORDZONE

Look! You can put two nouns together and make a **compound noun**. The first noun usually describes the second noun.

A **show** that's on **stage** is a *stage show*.
The **organiser** of a **festival** is a *festival organiser*.
A **festival** of **chocolate** is a *chocolate festival*.

→ Vocabulary File, page 155

5 Match the nouns (1–3) with the nouns (a–c) to make compound nouns.

1 neon   a park
2 theme   b lights
3 circus   c act

6 Find more examples from the texts.

A tour of the factory is a ...
A fan of ballet is a ...
A festival of music is a ...

Memorise

Add as many words as you can for each category.

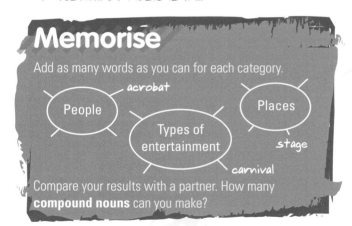

acrobat

People

Types of entertainment

Places

stage

carnival

Compare your results with a partner. How many **compound nouns** can you make?

Present perfect simple and continuous

GRAMMARZONE

Present perfect simple

A things or experiences in our lives up to now
I haven't been to a chocolate party before.

B situations or experiences that are still true up to now
There has never been so much chocolate in one place.

C actions that happened in the past (recently) and have results in the present
They have turned the event into a carnival.

Present perfect continuous

D actions or situations that started in the past and are continuing up to now
The festival has been running for years.

E actions in the recent past that have just now stopped
They've been looking forward to this evening all summer ... .

➜ Grammar File, page 167

1 Find other examples of the present perfect simple and continuous in the texts on pages 40–41. Match them to the uses in the Grammarzone.

2 Choose the correct form to complete the sentences.

1 They *'ve been eating/have eaten* chocolate, and now they're covered in it!
2 *Have you been tasting/Have you tasted* the local ice cream? It's fabulous.
3 The main attraction *hasn't been changing/hasn't changed*. It's always the local pop group.
4 The parade *has been starting/has started*. Come on, let's go and watch it!
5 It *'s been raining/has rained* for hours and it looks like it's not going to stop.
6 The musicians *have been playing/have played* all evening. They're beginning to look very tired.

3 Complete the text with the correct form (present perfect simple or continuous) of the verbs in brackets.

World News

World News

Insects on menu at food festival

OVER the past few days food lovers 1) *have been arriving* (arrive) in Johannesburg for an unusual food festival. They 2) .... (come) to eat chocolate-coated bugs and fried insects!

The South African Chefs' Association 3) .... (plan) the menu for months. They say they want to introduce dishes such as tomato, onion and insect stew to a wider audience.

The festival 4) .... (bring) visitors from all over the world and the organisers believe it 5) .... (be) a big success.

'Insect-eating is a cultural practice that people today 6) .... (forget). This festival 7) .... (give) us the chance to prove how healthy and tasty they are.'

Time to talk

4 Do you think you would try chocolate insects? Why/Why not? What food have you eaten at festivals?

Making music

SKILL ZONE

Do you need to **decide if a statement is true or false?** Read the statements first and underline key information. Then listen carefully for words and phrases that give you the answer.

Get ideas

1 What sort of musical events do you like going to? Which of the events in the photos would you like to go to?

Time to listen

2 You are going to listen to an interview about preparations for a Hip Hop festival. Which of these words do you expect to hear?

art exhibition   competition   costumes   DJs
main stage   pop concert   rubbish   stalls

 3 Listen and check.

 4 Listen again and decide if the statements are true (T) or false (F).

1 This is the first International Hip Hop festival.
2 They've finished the preparations.
3 Last year they had the festival on the beach.
4 Last year they sold tickets for the festival.
5 The park is quite near the town centre.
6 The festival has lots of new attractions this year.
7 The graffiti artists can paint anywhere in the park.
8 There will be food from Greece and China at the festival.

5 Complete the sentences in your own words.

1 Last year local people were angry because …
2 The organisers have sold tickets in advance this year so that …
3 The festival is in a park this year because …
4 The festival organisers have organised a graffiti competition in order to …

Get ideas

1 What makes a good festival? What can go wrong at a festival?

2 Find the phrases that give reasons.

> **1** They've cancelled the festival because of financial problems.

> **2** The main reason is that the tickets are very expensive.

> **3** The crowd has been waiting for a long time in order to see the main attraction.

> **4** The organisers didn't plan the event carefully, and that's why they've lost money.

> **5** It's important to book top bands, because they attract a good audience.

Time to speak

3 Complete the answers to the questions with the Useful phrases. Then ask and answer the questions with a partner.

1 Why have a lot of people come to the festival?
 – … top bands are playing.
2 Why is the festival so good?
 – … is that they planned it very carefully.
3 Why aren't they playing at the moment?
 – It's … the rain.
4 Why are people standing here?
 – They're queuing … go to the loo!
5 Has the festival finished?
 – Yes, … people are leaving.

Useful phrases

Giving explanations and reasons

because of … because … … in order to …
… that's why … … that's because
The main reason … That means …

4 Ask and answer questions about the pictures with a partner. Use the ideas to help you.

1 set up / stalls?
Have you set up the stalls?
– rain all day
No, we haven't because it's been raining all day.

2 band / arrive?
 – van / broken down

3 why / not sell / many tickets?
 – expensive

4 why / acrobats / not practise?
 – cold on the stage

5 happen / mayor?
 – wind blow wig off / go home

6 why / not call TV station?
 – too much to do / forget

5 Write three questions, then ask and answer with a partner.

Do you like … – Yes, I do. / No, I don't.
Why/Why not? – The main reason is …

Adverbs

→ Vocabulary File, page 155

Do you want to **make an adverb** from an adjective? Add *-ly*. For adjectives ending in *-y*, drop the *-y* and add *-ily*.

bad (adj) – bad**ly** (adv)
tidy (adj) – tid**ily** (adv)

Learn the irregular adverbs.
early (adj) – early (adv)
fast (adj) – fast (adv)
hard (adj) – hard (adv)
good (adj) – well (adv)

1 Complete with the correct adverb.

adjective	adverb
1 bad	badly
2 easy	
3 fast	
4 hard	
5 quick	
6 loud	
7 sad	
8 quiet	
9 happy	
10 international	

2 Complete the sentences with the correct adverbs. Use the adjectives in brackets.

1 The performers moved ......quickly...... (quick) through the crowd.
2 The children started talking .... (loud) during the performance.
3 .... (sad), he was too old to dance.
4 She has worked .... (hard) for the festival.
5 You must get there .... (early) to see the show.
6 They're speaking .... (quiet) and I can't hear them.

3 Complete the sentences in your own words. Use the correct adverb.

1 The audience sat (quiet) ....
2 Everybody waited (patient) ....
3 He trains very (hard) ....
4 If you arrive (early) ....
5 The band from Canada (easy) ....
6 Don't walk so (fast) ....

 4 Complete the article with the correct form of the words in brackets.

Music

Wanted! Teenage pop sensation

The pressure is on! In an international
1) ...competition... (compete) to find the world's best teenage band, 1,100 wannabe stars are
2) .... (nervous) waiting for results. Soon
5 they will know if they are in the final group of six.

It hasn't been easy. A special team of DJs,
3) .... (music), songwriters and record
4)...................... (produce) has judged each act. These experts know the music industry 5) ....
10 (good) and they know what succeeds from indie to pop and 6) .... (tradition) to alternative music.

So how can the bands 7) .... (successful) convince these judges? Some have used lyrics to describe what interests teenagers today. Elena from
15 Georgia hopes her words help teenagers make
8) .... (decide) for themselves. Richard from France sings about teenage love of clothes and image, but says he's 9) .... (obvious) referring to himself! Finally, there's George who raps
20 10) .... (impress) in Greek and English about friendship and loyalty.

Other bands just offer great musical 11) ....
(entertain) and impress the judges with their enthusiasm and energy. The Go Band from Rio give a cool Hip Hop
25 12) .... (perform) while the six Colombians in the band Hop'n'Skip 13) .... (energy) show a love of rock 'n' roll.

If it's true that music can change the world, maybe the world will change for one of these six finalists tonight.

Direct and indirect objects

GRAMMARZONE

Word order: direct and indirect objects

Some verbs can have two objects. You can use different structures with these verbs:

A

Subject	Verb	Object (thing)	to/for	Object (person)
They	gave	a prize	to	the best band.
I	bought	tickets	for	everyone.

B

Subject	Verb	Object (person)	Object (thing)
They	gave	the best band	a prize.
I	bought	everyone	tickets.

C use *to* + object after certain verbs, e.g. *bring, give, lend, show,* etc.
use *for* + object after certain verbs, e.g. *buy, cook, make, play,* etc.

1 Put the words in the correct order to make sentences.

1 a drink / get / I / Can / for / anyone?
   Can I get a drink for anyone?
2 friends. / She's / meal / a special / for / cooking / her
3 the audience / The dancers / showed / some new movements.
4 played / the fans. / its best songs / for / The band
5 this costume / to / please? / Can you take / Michael
6 offered / The organisers / umbrellas / everyone / as it was so wet.

2 Complete the sentences. Use *to* or *for* if necessary.

1 The stallholders served ..... the children free drinks.
2 She owes lots of money ..... her dad because he paid for the tickets.
3 The band is going to sing *Happy Birthday* ..... that girl. She's sixteen today.
4 I'm going to buy a really nice present ..... my best friend.
5 Did she cook ..... him a cake?
6 The competition gave ..... the winner a cash prize.

3 Choose the correct answers to complete the text.

Ticket trouble!

I can't believe it! Only one week to go until the concert and my tickets haven't arrived. What a disaster! You see, Mum bought the tickets 1) *my birthday*/*for my birthday*. 'Have you sent 2) *to them*/*them* the money?' I asked her suspiciously. 'Of course!' she said. She sent a cheque 3) *to the organisers*/*the organisers* four weeks ago. Anyway I didn't hear anything so last week I wrote 4) *to them*/*them* an email. 'Don't worry,' came the reply. 'We have had a small problem with our computers. However, we've reserved the tickets 5) *for Mrs Armstrong*/*Mrs Armstrong*. As soon as the technicians have fixed the computers we'll send them 6) *to her*/*her* at 104 Park Lane, Manchester. Enjoy the festival.'

But guess what? I live at 104 Park Lane, Liverpool!

4 Complete the questions with *to* or *for* if necessary. Use the correct form of the verb.

1 Have you ever / send / anyone / a Valentine's card?
   Have you ever sent anyone a Valentine's card?
2 Have you ever / give / money / a street performer?
3 Have you ever / bake / anyone / a cake?
4 Have you ever / lend / money / anyone?
5 Have you ever / cook / your parents / anything special?
6 Have you ever / buy / anything / your teacher?

5 Ask and answer the questions with a friend.

Have you ever sent anyone a Valentine's card?
Yes, I have./No, I haven't.

Time to talk

6 Do you know any bands that have won a competition? Are they good bands?
Have you ever performed on stage? What was it like?

Get ideas

1 What is the best/worst festival you've been to? Why? What type of entertainment have you seen at festivals?

Find the right words

2 Complete posters (1–3) with the correct information. Use these words and phrases.

an unforgettable experience   bring your camera
circus workshops   competition   music festival
relax on the beach

2
WELCOME ALL FILM FANS!

Join us for this special film festival in the south of France. Come and watch the latest movies or 3) .... Try out the amazing local cakes and juices. Don't forget to 4) .... There will be some fascinating guests!

Festival begins Friday evening at 9p.m. and ends Sunday at 5p.m.

1
CARNIVAL
in the city!

It will be **ENORMOUS!**
Join us this Saturday for an exciting 1) ....
There will be bands from all over the world, dance parades and a 2) ....
for the best costume.
Free drink and hot dog for anyone in costume.

3
summer
festival!

Come along to Central Park this weekend for 5) .... There will be magic shows, 6) .... , great fireworks and fantastic Mexican food. Get there early! Performances start at 9a.m. on Saturday and 11a.m. on Sunday.

4 Find adjectives in the festival posters that match these meanings.

1 interesting
2 very good
3 big

3 Complete the missing information about the festivals.

	Festival 1	Festival 2	Festival 3
Type of event		film festival	
Where?			
What's it like?	enormous/ exciting		
Food?			
How long is it?			two days
Extra information	free drink		

5 Complete the sentences with the correct information.

Hi, Paul here, I've just arrived at the Carnival in the city ...

1 I've listened to ...
2 I've watched ...
3 I've eaten ...
4 I've won ...
5 It's ...

6 You have arrived at the Film Festival or the Summer Festival. Describe what you have seen on your first day.

I've just arrived at ....

Plan ahead

7 **Read the article quickly and choose the correct answer.**

a Isabelle's article is *polite and formal/chatty and friendly*.

b She wrote the article for *younger/older* readers.

CelebrityLife

Isabelle Martin has spent a day at the Film Festival in Cannes in the south of France.

1 Have you ever seen a famous person? You might not believe this but I've just seen Brad Pitt and Angelina Jolie!

2 I've come to the Cannes Film Festival. Cannes is a beautiful town in the south of France. It's on the coast and has fantastic beaches and cafés. The town has been organising film festivals since 1946. Lots of fascinating celebrities have come for the event. During the festival the streets are jammed with famous people, movie makers, journalists and photographers.

3 There's a great atmosphere here and I've had an exciting day. I've been watching everybody on the beach and taking photos. I haven't seen any films yet because I've been too busy with my camera! I've met Eddie Murphy. He does the voice of Donkey in *Shrek*. He's been working really hard during the festival but agreed to give me a special interview!

4 We've eaten really well. The food is beautifully prepared and everybody works so hard to make sure you're having a good time. Just a minute! I can hear clapping and shouting. I've got to go. I've had a most amazing experience. See you next year … .

8 **Read the article again and answer the questions.**

1 How does Isabelle start her article and why?
2 Is the style of the article formal or informal? Find examples.
3 What adjectives does Isabelle use to attract the reader?
4 What punctuation does Isabelle use?

9 **Think of a festival you've been to and complete the notes.**

> **Para 1:** Have you ever …? I've just …
> **Para 2:** I've come to …/I've arrived at …
> There are lots of … fantastic …,
> fascinating …
> and exciting ….
> **Para 3:** I've seen …/I've been watching …
> **Para 4:** I've had a … day/… experience!

Time to write *an article*

10 **Write an article describing your first day at a local festival. Write between 150 and 180 words. Use the Skillzone and Isabelle's article to help you.**

SKILLZONE

Are you **using the right style or register**? Make sure you:

- attract your reader at the beginning.
- use interesting adjectives.
- talk directly to the reader and sound friendly.

Time to watch *Scotland's fire festival*

11 **Watch the DVD and do the activities on page 155.**

Vocabulary

1 Choose the word or phrase (A, B, C or D) that best completes the sentence.

1 I can't .... to buy any new CDs this week.
A afford   **C** cost
B spend   **D** owe

2 Could you tell us the .... of the tickets for the concert?
A money   **C** price
B pay   **D** cash

3 Sam's dad offered to pay for the CD player with his ....
A pocket money   **C** change
B credit card   **D** cost

4 They're .... up their money for the summer holiday.
A spending   **C** owing
B saving   **D** earning

5 Can you .... me some money to buy a present?
A waste   **C** afford
B spend   **D** lend

2 Put the words into the correct category.

acrobat   audience   band   carnival   crowd
entertainer   festival   organiser   performer
show   stage   stalls

1 A person: .....*acrobat*..... ....
....
2 A group of people: ....
....
3 A place or object: ....
4 An event: ....

3 Make adverbs from the adjectives in the box and match them to the best verb.

fast   happy   hard   loud   quiet

1 We whispered .....*quietly*.......
2 He smiled ....
3 She shouted ....
4 They ran ....
5 I worked ....

4 Complete each sentence with the correct form of the word in capitals.

1 The bill for my mobile is ......*payable*....... monthly.   PAY
2 It is .... to switch off your mobile at night.   SENSE
3 Lack of sleep makes you feel ....   MOOD
4 I always put my clothes away .... in the cupboard.   TIDY
5 The costumes at the carnival are ....   COLOUR
6 It can be .... to take part in the Night of Fire celebrations.   DANGER
7 It's hard to get tickets for Glastonbury, but it's not ....   POSSIBLE
8 The audience was .... because the show was boring.   ENTHUSIASTIC
9 The dancers moved ....   QUICK
10 The acrobats performed really .... on stage.   GOOD
11 We arrived .... for the concert.   EARLY

5 Complete the sentences with compound nouns. Use these nouns.

circus   factory   lights   show   theme

1 I'd love to visit a **chocolate** .....*factory*...... this summer!
2 Last weekend we spent the day at a .... **park**.
3 The festival was decorated with **neon** ....
4 The tickets for the **stage** .... have sold out.
5 We saw an amazing .... **act** performing.

6 Match the phrasal verbs 1-8 to the correct meaning (a–h).

1 catch up (on)
2 end up
3 grow up
4 sort out
5 switch off
6 tidy up/clear up
7 set off
8 turn into

a become an adult
b finish in a particular situation
c organise things into groups (e.g. things you want/don't want)
d make up for what you've missed (e.g. school work, sleep, news)
e start a journey
f stop an electrical item
g become something different
h put things away neatly

Grammar

7 Complete the second sentence so that it has a similar meaning to the first sentence using the word given.

1 The weather forecast is for rain tomorrow.   WILL
It ....will rain...... tomorrow.

2 Do you want me to help you tidy up this mess?   SHALL
.... tidy up this mess?

3 We've arranged to take part in a local dance festival on Friday.   TAKING
We .... a local dance festival on Friday.

4 I'll remember to buy Mum's present tomorrow, I promise.   FORGET
I .... Mum's present tomorrow, I promise.

5 Alex is saving up his pocket money for a new computer game.   BUY
Alex .... a new computer game.

6 Our band is certain to win the music competition.   WILL
Our band .... the music competition.

8 Choose A, B, C or D to complete the sentences.

1 The concert .... starting now. It's not 9.00p.m. yet.
A can't be   **C** could be
B must be   **D** might be

2 The entertainers .... to be on stage soon.
A should   **C** must
B ought   **D** could

3 I've heard that Robbie Williams .... a surprise appearance.
A might make   **C** can't make
B should make   **D** must make

9 Complete the interview with the correct form (present perfect simple or continuous) of the verbs in brackets.

Reporter: I 1) 've just arrived.... (just arrived) at Wimbledon Tennis Club and I'm standing outside. The famous tennis tournament 2) .... (start) but some people 3) .... (not / buy) their tickets yet. Look at this queue! How long 4) .... (you / wait) here?

Max: We 5) .... (stand) in this queue since 5a.m.

Sam: And the weather's terrible, it 6) .... (rain) for hours! Still, there's a fantastic atmosphere here. We 7) .... (meet) some great people, too.

Reporter: Oh, I've just heard that Rafael Nadal and Roger Federer 8) .... (practise) on the centre court for the last ten minutes and their match 9) .... (start). I must get inside – I don't want to miss it!

10 Choose the word or phrase (A, B, C or D) that best completes the sentence.

1 His friend wrote the music ....
A him.   **C** to him.
B for him.   **D** of him.

2 The band ....
A us a special song played.
B a special song us played.
C played a special song us.
D played us a special song.

3 The musician .... for the next show.
A gave free tickets for them.
B gave to them free tickets.
C gave them free tickets.
D gave free tickets them.

11 Complete the text with one word which best fits each gap.

Have you ever 1) .....been............ to a really big concert? I 2) .... been waiting for years for my favourite band to play in our town and now Razorlight are really here! My dad has 3) .... two tickets for me and my best friend and finally the big day is here!

Nick is here at my house. 4) ....'ve both been getting ready for hours and we've been 5) .... to Razorlight's latest CD all afternoon, too. We've got our cameras, of course, because we're 6) .... lots of photos! It's going 7) .... be amazing!

It's 8.00p.m. and we're ready to set 8) .... , so the taxi should 9) .... here any minute. Oh, the taxi driver 10) .... just rung the doorbell, so it 11) .... be time to go now! I promise I 12) .... call you tomorrow so you can catch 13) .... on all the news!

Kate x

Did you remember all the vocabulary and grammar points?

→ Vocabulary File, pages 154 and 155
→ Grammar File, pages 166 and 167

5 Extreme behaviour!

Get ideas

1 How do you usually react to people's bad behaviour? Do you easily get angry? Do the quiz and compare your answers with a partner.

QUIZ

How do you react to unfair behaviour?

➤ **Check your answers below to see how well you solve problems.**

1 What would you do if someone accidentally made you fall over in the playground?
   A Hit the person hard.
   B Sit down and cry.
   C Give them a chance to apologise.

2 What would you do if an older boy wanted your money?
   A Fight him.
   B Give him the money.
   C Shout and try to run away.

3 If someone in your class always made rude comments about you, what would you do?
   A Get very angry.
   B Get upset, but not say anything.
   C Try not to react to the comments and tell an adult.

4 If you heard some kids saying horrible comments to your friend, what would you do?
   A Shout at the other kids.
   B Ignore it. Let your friend sort out the problem.
   C Help your friend and tell the other kids to stop it.

Time to read

2 Read Mike's letter and answer the questions.
   1 Why wasn't Mike's brother happy at his school?
   2 Why did Mike get involved?
   3 What is Mike worried about now?

3 Read Dan's reply to Mike's letter. What does Dan think are the two problems with fighting bullies?

4 Read the two letters again. Choose from the sentences (A–G) the one which fits each gap (1–6). There is one extra sentence.

   A He was laughing at my brother and suddenly I felt really angry.
   B Bullies hate that!
   C They said rude things and called him names.
   D Bullies usually repeat their behaviour – it becomes a habit.
   E It's still bothering me, so I'm writing to ask for some advice.
   F I was in terrible pain after he hit me.
   G I'm not usually violent. Was I right or wrong?

Do you need to **put sentences back into a text**? Look for reference words that help you work out how the text fits together. Match words in the sentences before and after the gap with words in the missing sentences.

5 Find words in the text that match these meanings.
   1 a long time (line 4)
   2 from a high social class (line 6)
   3 a lot (line 9)
   4 friends (line 17)
   5 push (line 17)
   6 walked (quickly and angrily) (line 24)
   7 asked for (line 25)
   8 horrible (line 30)

PROBLEMS

FRIENDS & FAMILY
Was I a bully, too?

TURN OVER FOR
MORE ADVICE

Dear Dan,
My brother Sam and I moved to a new
secondary school a year ago. At first we
hated it because it took us ages to make
5 new friends. Some kids at our school
are quite posh, but that doesn't
mean that they're nice! For about
six months my brother Sam had
loads of problems. I tried to
10 protect him, but I don't know
if I did the right thing. (1) E..
Let me explain …
Some kids teased Sam. (2) ..... .
A boy called Jake, who was
15 older than Sam, was the worst
bully. Sometimes, he and his
mates would shove Sam in the
corridors or throw his bag on the floor.
Anyway, one day last month Sam and his
20 friends were standing in a queue in the school
canteen. Jake sometimes expects younger
kids to give up their place in the queue or
hand over some of their dinner money. That
day Jake marched up to Sam and his friends
25 and demanded 50p. 'If you don't give us the
money, I'll get you after school.' I saw what
was happening. (3) ..... . I felt responsible for
my brother, so I pushed Jake out of the way.
Unfortunately, he fell and banged his head on
30 the wall with a revolting thump.
Jake hasn't bothered Sam since that day, but
sometimes I feel guilty. (4) ..... . Do you think I
was a bully, too?
Mike, 14, Manchester

FACT!
a report from
the USA says
that 86% of 11–15
year-olds worry
about teasing and
bullying.

Dear Mike,
If I were you, I'd forget about this and carry on with your 35
life as usual. If you fight back once, it doesn't
make you a bully I'm sure you'll agree.
(5) ..... . To be honest, I disapprove of
using violence to deal with bullies.
If the bullies fought back, you would 40
get hurt. Also, you would get into
trouble. Bullies often get bored if
you don't react, and they will usually
stop if you laugh at them. (6) ..... .
It's impossible for adults to help you 45
unless they know about it, so try to
tell a friend, a parent or a teacher about
any bullying. Most bullying is not illegal,
but it is very unfair and by law schools should
protect you. Don't forget that bullies may have 50
problems, too. Some are immature and others bully if
they feel insecure, so they might need help, too.
Everyone deals with things differently, but the important
lesson is the one you and your brother learned; if you
believe in yourself, the bullies will soon leave you alone. 55
Good luck!
Dan

Summarise

Complete the sentences in your own words.
Mike asked for advice about …
Mike was worried that …
Dan advised Mike …
Dan suggested that …

Time to talk

6 **Do you agree with the advice that Dan gives? Why/
Why not?**

Coming up … *Solving a problem* on DVD. See page 61.

Right and wrong

WORDZONE

Do you want to make an adjective or a verb **negative**? Add a new beginning.

*logical – **il**logical*
*regular – **ir**regular*
*obey – **dis**obey*

→ Vocabulary File, page 156

1 Complete the table. Use the letters on page 53 to help you.

	positive	negative
1	honest	dishonest
2	legal	....
3	....	irresponsible
4	....	disagree
5	approve	....

2 Choose the correct form to complete the sentences so they are true for you. Compare with a partner.

1 I *approve/disapprove* of getting married when you're a teenager.
2 I think smoking should be *legal/illegal* when you're fifteen.
3 I *agree/disagree* that you should always wear a seatbelt in a car.
4 I think if teenagers want a tattoo or body-piercing, they should be *honest/dishonest* with their parents.
5 I think most teenagers usually *obey/disobey* the school rules.
6 I think it's *logical/illogical* to allow young teenagers to work.

3 Complete the article below. Use suitable words from Exercise 1. Which of these laws are the same/different in your country?

4 Complete the definitions with a bold word or phrase from Exercise 3.

1 The ....law........ is a system of rules that people in a country must obey.
2 A .... is the person who decides how to punish people.
3 A judge makes legal decisions in ....
4 If something is .... it is illegal.
5 A .... is a sum of money you pay if you break the law.
6 Criminals go to .... as a punishment.
7 A .... is something you can legally do.

Memorise

Write four adjectives or verbs from Exercises 2 and 3. Work with a partner. Exchange lists with your partner and write the opposites. Then compare your lists.

What's **legal** for young people in the UK?

Age 10: You have the (1) ......legal...... **right** to choose your own religion.

Age 13: It's 2) .... for you to work all day, but it's OK to work for a few hours a week.

Age 14: You are 3) .... for having your seatbelt fastened in a car. It's **against the law** for you to leave your belt unfastened. You may have to pay a **fine** of £20 if you leave it undone.

Age 16: You can get married, but you must check with at least one of your parents. If they 4) .... , then you'll have to wait!

Age 17: You can't have a tattoo or body piercing unless your parents are with you and they 5) .... If someone gives you a tattoo without your parents' permission, they will have to go to **court** and the **judge** may fine them or send them to **prison**. You can have a driver's licence, but you must 6) .... the law and have an adult with you.

Age 18: By **law**, you are now an adult. Many more things are now 7) .... for you. You can get married without asking your parents, have a bank account and you can vote. You can buy cigarettes, but you must be 8) .... about your age. Take an ID card or a copy of your birth certificate as proof. And remember, they're very bad for your health!

Conditionals: zero, first, second

GRAMMARZONE

Zero conditional

A *if/when* + present simple + present simple for a general truth
Bullies often get bored if you don't react.

First conditional

B *if* + present simple + *will/can/could/may/might* for a possible action in the future
If you don't give us the money, we'll get you after school.

Second conditional

C *if* + past simple + *would/could/might* for an imaginary/impossible situation in the present
If the bullies fought back, you would get into trouble.

D giving advice: *If I were you, I'd …*
If I were you, I'd forget about this.

unless = if … not/except if …
It's impossible for adults to help you unless they know about it.

When the *if*-clause comes first, we use a comma after it.

→ Grammar File, page 168

1 Find another example of zero, first or second conditional in the letters on page 53.

2 Choose the correct verb form to complete the sentences. Add a comma in the correct place where necessary.

1 If friends argue, they *say/said* sorry afterwards.
2 Behaviour may be bullying if it *happens/will happen* regularly over a period of time.
3 If people *tease/teased* you in a friendly way it is not bullying.
4 Behaviour is not bullying if both people *could agree/agree* that it is OK.
5 If we *see/saw* people teasing a friend we will try to stop them.
6 Teasing isn't a problem unless someone *will feel/feels* unhappy.
7 If you take your ID it will *prove/proved* your age.

3 Complete the sentences with the correct form of the verbs in brackets.

1 If I ....*wanted*........ (want) to look different, I would ....*dye*.......... (dye) my hair bright red!
2 We wouldn't .... (stay) out late unless our parents .... (agree).
3 I would .... (tell) my mum or dad if I .... (have) a problem at school.
4 She wouldn't .... (go) to the party unless her dad .... (drive) her home.
5 If my friend .... (have) a ring in her eyebrow, I'd .... (want) one, too.

4 Complete the second sentence so that it has a similar meaning to the first sentence using the word given.

1 If you don't do your homework, you can't go out tonight.
You can't go out tonight .... UNLESS homework.
2 Jack doesn't behave badly unless he's bored.
Jack doesn't behave badly .... IF bored.
3 My sister can't get a driving licence unless she has driving lessons.
My sister can't get a driving licence IF .... driving lessons.
4 Your teacher wouldn't get angry if you weren't shouting.
Your teacher wouldn't get angry UNLESS .... shouting.

5 Complete the sentences so that they are true for you.

1 If I could meet someone famous, ...
2 If my school abolished homework, ...
3 I would buy my teacher a fantastic present if ....
4 My English would improve if ....
5 I wouldn't go to another country without my family unless ....

Time to talk

6 If you could visit any country in the world, where would you go? Why?

body art

FACT!
Tattooing is a very old art, going back ten thousand years. Tattoos are very popular with sailors. Henna tattoos are temporary, and fade in two or three weeks. Celebrities such as David Beckham and Lena Headey have helped make tattoos into a fashion statement.

Get ideas

1 Why do people have tattoos? Do you know any people with tattoos? Who are they?

Time to listen

1.12 **2** Listen and choose the reason(s) why Julie had a tattoo. Then compare your answers with a partner.

Julie had a tattoo …
1 … because her friends told her to.
2 … because it was fashionable.
3 … because she wanted to remember somebody.
4 … because she likes tattoos.

1.13 **3** You will hear four people talking about tattoos. Listen and match the statements (A–E) with the speakers (1–4). There is one extra statement.

1 Amanda   2 Tony   3 Sandra   4 Dr Armstrong

A Tattoos can cause long-term problems.
B Young people don't realise how dangerous tattoos can be.
C Tattoos can be attractive if done well.
D Young people must decide for themselves and not be influenced by others.
E Only doctors should do tattoos.

SKILL ZONE

Do you need to **match speakers with statements?** First try to understand the main idea. Then choose the speaker you think fits each statement. Finally, listen again for phrases or expressions that confirm your answer.

Get ideas

1 Do you and your friends have the same opinions about: music? school? clothes?
Is it important to have the same opinions as your friends? Why/Why not?

2 Read the conversation and answer the questions. What reasons do Ben and Elena give for ...

1 disliking permanent tattoos: look awful, ...
2 preferring temporary tattoos: look nice, ...

Elena: Well, 1) ~~I really think~~ that girl was silly to have a tattoo of Winnie the Pooh. She's too young and it's huge — it just looks awful.

Ben: 2) .... I don't think it's a good idea to have permanent tattoos. What happens if you change your mind? If you ask me they're a bad idea full stop!

Elena: Exactly! Personally 3) .... those henna tattoos. Some of them look really nice and they're not harmful.

Ben: 4) .... You can try lots of different designs too and see which one you prefer. Hey, why don't we go and get one on Saturday?

Elena: Mmm, 5) .... that's such a good idea. Let's think about it!

3 Think of some more reasons and compare your ideas with a partner.

4 Complete the conversation in Exercise 2 with phrases from Useful phrases.

5 Mark the stressed words (important words) in the conversation in Exercise 2. Then listen and check.

Time to speak

6 Practise the conversation in Exercise 2 with a partner.

SKILL ZONE

Are you giving an opinion? It's a good idea to support your ideas by explaining why you like/dislike something. Always give reasons for agreeing/disagreeing with someone.

7 Choose one of the statements and discuss with a partner.

> Tattoos and piercings are just another way of decorating your body like make-up or clothes.

> Young people only want tattoos because famous people have them.

> Temporary tattoos are better than permanent ones because you can change the design when you change your clothes.

> Some tattoos look cool but it can be difficult to get a good job if you're covered in them.

8 Join up with another pair and continue your conversation. How long can you keep the discussion going?

Useful phrases

Giving your opinion
I'm not sure.
I think ...
I prefer ...
If you ask me ...
I _really_ think ...
I feel _really strongly_ about this.

Agreeing
Yes, you're right.
Exactly!
I agree completely.

Disagreeing
I don't agree.
I don't think ...

Verbs with prepositions

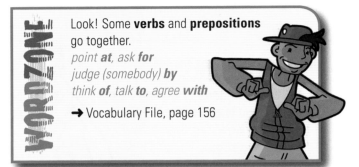

WORDZONE

Look! Some **verbs** and **prepositions** go together.
*point **at**, ask **for***
*judge (somebody) **by***
*think **of**, talk **to**, agree **with***

→ Vocabulary File, page 156

1 Match the verbs with the prepositions.

argue	
look	
talk	at
blame (sb)	for
shout	of
laugh	to
think	by
judge (sb)	with
stare	

2 Choose the correct prepositions to complete the sentences.

1 Nobody ever laughs *for/at* my jokes.
2 I'm going to talk *at/to* her this evening to find out what's wrong.
3 Don't look *to/at* me like that!
4 I try to judge people *for/by* their behaviour and not their appearance.
5 He was so angry he started shouting *to/at* her.
6 I can't think *for/of* one good reason for having a tattoo.
7 Everybody stared *to/at* him when he walked into the room.
8 She blamed her new hairdresser *to/for* her pink hair.

3 Complete the sentences with the correct form of the verbs from Exercise 1.

1 You can't .... your friends for the tattoo when it was your decision.
2 The music was so loud I had to .... at my friends so that they could hear me.
3 What do you .... of my latest idea?
4 I tried to .... to her but she didn't say much.
5 If you .... at my new haircut, I'll kill you!

4 Complete the text with one word which best fits each gap.

Call me what you want but I'm me!

Becci, 15, from England says:
'Some people stare 1) ....at............ me because I don't look like them. My clothes are different and my hair's dyed so they think I'm a troublemaker. Sometimes they blame me 2) .... the problems at school and that's so unfair! Perhaps I dress differently but that doesn't mean I'm a horrible person. I think 3) .... my clothes as a way of expressing my individuality – I don't see why it's such a big thing. The way some people react often surprises me – they laugh 4) .... me and sometimes won't talk 5) .... me in class. Once on the school bus somebody started shouting insults 6) .... me and everybody thought it was funny – I mean, that's really out of order, totally unacceptable. I just want to say that other people won't stop me wearing what I want to wear. It's their problem!'

Sarah, 14, from Scotland, has a different point of view:
I disagree 7) .... Becci. I think she's too angry about people looking at her. If she wears strange black clothes and scary make-up, then people will look 8) .... her because she's different. Personally, I'm just not brave enough to dress like Becci, but I don't want people to judge me 9) .... my appearance!

so, such a, too, not ... enough

GRAMMARZONE

so + adjective/adverb

A emphasises the adjective or adverb
That's so unfair!

such a + adjective + noun

B emphasises the adjective before the noun
I don't see why it's such a big thing.

too + adjective/adverb

C means 'more than is acceptable or possible'
I think she's too angry about people looking at her.

not + adjective/adverb + **enough**

D means 'less than is acceptable or possible'
Personally, I'm just not brave enough to dress like Becci.

→ Grammar File, page 168

1 **Complete the sentences with *so, such* or *such a*.**

1 Becci wears ......**such**........ strange clothes that people laugh at her.
2 It's .... embarrassing when you go to school with a new haircut and everybody stares at you.
3 Dressing in black and putting on lots of weird make-up must be .... good fun.
4 The teacher was .... angry about the bullying that he decided to have a meeting with the parents.
5 The school sees graffiti as .... big problem it's going to start fining parents.
6 You look .... funny in those new clothes – where did you buy them?

2 **Complete the answers to the questions. Use *too* or *not ... enough* and the adjective in brackets.**

1 Do you think seventeen is a good age to learn to drive? No, it's ......**too**.......... (young).
2 Have you seen that new horror film? No, I'm .... (brave).
3 Does she like being the centre of attention? No, she's .... (shy).
4 Can you ride a motorbike? No, I'm .... (old).
5 Do you like my new skirt? No, it's .... (short).
6 Have you finished this exercise? No, it's .... (difficult).

3 **Complete the sentences in your own words.**

1 It's so embarrassing when . . .
2 I had such a good time at . . .
3 I'm not old enough to . . .
4 I'm not brave enough to . . .
5 People think they're so cool when . . .

4 **Complete the second sentence so that it has a similar meaning to the first sentence using the word given.**

1 The concert was so noisy that I left with a headache.   SUCH
It was .... I left with a headache.
2 She's too young to have her nose pierced.   ENOUGH
She's .... to have her nose pierced.
3 That tattoo is so awful!   SUCH
That is ....
4 It was such a difficult exam I knew I'd fail.   SO
The exam .... I knew I'd fail.
5 You speak so quietly I can never hear you on the phone.   SUCH
You're .... I can never hear you on the phone.
6 My books are too big for my bag.   BIG
My bag .... for my books.

5 **Complete the text with *so, such, too, enough*.**

Last week I went to a fair with a friend and a man was doing tattoos. I'm not old 1) .... to have a real tattoo but these were temporary ones. The designs were really pretty and not 2) .... big. I chose to have a small butterfly on my arm and my friend had a flower. It was 3) .... good fun and everybody said they looked like the real thing. When I got home Mum was 4) .... shocked! She thought it was 5) .... good to be a temporary tattoo. If I had another tattoo I'd have some Chinese writing. That would be 6) .... cool!

Time to talk

6 **When are you old enough to do the following? Compare your ideas with a partner.**

- Choose clothes you want to wear.
- Choose who your real friends are.

Get ideas

1 Why do you think people write to magazines? Would you write to a magazine for advice? Who do you usually ask for advice?

2 Read Kate's letter to the Problems column of a magazine. Complete the photo story with these phrases.

Can't she   Can't you   How about   should
shouldn't   stop   Try not to   Why doesn't he

Find the right words

3 Which of these phrases are polite or not polite?

a Stop making a mess.

b My advice would be to tidy up.

c Can't you tidy up?

d You must tidy up.

e How about tidying up?

f Tidy up right now!

g Have you thought of tidying up?

h You could tidy up.

4 Work with a partner. Decide what advice you would give Kate. Write three ideas using polite phrases.

1 You could ....
2 Why don't you ....
3 ....

5 Read Dan's reply and answer the questions.

1 Does his letter use many short forms or full forms?
2 Is the style formal, not very formal or completely informal?
3 Are any of the phrases friendly or unfriendly? Which ones?
4 Is there a difference between the phrases used in the photo story and the phrases in Dan's reply?
5 Was Dan's advice good? Did you think of a better piece of advice?

Plan ahead

6 Read Andy's letter to the Problems column and underline the phrases that describe his problem.

> **Dear Dan,**
> I'm fourteen and two of my closest friends are nearly sixteen. Recently they've started smoking cigarettes in secret, maybe one or two cigarettes a day. They offer me one sometimes and it's hard to say 'no'. I'm worried that they might tease me if I don't join in.
> Andy

Problems

Ask Dan ?

Dear Dan,
Sam, my younger brother, is such a pain! He goes through my things and he even nicks stuff. He's so annoying! Then he tells our mum that I'm being horrible when I catch him. She always takes his side 'coz he's younger than me. (1) Can't she understand that I need my own space sometimes?
Kate

Can I borrow this CD?

You never bring them back, so no.

If she doesn't lend it to me, I'll just have to nick it!

I knew he'd steal it! (2) .... listen to me.

I wish Mum understood me. I'm so fed up.

7 Write what you would do if you were in Andy's situation. Write three or four sentences.

If I were in Andy's situation, I would ___ .

8 You are planning to write a reply to Andy. Choose the statements you agree with.

1 Use formal language.
2 Start your letter in a friendly way.
3 Briefly mention the writer's problem.
4 Show your understanding of the problem and look at it from another person's point of view.
5 Talk about similar problems you have had.
6 Make your letter funny and entertaining.
7 Briefly discuss how to deal with people's reactions.
8 Finish your reply on a positive note!

Time to write *a letter of advice*

9 Write your opening paragraph. Swap with a friend and give your comments.

10 Complete your reply to Andy. Use your ideas from Exercises 8 and 9.

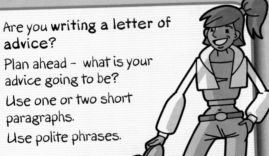

SKILLZONE

Are you writing a letter of advice?

Plan ahead - what is your advice going to be?

Use one or two short paragraphs.

Use polite phrases.

Time to watch *Solving a problem*

11 Watch the DVD and do the activities on page 156.

Next morning ...

Mum, please tell Sam to (3) .... pinching my things.

Oi! That's my diary!

(4) .... be nice, Kate? (5) .... sharing for a change!

Well you (6) .... keep it hidden!

Sam says you shouted at him. (7) .... be horrible!

I can't believe it! He (8) .... take my things. He's the one in the wrong.

Dear Kate,

Thank you for your letter. You sound quite fed up with your brother taking your things! Have you thought of asking your mum to talk to him? You could tell her that you love your brother but that he doesn't always take care of your things.

Also, have you thought about why your brother is doing this? Maybe he is jealous of your CD collection. If he had some more CDs of his own, perhaps he wouldn't borrow yours. Could you and your mum buy him a few CDs for his birthday?

Finally, why don't you talk to your brother, as well? Explain that it's polite to ask first. After all, you don't borrow his things, do you? You could agree to let him borrow one thing if he asks nicely ... . If this doesn't solve the problem, maybe you should put a lock on your bedroom door!

I hope this advice helps you.

Best of luck,

Dan

Get ideas

1 Do you recognise any of these games? What are the most popular computer games for boys/girls in your class?

Time to read

2 Look at the photos and the title of the magazine review on page 63 and answer the questions.

1 What is the review about?
2 Does this game look exciting? Can you guess which one it is?

3 Match the headings (A–F) with the paragraphs (1–6).

A What's bad about it?
B What's good about it?
C Introduction
D Conclusion and recommendation
E Why choose this to review?
F Background and more detailed description

4 Read the text and decide if the statements are true (T) or false (F).

1 The review is about a very popular game.
2 Many computer games require speed and attention.
3 Game testers liked Will's first idea for *The Sims*.
4 *The Sims'* characters are very predictable.
5 The reviewer dislikes teaching Sims what to do.
6 The majority of *Sims* players are male.

5 Find words in the text that match these meanings.

1 having many different uses (line 9)
2 the aim that you try hard to achieve (line 14)
3 involving communication between a computer or TV and the person using it (line 16)
4 a person who loves reading (line 22)
5 to react to something (line 34)
6 a group of things that are different, but of the same general type (line 39)

SKILL ZONE Do you need to focus on specific information? It's a good idea to underline key words in the questions and look for similar information in the text. Ignore any extra facts that don't relate to the question.

Summarise

Explain in your own words:
- What is different about *The Sims*?
  The Sims is different from other games because …
- What *The Sims* do: *The Sims …*
- The reviewer's opinion of The Sims.
  The reviewer likes … but …

Time to talk

6 Have you ever played *The Sims*? Was it fun? In your opinion, what makes a good computer game?

◻◻▷ GAMES

The game that made history

▷ **1** Action and excitement, thrills and challenges: surely these are the ingredients that keep everybody hooked on computer games? Wrong! One of the best-selling computer games has none of these ingredients. Have you ever enjoyed putting out the rubbish? What about sleeping or studying?
5 It all sounds really dull, but that's what you get in this game. In case you haven't guessed yet, I'm talking about *The Sims*. In fact the publishers didn't think it would sell very well, but they were wrong! *The Sims* has sold several million copies worldwide since it came out in 2000. Of course, part of the reason for this is that computer games have become more popular. Now they're very versatile: you can
10 play *The Sims* online or use a portable console to play anywhere, anytime. I've had a console for about a year now, and it's definitely my favourite hobby!

2 To understand why I chose to review *The Sims*, you need to know a bit about the history of computer games. Most of my friends like traditional games which involve sports or battles. In these games the objective is clear: you win by scoring more
15 points than your opponent. You need fast reactions and good concentration, too, as most games are very interactive and respond to lots of different input from the user. Games have changed a lot over the past few years. Now most action-packed films, like *Harry Potter* and *Lord of the Rings*, exist as computer games. Why? Because good games usually need a hero and a battle between good and evil.
20 However, none of these ideas influenced Will Wright, the man who created *The Sims*. He wanted to create a 'real' world.

3 As a boy, Will was a quiet, intelligent bookworm who wanted to be an astronaut. He still collects robots and pieces of space equipment! Will's interest in unusual things eventually led him to games design. *The Sims* began when Will created a
25 game to design a dream home with beautiful graphics. When players tested it, they were disappointed that there was no-one to live in the homes, so Will created little people for this new world. The game testers loved it and so *The Sims* was born. There are loads of different Sims games, but the best version I've ever played is *The Sims 2*, because the artificial intelligence makes the characters even more real.

30 **4** I would recommend this game for lots of different reasons. My sister and I love it because you can create characters who look like you and your friends. We've just made a Sim who looks like my teacher! In many ways Sims are just like real people. You can even programme their personalities, but their moods can change, so one Sim may respond differently each time you play.

35 **5** My only criticism of *The Sims* is that you need a lot of patience. Sims are very hard to train – you have to wake them up and make them work and teach them to clean their homes. They don't always do what you want.

6 I would like to summarise by adding that one of *The Sims'* best features is the ability to create your own 'story' world, with a huge range of characters. This might
40 be why around 60 percent of Sims players are girls and women. In fact, *The Sims* is so popular that people say Will Wright has completely changed computer gaming. If you haven't already played this game, you should definitely try it! ■

Coming up ... *Computer games* on DVD. See page 71.

Computers and the internet

1 Decide whether these words from the review on page 63 are nouns (n) or adjectives (a). Then complete the definitions.

1 best-selling ..a.. something which …
..is very popular...

2 online ..... connected to ....

3 portable ..... something which ....

4 console ..... an electronic device which
....

5 input ..... information which ....

6 graphics ..... the pictures and designs
....

7 game-testers ..... people who ....

8 artificial ..... something which ....

2 Label the computer with these words.

keyboard   laptop   memory stick   mouse   screen

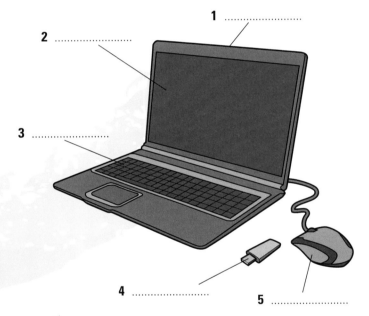

3 Complete the sentences with words from Exercises 1 and 2.

1 A laptop computer is .... because it's small and light.

2 The .... on a Gameboy console is about 5x7 centimetres.

3 We usually use a .... to input information into a computer.

4 Computers also have a .... to move around the screen and click on information.

5 Some .... spend several hours a day in front of a screen.

6 If you want to send an email, you need to go .... first.

WORDZONE

Look! You can put two words together to make **compound nouns and adjectives**!

A **game** that you play on **computer** is a *computer game* (n)

Something that is **friendly** to **users** is *user-friendly* (adj)

Something you **hold** in your **hand** is *hand-held* (adj)

→ Vocabulary File, page 157

4 Complete the text with compound words. Use these adjectives to help you.

built   hand   hi   old   touch   user   well   wide

Computers have been around for over sixty years and they have changed our lives. It is a 1) ....well.........-**known** fact that the first modern computer, ENIAC (electronic numerical integrator and computer), began operating in the USA in 1945. This huge machine was the size of a large room. It was also very slow and so complicated to use that only an expert could operate it. That's very different from modern PCs which are so 2) .... -**friendly** that anyone can use them.

During the 1970s, tiny electronic microchips became more common. By the 1980s and 90s, home computers were becoming smaller, faster and cheaper. As a result, more people bought them, so computers became more 3) ....**spread**.

Since then, new developments have made the first PCs look 4) ....-**fashioned**. The latest consoles are small and portable. Modern computers also often have 5) ....-**sensitive** screens, so you don't need a mouse or keyboard, you just touch the screen.

New mobile phones are much more 6) ....-**tech** than ones even just a few years old, so they can do a lot more than make calls and send text messages. In the 1970s no one could imagine computers small enough to carry, but now, 7) ....-**held** devices with internet access are very common. These gadgets often include tiny 8) ....-**in** keyboards that are part of the structure. You can download music or send and receive emails wherever you are!

Memorise

In groups: Choose the most difficult **computer words** (Group A) or **compound nouns or adjectives** (Group B). Write a list and close your books. Take it in turns to call out a word for the other team to spell on the board. The group with the most correct words is the winner.

Past simple and present perfect simple

GRAMMARZONE

Past simple

A for an action that finished at a definite point in the past
The Sims came out in 2000.

Present perfect simple

B for a past action, if we are not interested in when it happened
Games have changed a lot over the past few years.

Present perfect with adverbs

C *just* for very recent events
We've just made a new Sim!

D *yet* for something we expect to happen
Haven't you guessed yet?

E *already* for something that has happened before now
I've already bought the latest Sims game.

F *since* refers to a point in time
This game has sold several million copies since 2000.

G *for* refers to a period of time
I've had a console for about a year.

H *ever* and *never* for 'any time up to now'
Have you ever enjoyed putting out the rubbish?
(No, I've never enjoyed doing that!)

→ Grammar File, page 169

1 Find other examples of the present perfect in the review on page 63 and match them with the grammar points in the Grammarzone.

2 Put the conversation in the correct order. Write PS (past simple) or PP (present perfect) next to each line.

a ..1.. Have you used a computer recently? PP

b ..... My parents haven't used one, but my grandad has. .....

c ..... Yes, I have. I used one at school. .....

d ..... Oh. Did he enjoy it? .....

e ..... What did you use it for? .....

f ..... Have your parents or grandparents ever used a computer? .....

g ..... Yes. He played a racing game and he loved it. Now he wants a console of his own! .....

h ..... I did some research for a project. .....

3 Complete the texts with the correct form (past simple or present perfect simple) of the verbs in brackets.

▼ **Messages**
Displaying all messages   See all

Dear Henry,
We 1) have just bought (just/buy) our first computer! I 2) .... (already/use) it to do my homework, but I 3) .... (not/play) any games on it yet! My problem is that yesterday I 4) .... (want) to buy a computer game, but my parents refused. They say these games are a waste of time. How can I persuade them to change their minds?
Jimmy

Dear Jimmy,
5) .... (your parents/ever/play) a computer game? Maybe that would persuade them! Perhaps they think games are for teenagers? Actually I 6) .... (just/read) an article that says the biggest group of gamers are aged between twenty-five and thirty-four!
People who are worried about the content of games should check the age ratings on the box. All the big games companies 7) .... (use) this system for years as it follows common guidelines, similar to those on DVDs.
Finally, you can tell your parents that scientists 8) .... (do) lots of research on this subject. A few years ago, one study 9) .... (show) that 'Gamers were more successful academically,' i.e., they often did better at school. The report also 10) .... (say) that gaming is 'as rich an experience as reading a book and … a more challenging activity than watching TV'.
I hope that helps!
Henry

Post

Time to talk

4 Have you/your parents/your grandparents ever used a computer? When and why? Is your attitude to computers different from your parents' or grandparents'?

'Why don't we ...?'

Get ideas

1 Have you done any of these things recently? When? Who with? How much do you enjoy doing these activities?

Fantastic

go to the cinema?

read magazines?

play board games?

listen to music?

play a sport?

Terrible

Time to listen

1.15 **2** Put the words and phrases into the correct column. Then listen to conversation 1. Which words and phrases do you hear?

action-packed amazing awful boring cool
don't mind good hate love maybe
not keen why not? can't stand

Fantastic	OK	Terrible
action-packed	don't mind	awful

1.16 **3** Listen to conversation 1 again and choose the best answer, A, B or C.

1 What is Anya's reaction to the idea of staying in?
  A She doesn't mind.
  B She's not very interested.
  C She thinks it's a good suggestion.

2 What is Jack's opinion of *Spiderman* films?
  A He thinks they're exciting.
  B He's fed up with them.
  C He says they're OK.

1.17 **4** Listen to conversation 2. For each question, choose the best answer, A, B or C.

1 You hear a girl talking to her sister. What are they doing?
  A suggesting **B** apologising **C** arguing

2 What is Carla's opinion of chess?
  A She dislikes it.
  B She thinks it's a good game.
  C She says it's OK.

1.18 **5** Listen to conversation 3. For each question, choose the best answer, A, B or C.

1 You hear a father and son talking. What is the father's attitude to his son's music?
  A He hates that music.
  B He's fed up with the noise.
  C He wants to know what it is.

2 The son reads a film review. What is the reviewer's opinion of the film?
  A excited **B** disappointed **C** bored

SKILL ZONE Do you need to answer questions about situations, attitudes and opinions? Read the questions and the options first. Then listen for the words, phrases and tone of voice that are similar to one of the options.

Get ideas

 Look at the findings of a recent survey.

- Can you think of any reasons for these results?
- As a class, find out who prefers going out and who prefers staying in.
- Are the results for your class similar to the survey?

Age	prefer going out	prefer staying at home
10-12	15%	85%
13-15	25%	75%
16-18	50%	50%
18+	80%	20%

Time to speak

2 **Work in groups. Ask and answer questions about going out or staying in. Use the ideas below to help you.**

- Do you prefer …?
- Why do you like …?
- What sort of things do you like doing …?

Reasons for going out

You can wear nice clothes.
You can see larger groups of friends.
You can go somewhere different.
It's more exciting.
You can't stay at home all the time.

Reasons for staying in

You don't need to dress up.
You can see one or two friends.
It's easy to organise.
It's more relaxing.
There are no crowds.

Adjectives to show your opinion

Good
amazing cool entertaining fantastic fascinating fun funny great interesting stunning

Bad
awful boring disappointing dull revolting terrible weird

3 **Complete the quiz for yourself. Then ask and answer the questions with a partner. Make a note of your partner's answers.**

A Have you been out with friends? **B** Yes, I have.

What have you done since last Saturday?

1 be / out with friends?
2 play / a game indoors?
3 see / a film?
4 watch / TV?
5 use / the internet?
6 read / a book or magazine?
7 do / sport?
8 listen / music?

4 **Ask specific questions about something your partner has done. Find out as much extra information as you can.**

- When / Where did you go / see / play it?
- What did you see / read / play?
- Who did you go with?
- What was it about / like?
- How long was it / did you …?
- What did you think of it?

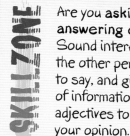

SKILLZONE
Are you asking and answering questions? Sound interested in what the other person has to say, and give plenty of information. Use adjectives to show your opinion.

Useful phrases

Really?   Oh!   Right!
It sounds cool!   Did/Didn't you?

Order of adjectives

WORDZONE

Do you want to use **more than one adjective** to describe a noun? Put them in this order:

your opinion *dynamic / exciting / expensive*
size *huge / tall / wide*
shape *round / square / moon-shaped*
age *modern / old / teenage*
colour *yellow / silver*
nationality *English / Greek / Polish*
material *leather / metal*

*Nadia Vole has a **blank**, **moon-shaped** face.*
*It's a **fast**, **modern** computer.*

→ Vocabulary File, page 157

1 Complete the sentences with the adjectives in brackets in their correct order.

1 Alex Rider is wearing a ....
.... jacket. (black / cool / leather)
2 He's got ....
.... hair. (blond / untidy / long)
3 He's riding a ....
quad bike. (metal / silver and black)

2 Write two sentences about Nadia Vole. Use two or three adjectives in each sentence and some ideas of your own.

Nadia Vole is ... . She is wearing ... .

modern   neat   elegant   mean   ugly   (un)fashionable
(un)friendly   short   tall   long   dark   blond(e)   red
black   grey

3 Read the report below and choose the best answer, A, B, C or D.

	A	B	C	D
1	cheerful	comfortable	careful	correct
2	fresh	young	new	fast
3	just	yet	already	since
4	cool	freezing	icy	cold
5	active	energetic	dramatic	interactive
6	never	ever	always	usually
7	frightened	scary	terrified	afraid
8	online	hi-tech	input	microchip
9	everyday	normal	common	plain
10	just	yet	already	since
11	just	yet	already	since

4 Read the report again and underline places where the author uses more than one adjective.

BOOKS v. FILMS

Are you a bookworm? I love staying at home and sitting in a big 1) .B.. armchair with a good book. Some books can take you to a different world with amazing 2) ..... characters.

However, I've changed my mind about books 3) ...... I saw *Operation Stormbreaker*. It's an action-packed thriller with a dynamic teenage hero played by Alex Pettyfer – he's really 4) ..... ! I've decided that films are much more 5) ..... than books!

I've already read the book of the film twice, but a few of my friends have 6) ..... read it! The main plot involves a teenage spy, Alex Rider, and several villains. My favourite is Nadia Vole, who has 'a strangely blank, moon-shaped face' and wire-framed spectacles. I was disappointed because in the film she is not quite so 7) ..... ! The main villain, Mr Sayle, wants to give an expensive, 8) ..... 'Stormbreaker' computer to every school in the country. These computers are '9) ..... black with a white lightning bolt down one side'. Alex has 10) ..... switched on a Stormbreaker when he notices its speed and power, but unfortunately every Stormbreaker contains a deadly virus … but I don't want to spoil the story in case you haven't seen it 11) ..... !

Nadia Vole

Countable and uncountable nouns; quantifiers

GRAMMAR ZONE

Countable nouns

A Most nouns are countable. Individual objects, people or ideas can have a singular and plural form.
Operation Stormbreaker is a thriller . . .
There are several villains.

Uncountable nouns

B Things we think of as a single mass and abstract ideas. There is no plural form for uncountable nouns.
Alex notices the computer's speed and power.
His advice was very useful.

Quantifiers

C use *much, a little, a bit of* with uncountable nouns only

D use *some, any, a lot of, lots of, plenty of* with countable and uncountable nouns

E use *many, a few (of), several* with countable nouns only

→ Grammar File, page 169

1 **Choose the correct word to complete each sentence.**

1 How *much/many* time do you spend watching TV?
2 I've bought *a little/a few* good computer games this year.
3 We often listen to *several/a bit of* music in the evening.
4 I need *some/many* paper to write a story.
5 I've got *plenty of/much* CDs, so you can borrow some.
6 I don't need *an/any* advice. I know what I want.
7 There's *a lot/much* of traffic today.
8 *Is/Are* there any information about the accident?

2 **Complete the text with these words.**

a advice an any few fun lots many
paper people plenty several some

How 1) ......*many*...... people want to write? Loads. But only a 2) .... of them actually become writers. Are there any reasons for this? We spent 3) .... time with the author of Stormbreaker, Anthony Horowitz, and asked him 4) .... of questions. He made 5) .... suggestions to help young writers.

· ·

Interviewer: Do you have 6) .... tips for would-be writers?

A H: This is something I'm asked quite often and my 7) .... is fairly simple: 1 The more you read, the better you'll write. The more you write, the better you'll write. 2 Believe in yourself. The only difference between 8) .... successful writer and 9) .... unsuccessful writer is that the unsuccessful writer gives up. 3 Have 10) .... ! You need something to write about, so make sure you have 11) .... of experience. Travel. Meet 12) .... Do irresponsible things. If you sit in a dark room staring at a piece of 13) .... you'll only be able to write about someone who sits in a dark room staring at a piece of paper.'

3 **Choose the word or phrase (A, B, C or D) that best completes the sentence.**

FACT FILE

1 Anthony Horowitz has written .... popular novels for teenagers.
   A many   **B** lots   **C** any   **D** a little
2 When he was younger, Anthony and his mother didn't have .... money.
   A some   **B** a bit of   **C** plenty   **D** much
3 Aged 18, Anthony travelled the world and had .... of adventures.
   A several   **B** lots   **C** a few   **D** some
4 Anthony writes with an old-fashioned pen so he needs .... ink.
   A much   **B** any   **C** several   **D** plenty of
5 If Anthony has .... spare time, he plays the piano.
   A any   **B** much   **C** many   **D** a few

Time to talk

4 **Would you like to be a writer? What would you write about? Do you prefer to go and watch a film or stay in and read a book?**

Get ideas

 1 Which of these books would you choose to read? Why? Can you match the books (A–C) to these genres (types of book)?

Action/adventure   Horror/ghost stories   Non-fiction
Romance   Science fiction   Spy story   Thriller

A — PENGUIN READERS — The Strange Case of Dr Jekyll and Mr Hyde — Robert Louis Stevenson

B — PENGUIN READERS — Girl Meets Boy — Derek Strange

C — PENGUIN READERS — 2001: A Space Odyssey — Arthur C. Clarke

Find the right words

 2 Read the writing task and the reviews that two students, Adam and Natasha, wrote. Answer the questions.

1 Which are the key points in the task?
2 Which review included all the key points?
3 Which book, *Stormbreaker* or *Clean Break*, would you choose to read? Why?

> You have agreed to write a review of a book for the entertainment section of an international student magazine.
> Describe the book you have chosen, and say what the strengths and weaknesses are. Write your review in 120–180 words.

 3 Adam and Natasha have organised their reviews differently. Which of them does best in each of these areas?

1 using good linking phrases
2 arranging paragraphs
3 describing their chosen title
4 answering the question fully

 4 Find the adjectives used in each review and answer the questions.

1 Which writer uses adjectives to describe plot and characters?
2 Which writer does not repeat any adjectives?

what's **HOT**

BOOKS

Stormbreaker
by Anthony Horowitz

Do you enjoy mystery or horror books, thrillers and spy stories? If so, you'll love this series.
The main character is a boy called Alex who has just discovered that his uncle, Ian Rider, is dead. In the first book, Alex is 14, and a whole series of strange events begins as he becomes a spy. Alex has been brought up by his

uncle, but he begins to realise a strange fact – how little he actually knew about his uncle. Moreover, when he finds his uncle's car there is something very mysterious about it.

Alex desperately wants to find out more about the circumstances of Ian Rider's death. As a result, when secret spies from MI6 meet him and offer to train

him, he takes up their offer. In spite of his worries, he agrees to go to Stormbreaker headquarters – where he meets the mysterious Nadia Vole – is she a friend … or perhaps a deadly enemy? Do you want to find out what happens to Alex? Buy or borrow this book now – I strongly recommend it!

(Adam, 13)

what'sHOT

BOOKS

Clean Break
by Jacqueline Wilson

Jacqueline Wilson is a famous British children's author. In 2005 she became the 'children's laureate', a job which involves meeting children and encouraging them to read. I borrowed *Clean Break* from our class library to discover why she's so popular.

I thought it might be rather young for me as it's for 12–14 year-olds. However, the book deals with family problems and relationships, so it was quite interesting. The main character, Em, worries about her mother and father. She tries to be optimistic, but the problems at home affect her badly. Will her problems have a happy ending?

I haven't read many books about such personal problems and I thought this was a strength of the book. I got an idea of other people's lives and it made me think how I would deal with those problems. The biggest weakness is that boys wouldn't enjoy this book.

Most of the story seemed quite realistic. It was easy to read and there was plenty of humour, so I would definitely recommend it to anyone!

(Natasha, 14)

Plan ahead

5 **Decide what your review will be about. With a partner, answer these questions.**

1 Which book, film or game would be most interesting to write about?
2 Which do you know most about?
3 Do you have strong feelings (good or bad) about any of them?

6 **Make notes for each paragraph of your review.**

Para 1 A brief introduction and background, including the genre (type) and reasons you chose to review this particular title.

Para 2 A description of the main characters and their relationships to one another.

Para 3 A summary of the plot/game, including strengths and weaknesses.

Para 4 A personal opinion and summary of who else might like to read, see or play it.

7 **Discuss your plan with a partner.**

Time to write *a review*

8 **Write your review for the task in Exercise 2 on page 70.**

SKILL ZONE

Are you writing a review?
Read the task carefully and make sure you understand the relevant points.
Start by making some notes.
Organise your work – use a new paragraph for each main topic.
Use linking words and phrases.

Time to watch *Computer games*

9 **Watch the DVD and do the exercises on page 157.**

Vocabulary

1 Choose the correct word to complete the sentences.

1 It's *responsible/<u>legal</u>* for ten-year-olds to choose their own religion.
2 It's *illegal/dishonest* for a thirteen-year-old to drive a car.
3 A judge may send someone to *prison/court* as a punishment.
4 A *court/fine* is a punishment for breaking the law.
5 At eighteen you have the *right/law* to get married.
6 Bullies are often *illegal/immature*.
7 A judge makes decisions in *court/prison*.

2 Match the parts of a computer (a–d) with the uses (1–4).

a keyboard   **b** memory stick   **c** mouse   **d** screen

1 to move around and select information by clicking on it
2 to show pictures and information
3 to input information into the computer
4 to save information or move it from one computer to another

3 Complete the emails with the correct prepositions. You may use some more than once.

at   for   of   to   with

From: Evi To: Dan
Subject: Friends

Dear Dan,

Do you think it's OK to argue 1) ....with........ your friends? I often ask 2) .... my best friend's opinion on my clothes or CDs. I like to know what she thinks 3) .... my things, but sometimes she disagrees with me about what is good!

Of course we don't shout 4) .... each other, but I sometimes I worry that we have such different opinions!

Evi

From: Dan To: Evi
Subject: Re: Friends

Dear Evi,

It can be quite healthy to argue. You can't agree 5) .... your friend all the time! I'm sure you don't blame her 6) .... expressing her opinion, do you? Maybe you should talk 7) .... each other about it.

Dan

4 Write the negative of these words. Use the correct prefix *dis-, il-, in-, im-, ir-, in-*. Then complete the sentences with a suitable word (positive or negative).

.....agree   .....legal   .....secure   .....mature   .....obey
.....regular   .....patient   .....logical   .....dependent
.....responsible

1 I'm sorry, I really ....*disagree*.... with what you're saying.
2 Adam is my older brother but he's so .... he acts like a five-year-old!
3 Kate is very .... so she likes to organise her own life.
4 I always do my homework in a hurry because I'm so ....
5 That shop opens at .... times, so you never know if it will be open.
6 If you .... the teacher you'll get into trouble.
7 This Maths problem doesn't make sense, it's ....
8 If people tease you it can make you feel ....
9 Luke is really .... You can't rely on him.
10 In some countries smoking is .... in public places.

5 Complete the notice with the correct prepositions.

at   in   on   out   with

Rules for
success
in the gym

Always believe 1) ..*in*.. yourself.

Learn to laugh 2) ...... your mistakes.

Carry 3) ...... with your practice session, even if people are watching.

You need to learn how to deal 4) .... having an audience.

Your trainer will help you to sort 5) ...... any problems.

Grammar

6 Match the beginnings (1–6) with the endings (a–f).

1 If characters are predictable,   **a** you'll get headaches.
2 If *The Sims* is popular,   **b** you'll love *Sims 2 Pets*.
3 If you don't have a rest,   **c** it's because girls like it, too.
4 If I bought a new computer,   **d** I would buy a laptop.
5 If I had only one computer game,   **e** you know what they do.
6 If you like computer games,   **f** it would be *The Sims*.

7 Write sentences using *too* and *not … enough*.

1 Teacher (he): strict / kind when we forget our homework.
   My teacher is too strict when we forget our homework. He isn't kind enough when we forget our homework.
2 Friend (she): shy / confident to speak in class.
3 Brother: scared of the dark / brave to sleep without a light on.
4 Sister's hairstyle: weird / acceptable, so the teacher sent her home.
5 I: young / old to drive a car.

8 Write sentences using *so* or *such a*.

1 Sam's got / weird / tattoo.
   Sam's got such a weird tattoo!
2 Joe's pierced nose looked / silly / that we laughed at him.
3 Jenny was wearing / strange dress.
4 Mike's hair was / long / that his dad cut it.

9 It's 8.05p.m. Look at Jim's notes and write about what he's done today.

Go to karate class. ✓
Finish English homework. ✓
Watch Science programme 7.30–8.00pm. ✓
Send email to Richard. ✗
Do Maths homework ✗
Pack school bag for tomorrow ✓
Phone Gran at 8p.m. ✓

already
1 Jim has already been to karate class.
2 ....
3 ....

just
4 ....
5 ....

not / yet
6 ....
7 ....

10 Write sentences. Put the words in the correct order.

1 My granddad / old / man. / an / unusual / is
   My granddad is an unusual old man.
2 white / hair. / long / got / He's
3 sunglasses. / He / wears / cool / often / Italian
4 French / jacket. / He's / expensive / got / an / leather
5 noisy / rides / a /ancient / black / motorbike. / He

11 Complete the text with one word which best fits each gap.

Have you 1) ....ever.......... wondered if there are any good websites for young people? We 2) .... found some sites which will keep you entertained for hours.

Runescape >>
If you like solving problems you 3) .... love this website. It's a virtual world full of fascinating places, so you'll never get bored! But beware. Some of the tasks are 4) .... difficult that they're almost impossible! Don't stop trying though – there are lots of exciting things to find! If you need help, you can talk 5) .... friends online, too!

Newsround >>
Just go online to learn the latest fascinating facts from around the world. Also, if you miss the TV news you 6) .... be able to download the latest podcasts to watch programmes on your computer. There's lots to read, as well. In fact, we think there are 7) .... many articles and not 8) .... video clips or games.

Marapets >>
9) .... you want some pets of your own, try this website. The activities are 10) .... fun that you might spend hours on this site. You can even invent your own pets of all shapes and sizes. You can also 11) .... emails to your mates using the website.

Remember! Have you asked 12) .... permission to use a website? Always check with an adult first.

Did you remember all the vocabulary and grammar points?

→ Vocabulary File, pages 156 and 157
→ Grammar File, pages 168 and 169

7 # Horrible history

Get ideas

 1 Do you enjoy watching films about people from history? Have you seen any films about pirates? What do you think life was like for pirates?

Time to read

 2 Read the article on page 75 and match the topics (A–D) with the correct paragraphs (1–4).

A Who chose to be pirates?   B Food and drink
C Life on a pirate ship   D Free time

 3 Read the text again and choose the best answer, A, B, C or D.

1 What is a pirate's life like in films?
   A It's romantic.
   B It's fun.
   C It's hard.
   D It's dangerous.

2 What did pirates do with their treasure?
   A They hid it.
   B They kept it.
   C They sold it.
   D They gave it away.

3 Why was the food so bad?
   A Because the rats had eaten it.
   B Because it didn't taste of anything.
   C Because there wasn't much of it.
   D Because it wasn't cooked very well.

4 When did the pirates find the animals on board?
   A After leaving the ports.
   B On their way to the ports.
   C Before leaving the ports.
   D During their stay in a ports.

5 Why were pirates bored on board ship?
   A Because the voyages were very long.
   B Because there was nothing to do.
   C Because they wanted to rob more ships.
   D Because they didn't like sewing.

6 What did pirates say when they got home?
   A That they had tried to escape.
   B That they had had a good time and made money.
   C That they had met exciting people.
   D That they had had a hard time.

 4 Match the words in the text to the correct definition.

1 people who kill other people (line 7)
2 valuable stones (line 10)
3 the end of someone's life (line 12)
4 very dirty (line 15)
5 liquid that comes through your skin when you are very hot (line 16)
6 old and in bad condition (line 22)
7 producing something that can kill you or make you ill if you touch it or eat it (line 28)
8 a computer system that shows you where to go (line 32)
9 used a needle and thread to make something (line 35)
10 coloured substances you put on your face (line 38)

Summarise

In your own words, describe:
• life on a pirate ship *Life on a pirate ship was …*
• the food and drink *Pirates ate … they didn't eat …*
• what pirates did *When they weren't working, pirates …*

Time to talk

5 What was the best/worst thing about life as a pirate? Would you choose to be a pirate if you lived in the past?

Historical truth or
HOLLYWOOD FICTION?

1 **P**irates of the Caribbean is a great film, but don't believe everything you see about the life of an eighteenth-century pirate! The filmmakers clearly hadn't studied history before they made the film. In the
05 film, a pirate's life seems exciting and Johnny Depp looks romantic, but in real life pirates weren't romantic at all, they were robbers and murderers. They attacked ships, killed sailors and took anything valuable. And it's no good looking for hidden treasure, because as soon as they
10 got into port, they sold the jewels or gold they had stolen. A pirate's life involved danger, violence and an early death, so perhaps it was a bit too exciting at times. It was certainly a hard life, because pirate ships weren't like the luxury cruise ships we see nowadays in the Caribbean.
15 Three hundred years ago ships were filthy and cramped. The smell of human sweat on board ship was unimaginable. There wasn't much privacy, there weren't any toilets and lots of pirates had stomach problems!
2 Pirates often suffered from stomachache because of
20 their terrible food. There wasn't any choice, there wasn't very much and what they had was usually dry and tasteless or rotten. Fresh water was a luxury and fresh fruit was definitely not on the menu. Often, when the cook went to the cupboard he found that rats had eaten most of
25 the food. Some ships had thousands of rats on board and they were hungry! Rats weren't the only travelling companions. When they left the tropical ports, sailors often found that snakes, poisonous spiders and scorpions had come with them and everyone had fleas.

Menu
~~Pizza~~ Rotten fish or meat
~~Fresh fruit~~ Biscuits with insects

30 **3** When they weren't robbing other ships, pirates had time – and lots of it. Without twenty-first century technology such as satellite navigation to plan the route and DVDs to entertain you, voyages were long and boring. Pirates who had finished their work sat around,
35 played cards and sewed. By the time they got home most had become experts at making their own clothes! They probably didn't look as good as Johnny Depp with his high boots and exotic make-up but many liked to look smart when they weren't on board ship.
40 **4** Life at sea was hard, boring, dangerous and dirty, so why did men choose to become pirates? In the 1700s, life on land was just as bad. A pirate's life probably sounded exciting. When they got home pirates told stories of how
45 they had been visiting beautiful places and having lots of adventures. They had stolen treasure and now they were rich. That probably sounded attractive to poor young men
50 who had been working on farms for very little money. You won't learn much about the life of an eighteenth-century pirate
55 from Johnny Depp!

FACTS >>

As early as AD 100, the Greek historian Plutarch described pirates as those who illegally attacked ships and maritime cities.

- -

Pirates received money if they lost a body part. They got most money if they lost their right arm or leg.

- -

Modern pirates exist and they use mobile phones and speedboats to follow larger ships.

Coming up … *Pirate legends* on DVD. See page 83.

Dates and times

1 Match the time expressions (1–8) with the definitions (a–h).

1	a century	a	before the birth of Christ
2	AD	b	from 1600 to 1699
3	a decade	c	a thousand years
4	BC	d	a hundred years
5	a millennium	e	more than one century
6	a fortnight	f	ten years
7	the 1600s	g	after the birth of Christ
8	centuries	h	two weeks

2 Complete the table.

Ordinal numbers

1st	first	11th	
2nd		12th	twelfth
3rd		13th	
4th		14th	
5th	fifth	15th	
6th		16th	
7th		17th	
8th		18th	
9th		19th	
10th	tenth	20th	

VOXAZONE

Do you want to **write dates**? Write:
17th May 1905/17 May 1905
23rd April 2001/23 April 2001
the 1950s, the 1700s

Do you want to **say dates**? Say:
The *seventeenth of May nineteen-oh-five*
The *twenty-third of April, two thousand and one*
The nineteen fifties, the seventeen hundreds

→ Vocabulary File, page 158

3 Practise saying the dates.
1 19 July
2 1900s
3 5 January 1922
4 15/04/1937
5 1920s
6 3 March 1941

4 Ask and answer the questions with a partner.
1 What is the date tomorrow?
2 What will be the date in three days' time?
3 What is your date of birth?
4 Think of a date in history. Why is it important?

5 Complete the sentences with the correct preposition.
1 Children had to work very hard *in/on* the Middle Ages.
2 The ship left *in/on* 12 May 1756.
3 He went to France *in/on* 1802.
4 Children worked on ships *in/on* the 1600s.
5 Pirates sailed the Caribbean *between/from* 1620 to 1740.
6 The pirate Morgan controlled Port Royal *during/for* fifteen years.

6 Find the time expressions in these sentences.
1 The word pirate (peirato) dates <u>from about 140 BC</u>.
2 The pirates sometimes went back to their families at the end of a voyage.
3 The pirates arrived on the island in 1705 and left it four years later.
4 In the mid 1700s pirates didn't have the advantages of twenty-first century medicine.
5 Until the end of the eighteenth century, ships had no scientific method of calculating distance.
6 Injured pirates received financial help decades before sailors did.
7 The pirates hated the captain and in the end they forced him to leave the ship.

7 Complete the sentences in your own words. Use a suitable time expression.
1 Schools .... are much better than they were ....
2 I can't imagine what life was like ....
3 There weren't any computers ....
4 In the .... people used horses not cars.
5 I started school in ....
6 People didn't write emails ....
7 Mobile phones became popular ....

Memorise

How many **time expressions** can you remember? Write a list and compare with a partner.

Past perfect simple and continuous

GRAMMARZONE

Past perfect simple

A an action that happened before another action in the past
Pirates who had finished their work, sat around and played cards or sewed.

Past	↓		↓	Now
◄	finished their work		sat around and … played cards	▼

Past perfect continuous

B an action that was in progress in the past before another action happened or interrupted it
Pirates recruited poor young men who had been working on farms for little or no money.

Past		↓	Now
◄—had been working —►		recruited	▼

→ Grammar File, page 170

1 **Find which took place first in each sentence.**

1 The ship <u>had left</u> by the time the young pirates arrived at the harbour.
2 The chef had been preparing the Captain's dinner when he suddenly fell ill.
3 The Captain said that when the storm started he'd been reading his map.
4 It was obvious the young boys hadn't been eating much because they were so thin.
5 He couldn't eat any cake because the rats had eaten it.
6 The pirates fell asleep quickly because they had worked so hard.

2 **Complete the sentences with the correct form of the verbs.**

1 When the Captain *arrived/had arrived*, the pirates *had played/had been playing* music for nearly an hour.
2 The men *had done/had been cleaning* the ship all morning and still *hadn't finished/didn't finish* it when the Captain *had come/came* to inspect it.
3 When John *woke up/had woken up* he couldn't remember if he *had had/had* a dream about his family at home.
4 At the end of the evening they *were/had been* really tired because they *have danced/had been dancing* all night.
5 The voyage was cancelled but David *had already decided/already decided* he *didn't want/hadn't wanted* to be a pirate.

3 **Complete the text with the correct form (past perfect simple or continuous) of the verbs in brackets.**

A pirate's dream

Patrick 1) ...*had been dreaming*... (dream) about food when he suddenly woke up. In his dream he 2) .... (work) hard. For dinner he 3) .... (eat) two large plates of hot sausages and potatoes. A waiter 4) .... (bring) him two bowls of ice cream and chocolate sauce. Then he had 5) .... (say) something to Patrick and that was when he 6) .... (wake up). Next to him was a plate of food that smelled horrible. It 7) .... (be) a terrible dream.

4 **Complete the sentences with your ideas. Use the correct form of the past perfect simple or continuous.**

1 She didn't do her homework because ....
2 He didn't play in the basketball match because ....
3 Before they came to the party they ....
4 By the time his parents arrived home ....
5 We were really cold when we finally got on the bus because ....
6 When I woke up this morning it was all white outside because ....

Time to talk

5 **What do you know about life in the eighteenth century? What are the best things about life in the twenty-first century?**

Messages from the past

Get ideas

1 What are the people in the photo doing? Why? Are the objects similar to things we use today?

2 Match the words with the photos.

bone   coins   pottery   jewellery
skull   teeth   tools   weapon   arrows

3 What information do you think these objects give about the past?

Time to listen

1.19 4 You are going to listen to a radio interview in four parts. After each part you will hear two questions. For each question, choose the best answer, A, B or C.

1 A northern England
   B New England
   C New York

2 A his High School friends
   B his History teacher
   C archaeology students

3 A a dead man
   B a man's skull
   C a frightening object

4 A quickly
   B powerfully
   C naturally

5 A when he was getting into the fort
   B when he was running to the fort
   C when he was running to the Romans

6 A around AD 33
   B around AD 43
   C around AD 53

7 A about one hundred
   B less than one hundred
   C several hundred

8 A They had all died.
   B The site was deserted.
   C The locals thought there were ghosts there.

SKILL ZONE

Do you need to **make notes**?
Write as quickly as you can.
Write down the dates, names or places that you hear.
Use abbreviations:
yr instead of *year*,
m instead of *metre*.

1.20 5 Listen again and complete the notes.

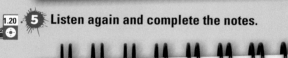

1 Place: Hill fort in ....
2 Battle between English and
   ....
3 Area deserted for ....
4 Local people saw ....

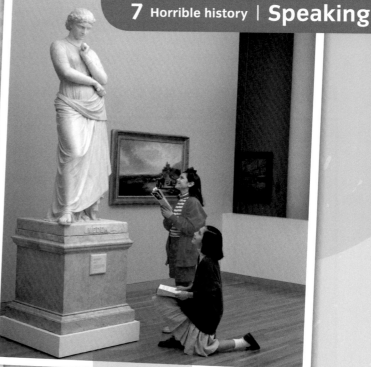

Get ideas

1 Look at the photos. Which place do you think is more useful for learning about the past? Which of these words can you use to describe each photo?

boxes   chair   daytime   gallery   house
jacket   mirror   organised   paintings   quiet
statue   untidy

2 Look at the photos again and answer the questions for each one.

1 Where is it?

Photo 1 – in a house. Photo 2 – in a museum.

2 Is it day/night?
3 What interesting objects are there?
4 How old are the objects in the photos?
5 Who used these objects?

Time to speak

3 Choose a photo and describe it to your partner. Use the questions in Exercise 2 to help you.

> The first picture is in a house. It's daytime because there's light outside.

4 Compare your photos with a partner. Use the Useful phrases to help you.

Useful phrases

Beginning your description
Well, the first/second photo shows …
This looks like a museum, an exhibition, a house …

Introducing your ideas
I think/I don't think …
It must be …

Talking about people
He/She/They seem to be …
He/She/They look …

When you're not sure
I can't make out …
I'm not really sure, perhaps …

Contrasting
The first picture is … but the second one is …
In this picture I can see … However, in the other one there's a …

5 Take turns in class to describe the photos and compare them.

SKILL ZONE

Do you need to **compare photos?** Look for things that are the same, and things that are different in each photo. Think about: the people, the place, the time of day, the atmosphere. Say whether these things are the same in both pictures, or different.

Expressions using time

WORDZONE

Look at some useful **time expressions**.

at the time = a particular moment in the past when something happened

by the time = the point in time when something happens

in time = after a period of time, especially after a gradual process of change

from time to time = sometimes, but not regularly or very often

most of the time = almost always

on time = at the correct time, the time that was arranged

➜ Vocabulary File, page 158

1 Match the beginnings (1–6) with the endings (a–f). Find the time expressions.

1 Most of the time …
2 The prisoners didn't say anything at the time …
3 If a prisoner didn't start work …
4 The food was bad …
5 By the time the prison closed, …
6 From time to time …

a … the prisoners would try to escape.
b … but the prisoners got used to it in time.
c … thousands of prisoners had died.
d … because they were too frightened.
e … the prisoners were too ill to work.
f … on time, the guards punished him.

2 Complete the sentences with the correct form of the verbs.

find   save   spend   take   waste

1 The prisoners .... most of their time doing physical work on the island.
2 The guards watched to see if the prisoners were .... time.
3 The men could never .... the time to plan their escape.
4 The men wanted to escape but knew that they had to .... their time and plan carefully.
5 The prisoners knew that they could .... time if they left by boat.

Wish you were here!

What a lovely place for a holiday! The blue skies, beautiful beaches and exotic palm trees look perfect. But 200 years 1) ..A.. this was not a popular holiday destination! Devil's Island was a prison.

The island belongs to French Guiana and the sea that surrounds it is wild and dangerous. Most of the 2) ..... the climate is hot and humid. Emperor Napoleon III built the prison in the 3) ..... 1800s. At that time the remote location seemed perfect for serious criminals. However, 4) ..... the next century it became one of the most famous prisons in history.

Times were very hard and 5) ..... prisoners weren't able to work because they were so ill. Many prisoners who could swim tried to escape but thousands died in the dangerous sea. In contrast, the director of the prison 6) ..... his time in a house on the hill where he was able to write his postcards in a nice breeze!

When the prison closed 7) ..... 1946 it had seen more than 80,000 prisoners and only 30,000 had survived the experience. The survivors had to stay in French Guiana for the 8) ..... of their lives.

Nearly thirty years 9) ..... the film *Papillon* made Devil's Island famous again. It tells the thrilling story of Henri Charrière who could swim but wasn't able to escape!

3 Read the travel guide and choose the correct answer, A, B, C or D.

1 **A** ago	**B** since	**C** later	**D** before
2 **A** month	**B** time	**C** while	**D** summer
3 **A** mid	**B** middle	**C** next	**D** later
4 **A** at	**B** during	**C** after	**D** by
5 **A** always	**B** times	**C** often	**D** forever
6 **A** took	**B** made	**C** wasted	**D** spent
7 **A** by	**B** in	**C** at	**D** on
8 **A** rest	**B** remainder	**C** end	**D** finish
9 **A** since	**B** after	**C** later	**D** before

Ability (modal verbs)

GRAMMARZONE

can, be able to

A use *can* or *am/is/are able to* for present ability
It tells the thrilling story of Henri Charrière, who can swim (or is able to swim).

will be able to

B use *will be able to* for future ability
He'll be able to swim well after he's had some lessons.

could, were able to

C use *could/was/were able to* for general ability in the past
Many prisoners, who could swim (or were able to swim) . . .

was/were able to

D use *was/were able to* for a single completed action in the past
Henri Charrière wasn't able to escape from Devil's Island

➔ Grammar File, page 170

1 **Choose the correct form to complete the sentences.**

1 He's a good captain and he *can/could* read maps well.
2 In the eighteenth century most of the pirates *can/could* sew.
3 The prisoners *can't/weren't able to* survive long because it was so hot.
4 Women and children who *can/can't* run fast must stay in the fort.
5 He said he *can't/couldn't* work any more because his back was aching.
6 For those who *can/can't* swim it's impossible to leave the island.

2 **Complete the sentences with the correct form of** *can/can't* **or** *(be) able to.*

1 .... you sew your own clothes?
2 If they can't swim, they won't .... escape from the island.
3 They .... hear the Captain. Ask him if he .... speak up, please?
4 I've never .... work in hot weather.
5 You .... join the ship if you want. We need more young men.
6 Ask the Captain. He will .... help you.

3 **Make questions from the prompts then ask and answer them with a partner.**

1 can / speak / French?
   Can you speak French?
2 would like / be able to / dance really well?
3 be able to / speak English fluently / next year?
4 could / write / five years old?
5 be able / help / my homework / tonight?
6 can / remember / learn / today?

4 **Complete the second sentence so that it has a similar meaning to the first sentence using the word given.**

1 The interviewer heard a child's voice and then he saw the ghost.   AFTER
   The interviewer saw the ghost .... a child's voice.

2 They started looking for the skulls this morning and they're still looking now.   BEEN
   They .... for the skulls all day.

3 The prisoners stopped because they were tired.   CONTINUE
   The prisoners .... until they'd had a rest.

4 He hadn't forgotten how hard it was on the island.   REMEMBER
   He .... how hard it was on the island.

5 It was his first visit to Devil's Island.   HAD
   It was the first time .... Devil's Island.

6 There was a lot of talk about the best way to escape.   BEEN
   They .... a lot about the best way to escape.

7 The archaeologists wanted to find out about the battle before they went home.   HAD
   The archaeologists wouldn't go home until they .... about the battle.

8 Could Johnny Depp fight like a real pirate?   ABLE
   Was .... like a real pirate?

Time to talk

5 **Do you know of any islands that are prisons? Why do stories about prisons make good films?**

81

Get ideas

1 Do you like hearing about when your parents/grandparents were young? Why/Why not? What family stories have you heard about life 40, 50, 60 years ago?

Plan ahead

2 Match the notes (a–g) with the topics below.

a went to cinema/theatre
b jazz musician
c grandad
d lived in village then city
e big school, lots of friends
f the 1940s
g not enough to eat

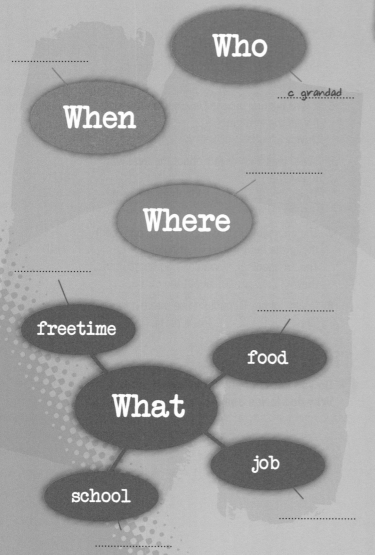

3 Read the article on page 83 and put the notes a–g in Exercise 2 in the correct order.

1 – c

4 Read the article again and complete the sentences.

1 He moved to the city because …
2 At his new school he …
3 In his free time …
4 There wasn't enough food …
5 He learnt … which his dad …
6 He worked in clubs then …

5 Find examples of the past perfect simple and past perfect continuous.

Find the right words

6 Find the dates and time expressions in the article. Do they describe the past, the present or both?

7 Write a paragraph (50–60 words) to describe a family story. Use the questions to help you.

- Who told you the story?
- Who is it about?
- When did it happen?
- Where did it happen?
- What are the main facts of the story?
- What happened at the end?

Then and now

STAR ARTICLE

By Philip Mason, Class 2B

1 What was life like sixty years ago? My grandad has always fascinated me with his stories. He was my age in the 1940s.

2 Until 1948 he had been living in a quiet village but when his dad found a job in the city, the family moved. He hadn't wanted to leave but in time he loved his new life. He went to a bigger school and soon found friends. Some had come from other countries and could speak different languages. They didn't play computer games or watch TV like we do but went out more to the cinema and theatre.

3 He said the worst thing was the food. Most of the time there wasn't enough of it and they couldn't always buy nice things to eat. Nowadays I can't imagine going to the kitchen and not finding a biscuit!

4 Grandad loved music and, before they moved to the city, his dad had given him a trumpet. He learnt how to play and started busking in the city centre. He played in the street and people gave him money. After he had left school he found work in clubs and a few years later he became a professional musician. He's 82 now and can still play great jazz!

Time to write *an article*

SKILLZONE

Do you want to write an article?
Make sure you organise your notes.
Think of ideas and write them down.
Add a key detail to each idea.
Add extra details e.g. personal experience, something funny.
Put your notes in order and divide them into four paragraphs.
Check your article when you've finished it.

8 Write your own article *'Then and now'* for the school magazine. Think about stories that you've heard from people you know. Write about 150–180 words. Use the Skillzone to help you.

Time to watch *Pirate legends*

9 Watch the DVD and do the activities on page 158.

Get ideas

1 What robots do you know about? What can they do? Which of these things might be easy or difficult for a robot to do?

dance   kick a ball   pick up things   see things
talk   walk   walk up or down steps

2 Look at the photos. Which robot do you think would be:

a most fun to use?   **b** most useful to scientists?

Time to read

3 Read the article quickly and match the photos (A–D) with the paragraphs (1–4).

SKILL ZONE

Do you need to find information quickly? Use titles, headings, photographs and the first sentence of each paragraph to predict where you will find it.

4 Read the article again and match these words and phrases with the robots.

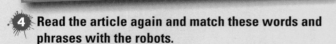
aggressive   dull   tail   team   university

1 Aibo   **2** Robosapien   **3** Roboraptor   **4** EduBot

5 Match questions (a–j) with the robots described in paragraphs 1–4.

a Which robot is most similar to a person? .....
b Which robot was often used by scientists? .....
c Which robot has not yet been used by researchers? .....
d Which robot is no longer being made? .....
e Which robot has a site on the internet specially for researchers? .....
f Which robot has been improved? .....
g Which robot could play football very well? .....
h Which robot has been designed for scientific purposes only? .....
i Which robot can carry things in its mouth? .....
j Which robot doesn't look interesting? .....

6 Complete each sentence using a word or phrase from the article.

1 The science of **r** .... researches and develops robots. (para 1)
2 If a robot acts or looks like a person it is **h** .... (para 2)
3 A **b** .... is a rectangular block which we use for building. (para 4)
4 If something is **e** .... it is absolutely necessary. (para 1)
5 A **c** .... object is made for sale in the shops. (para 2)
6 You can send instructions to a computer using a **j** .... (para 3)
7 **S** .... can detect sound or movement. (para 2)
8 You can send instructions to a **r** .... object from a distance. (para 3)

Summarise

Explain in your own words:
- the problem with Aibo, and some possible solutions
The problem is …
One solution is …
Another answer to the problem is …

Time to talk

7 Have you changed your mind about which robot is most fun to use? Why? Do you know of any other scientific uses for robots?

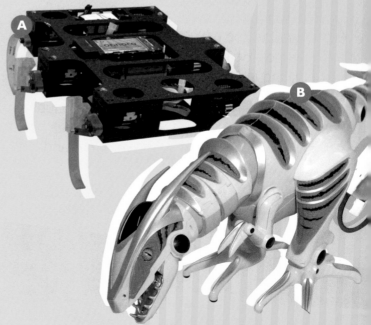

WHAT CAN TAKE AIBO'S PLACE?

1 Aibo the robot dog

Aibo, the robot dog was 'born' in 1999 and many children loved it like a pet. Aibo is equipped with a camera, sensors, a computer chip and the ability to walk. It can also be trained, like a real dog. Although Aibo was not designed as a research tool, scientists were also attracted by it. Aibo had all the things they needed to test Artificial Intelligence programs. Robotics scientists entered teams of Aibos for the 'World Cup' of robot football: the RoboCup Challenge. They used the competition to develop and improve their programs. For example, speed is essential in football, so scientists developed programs to make the robot dogs faster. So it wasn't only children who were disappointed by Sony's decision to stop producing Aibo. Scientists urgently needed another inexpensive, programmable robot to fill Aibo's shoes – or football boots!

2 Robosapien

One possibility is Robosapien, a humanoid commercial robot. It was invented by Mark Tilden, and is built by WowWee. The first Robosapien did not have as much power or as many sensors as Aibo. However, scientists were pleased to discover that it was designed so that it could be improved. Two Robosapiens that have been improved have already played in the RoboCup competition. With radar vision, Robosapien V2's 'eyes' can detect, recognise and remember objects but Robosapien isn't a great football player. Although it can control a football, it can't do a powerful kick for penalties without falling over!

3 Roboraptor the dinosaur

The Roboraptor, another robot created by Mark Tilden, is popular with children, but probably won't replace Aibo in the RoboCup. Roboraptor is a remote-controlled robotic dinosaur that's so intelligent it looks alive! Roboraptor has different moods, so it can be friendly or aggressive. It is controlled by a PlayStation-style joypad. Like Aibo, Roboraptor has been fitted with sensors so that it can see, hear and feel its environment. It has touch sensors in its head and tail and sonic sensors to detect sound and direction. Roboraptor can hold objects in its powerful jaws, too, which is clever but not very useful for playing football. Roboraptor's football career will be limited by another problem, too – it's hard to control its long tail and stop it scoring an own goal!

"The world was once ruled by dinosaurs – the universe will one day be ruled by robots."

4 An educational robot

One possible solution is a special robot for researchers that is being developed at the University of Pennsylvania. It's called EduBot and unfortunately it looks as dull as its name! It is shaped like a brick with six short 'legs'. However, when it moves, it's amazing. It can leap, run and jump straight up in the air. It is much faster than Aibo, but it can't control a football very well because its legs are so short. EduBot is being tested as a research tool and there is a useful website where scientists can compare results from their experiments. If researchers work together to design their own robots they won't be dependent on commercial companies in future.

"Will human footballers ever be beaten by robots? That's the RoboCup Challenge for 2050!"

Whichever replacement robotics experts choose, they have a lot of work to do. The aim of the RoboCup Challenge is to create a team of life-size robots which can beat human footballers by 2050! ∎

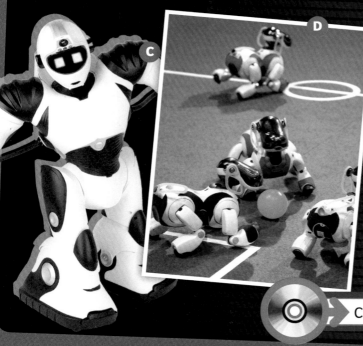

Coming up … *Robot challenges* on DVD. See page 93.

Science and communication

1 Choose the correct words from the article on page 85 to complete the sentences.

1 Scientists have to *test/detect* new robots to make sure they work properly.
2 When you have done a test, you need to check the *results/designs*.
3 To do any job, you need *programs/tools*, for example, scissors to cut paper.
4 I believe that every problem has a *solution/test*.
5 A sensor on a TV can *design/detect* signals from the remote control.
6 A *research tool/radar* can be used to 'see' where planes are.
7 If a researcher has a good design, the next step is to *develop/equip* it.
8 *Solution/Research* into new ideas is often done at universities.

2 Put these words into the correct category.

audible ears eyes feel hear hearing hold
listen look mouth nose scent see sonic
tongue visible vision visual

sight ....*eyes*....... ....
 ....
sound .....*audible*....... ....
 ....
smell ....
taste ....
touch ....

3 Complete the sentences with words from Exercise 2.

1 People use their sense of ....*sight*........ but robots use radar .... to 'see'.
2 In order to hold things in its hand, Robosapiens needs a sense of ....
3 Aibo's .... sensors give it a sense of hearing.
4 Dogs can hear things that are not .... to people.
5 A dog's .... is very sensitive, so it has an excellent sense of smell.
6 Different parts of the .... taste different types of food.

WORDZONE

Do you want to make **'people' nouns**?
Add different endings to nouns and verbs. The most common are *-er* and *-or*, but other endings are possible.
*explore (v) – explor***er**
*create (v) – creat***or**
*mountain (n) – mountain***eer**
*music (n) – music***ian**
*science (n) – scien***tist**

→ Vocabulary File, page 159

4 Write the correct 'people' nouns. Use the endings *-er, -or, -ist, -ian, -eer*.

1 design
2 invent
3 science
4 competition
5 research
6 engine
7 own
8 art
9 manufacture
10 mathematics
11 write
12 music

5 Complete the sentences with nouns from the table in Exercise 4.

1 The .... of the Aibo robot dog was a company called Sony.
2 Electronics .... often become interested in robotics.
3 It is the job of a .... to find out more information.
4 .... in the RoboCup come from many countries.
5 If you pay £80, you can become the .... of a Roboraptor.

6 Write a sentence about two famous people you know using words from Exercise 4.

Copernicus was a famous Polish astronomer,
scientist and mathematician.

Memorise

1 Complete the word map with as many **sense words** as you can remember.
Compare your results with a partner.

senses

2 Choose a word from Exercise 4. Ask your partner to say the **person noun**.

The passive

GRAMMARZONE

be + past participle (+ *by*)

	Subject	Action	Object
Active	*Mark Tilden*	*invented*	*the Robosapien*
Passive	*The Robosapien*	*was invented*	*by Mark Tilden (agent)*

A present simple
Roboraptor is controlled by a joypad.

B present continuous
EduBot is being tested.

C past simple
Robosapien was invented by Mark Tilden.

D past continuous
The website was being used every day.

E present perfect
Two Robosapiens have been improved.

F future
Roboraptor's football career will be limited by another problem …

➜ Grammar File, page 171

1 Find other examples of the passive in the article on page 85. Which tenses do they use?

2 Choose the correct form to complete the text below.

3 Rewrite the sentences in the passive.

1 Alessandro Volta invented the first electric battery.
The first electric battery
`was invented by Alessandro Volta` .

2 University students own this robot.
This robot ....

3 Will Wright designed *The Sims* computer game.
The Sims computer game ....

4 WowWee manufacture Robosapien and Roboraptor.
Robosapien and Roboraptor ....

5 Isaac Asimov wrote the book *I, Robot*.
The book *I, Robot* ....

4 Complete the sentences with the correct passive form of the verbs in brackets.

1 At first, the internet .... (use) by university researchers.
2 Millions of text messages .... (send) every day.
3 Contacting friends .... (make) easier by mobile phones.
4 The robot .... (develop) by scientists until the manufacturers stopped making it.
5 One day letters and emails .... (write) by robots.
6 Robots .... (improve) all the time.

Time to talk

5 Think of an everyday invention. What is it used for? Who is it used by? Would you use a robot to help you?

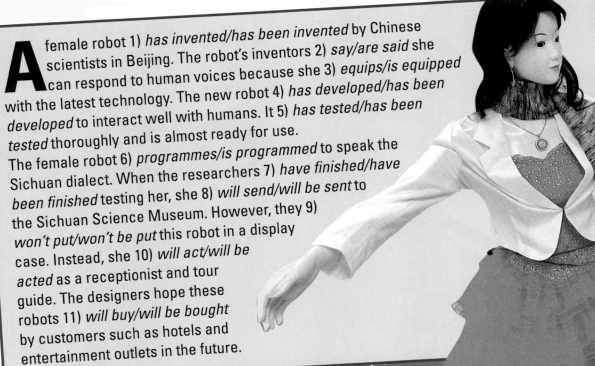

A female robot 1) *has invented/has been invented* by Chinese scientists in Beijing. The robot's inventors 2) *say/are said* she can respond to human voices because she 3) *equips/is equipped* with the latest technology. The new robot 4) *has developed/has been developed* to interact well with humans. It 5) *has tested/has been tested* thoroughly and is almost ready for use. The female robot 6) *programmes/is programmed* to speak the Sichuan dialect. When the researchers 7) *have finished/have been finished* testing her, she 8) *will send/will be sent* to the Sichuan Science Museum. However, they 9) *won't put/won't be put* this robot in a display case. Instead, she 10) *will act/will be acted* as a receptionist and tour guide. The designers hope these robots 11) *will buy/will be bought* by customers such as hotels and entertainment outlets in the future.

Write? Text? Phone?

Get ideas

1 How often do you use these ways to communicate with others? Which is the most/least popular in your class? Why?

 ... read a magazine?

... listen to the radio?

 ... watch TV?

... make a phone call?

... write a letter?

... send an email? @

Time to listen

2.2

2 Listen to four conversations and look at the pictures. After each conversation you will hear a question. For each question, choose the best answer, A, B or C.

1 A 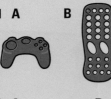 B C

2 A  B C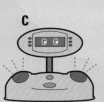

3 A  B C

4 A  B C

Need to choose the correct picture? Listen to the whole extract and try to pick the most important idea. Remember! Sometimes you may hear a word which sounds like the main topic, but it's not as important.

SKILL ZONE

2.3

3 Listen to three extracts from a TV programme and look at the pictures. After each extract you will hear a question. For each question, choose the best answer, A, B or C.

1 A **1876** B **1776** C **1866**

2 A B  C
詹姆斯

ΙAHON
IVSMFDVOCVI
PECTACVLADA

3 A B C

Get ideas

1 Do you think English is important or useful for these forms of communication? Why/Why not?

TV   books   internet   films   phone   radio

2 Complete the questionnaire.

Modern Languages Questionnaire

1 Which languages can you speak?
Mandarin Chinese; Portuguese; Greek; Italian; German; French; Spanish; Turkish; other

2 Would you like to learn any other languages?

3 Why are you learning English?
A It's your choice.
B It's your parents' choice.
C It's on your school curriculum.

4 How do you practise your language skills outside the classroom?
• watching DVDs or TV
• reading magazines or websites
• speaking to foreign visitors or phoning friends
• sending letters or emails to pen friends
• listening to CDs or English radio

Return your completed questionnaire to the Head of Modern Languages for a chance to win a prize!

Time to speak

3 Ask and answer the questions from Exercise 2 with a partner. Do you agree?

4 Read the speech bubble and decide which object is being described.

> It's small and it looks as if it's made from plastic. Maybe it's quite expensive. It's not colourful, but I think it's quite attractive. It could be made in Japan or China, but I'm not sure ...

5 Choose an object in your classroom and describe it in detail, giving your opinion. Ask your partner to guess what it is.

SKILL ZONE

Are you describing a picture or an object?
• Say what you can see in detail.
• Try to guess what it could be.
• Give your opinion about it.

6 Discuss how attractive each object would be as a prize.

The most/least attractive prize is ...
It would/n't appeal to ...teenagers / children / adults / men / women

Useful phrases

It may/might/could be/is made of/from ...
metal, plastic, glass, cotton, silk, paper, card

Maybe/Possibly/Probably it was made in ...
Japan, China, the USA, South America, Europe

It looks (a bit) like .../It looks as if ...
In my opinion it's ugly/attractive/too bright/
dull/plain/useful

Phrasal verbs

VOCAB ZONE

Did you know? Some **phrasal verbs** have a new meaning that is different from the meaning of the two parts. You can use phrasal verbs to talk about communication and media.

My new MP3 player has **fallen apart**. (= stopped working)

The DVD player has **broken down**. (= stopped working)

→ Vocabulary File, page 159

1 Match the phrasal verbs (1–6) with the meanings (a–f).

1 switch (sth) on/off
2 break down
3 break up
4 speak up
5 cut off
6 turn (sth) up/down

a to lose a connection, especially on the phone
b to raise one's voice
c to have a bad phone connection/to end a relationship
d to start or stop something
e to increase or decrease
f to stop working

2 Complete each sentence to show the meaning of the phrasal verbs from Exercise 1.

1 .... has broken down!
2 Could you speak up ....
3 Shall I switch on .... ?
4 .... got cut off.
5 Please turn up ....
6 Did you remember to switch off .... ?
7 .... but it fell apart after two days!
8 I'll turn down ....

3 Complete the article with one word that best fits each gap.

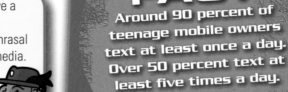

FACT
Around 90 percent of teenage mobile owners text at least once a day. Over 50 percent text at least five times a day.

Txts R gr8!

I spotted a bored teenager in a restaurant yesterday. He was switching 1) ......*on*........ his mobile to text his friends. 'You couldn't live 2) .... your mobile, could you?' his mother commented. It's true for most of us. We even keep spare phones in case one breaks 3) ....

> However, sometimes mobiles 4) .... used to avoid communication. The teenage boy was avoiding communication with his family. With a mobile you 5) .... allowed to avoid face-to-face contact. If you want to end a conversation, just say, 'Speak 6) .... ! I can't hear you. The line's breaking 7) .... !' Or you can say, 'It's a bad line, isn't it? Don't worry if we get cut 8) ....' Then you can switch your phone 9) .... !

> Speech 10) .... being replaced by texting. It is immediate, accessible and private. Texting is also a way of flirting. Surprisingly, a third of boys and a quarter of girls think it's OK to send a text message to break 11) .... with someone. The most common message which 12) .... sent by mobile is a social message: it shows people that you are popular, doesn't it?

C U L8r!

Question tags

GRAMMAR ZONE

Using question tags

auxilliary/modal verb + pronoun
She's French, isn't she?

A you are sure about something and you expect the other person to agree
It's a bad line, isn't it?

B you are not sure if something is true and you check if the information is correct
You speak Spanish, don't you?

C use a positive question tag, if you expect a negative answer
You couldn't live without your mobile, could you?

D use a negative question tag, if you expect an affirmative answer
It shows people that you are popular, doesn't it?

Positive or negative?

If the main sentence is positive, the tag is negative
The text message was from Jim, wasn't it?

If the main sentence is negative, the tag is positive
You didn't buy a new DVD player, did you?

→ Grammar File, page 171

1 Match the two phrases to make a question tag.

1	You're not going to use the computer now,	**a**	won't you?
2	He hasn't got a mobile,	**b**	shouldn't we?
3	They can send us an email,	**c**	did they?
4	We should phone them soon,	**d**	has he?
5	You'll write me a letter,	**e**	can't they?
6	They didn't watch that programme,	**f**	are you?

2 Complete the sentences with a question tag.

1 He isn't wearing those old jeans to school, ... ?
2 You didn't do your homework, ... ?
3 They've got a DVD player, ... ?
4 She hasn't listened to that CD yet, ... ?
5 They could meet us at the airport, ... ?
6 You mustn't be late for school, ... ?

3 Rewrite the questions as statements with a question tag, expecting negative answers.

1 Does your dad know how to send text messages?
Your dad doesn't know how to send text messages, does he?
2 Do you like *The Simpsons*?
3 Were they at home yesterday evening?
4 Has your sister got a mobile?
5 Can they speak English?
6 Did you walk to school today?

4 Rewrite the statements and question tags again, this time expecting an affirmative answer.

1 Does your dad know how to send text messages?
Your dad knows how to send text messages, doesn't he?

5 Choose the word or phrase (A, B or C) that best completes the sentence.

1 David, you haven't done your homework, ...
 A have you? **B** did you? **C** could you?

2 I think she takes sugar in her coffee, ...
 A can't she? **B** won't she? **C** doesn't she?

3 My motorbike .....
 A has broken up. **B** has broken down.
 C has spoken up.

4 We were talking on the phone, but we got .....
 A switched off **B** turned down **C** cut off

5 You won't forget to phone me, ...
 A would you? **B** will you? **C** were you?

6 We saw that film, ...
 A didn't we? **B** shouldn't we? **C** aren't we?

Time to talk

6 Write down some facts about your partner or your teacher. Ask question tags to check your facts.

Writing | Communication breakdown 8

Get ideas

1 Look at these problems. Have you ever had a problem like this? What happened?

1 Our TV stopped working after a bad thunderstorm. We couldn't switch it on because all the wires were burnt!
2 The battery on my mobile went dead and I couldn't recharge it.
3 My dad spent a whole day setting up our computer for broadband. But then we couldn't send or receive emails!
4 I bought a CD player, but it didn't work properly. I couldn't turn the volume up.
5 I couldn't work out how to download music onto my MP3 player, so I haven't used it yet!

2 Have you ever, or has anyone you know, written a letter of complaint or phoned a helpline? What about? What happened?

3 Read the letter of complaint and match it with one of the problems in Exercise 1.

Tom Parsons
25 The High Street
Newtown

Dear Sir/Madam

I am writing in connection with the CD player I bought last week. The problem is that it doesn't work properly. I am disappointed because it plays CDs, but I can't hear the music and I can't turn the volume up. The player is covered by a one-year guarantee so I would like you to replace it.

I look forward to hearing from you.

Yours faithfully,

Tom Parsons

Find the right words

4 Choose one of the communication problems in Exercise 1. Complete the short email asking for a solution.

a Is it covered by a one-year guarantee?
b Could it be replaced?
c Can it be repaired?
d Is there a Helpline number where I can get advice?

Reply | Reply All | Forward | Delete

To: **Service centre**
From: **Dan**
Subject: **Problem**

Dear Service Centre,
My problem is that ....
I hope this problem can be solved as soon as possible. ....
....

5 Read the letter of complaint and choose the best option to complete the sentences.

Dear Sir/Madam
1) *I'm really cross about/I'm writing in connection with* my new Spacebot. It's a fantastic robot but
2) *I've had a few technical problems with it/it's ridiculous because it's already useless.* Yesterday it broke down completely. Your advertisement promised that Spacebot would last for years, so
3) *I think you lied/as you can imagine I'm quite disappointed.* Is it covered by a guarantee? 4) *I would like you to replace my Spacebot or send a refund./I want my money back!*

Plan ahead

6 Marina has problems with her new mobile. Read the advert and Marina's notes, then complete the sentences.

FreeFriends

Sign up for the new FreeFriends mobile package.

Look at all the advantages:

- A top quality Smartphone 3 is included in the price.

> *I was sent a Smartphone 2 – the keypad is already falling apart!*

- Pay-as-you-go. It's easy! Our top-up card can be used in thousands of shops across the country.

> *I couldn't top up my card in any of our local shops.*

- Free texts to friends on the same service!

> *I was charged for my texts.*

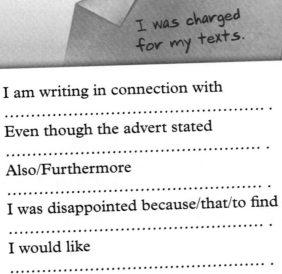

I am writing in connection with
....
Even though the advert stated
....
Also/Furthermore
....
I was disappointed because/that/to find
....
I would like
....

Time to write *a letter of complaint*

7 Use your notes from Exercise 6 and the Skillzone to write Marina's letter of complaint.

SKILLZONE

Are you writing a letter of complaint? Be polite!

Explain clearly what your problems are.

Tell the company what action you would like them to take.

End your letter by saying: *I look forward to hearing from you.*

Time to watch *Robot challenges*

8 Watch the DVD and do the activities on page 159.

Vocabulary

1 Complete the sentences with these expressions.

> a decade   a fortnight   BC   centuries   the 1700s
> the twentieth century

1 Women pirates in the ....the 1700s.... were just as dangerous as the men.
2 The internet must be one of the most important inventions of ....
3 By 4000 .... people were beginning to live in houses made of mud and wood.
4 The Cuban War of Independence lasted for .... from 1868 to 1878.
5 A month was a long time on the ship and after .... he was ready to go home.
6 Languages have developed over the .... because people of different nationalities have moved around from country to country.

2 Complete the sentences with the correct preposition.

> for   from   in   on   until   to

1 Mobile phones were developed in the 1960s but ......until........ the early 1990s they were too big to carry in your pocket.
2 The new World Wide Web project was publicised .... 6 August 1991.
3 The first emails were sent .... 1965.
4 Scientists worked on the design of the internet .... 1973 .... 1983.
5 Computer fans have been using the internet .... more than 15 years.

3 Choose the correct alternative to complete the sentences.

1 *Most of the time/By the time* people wrote letters because they couldn't communicate by phone.
2 At first I didn't like using my mobile phone but *in time/on time* I got used to it.
3 *By the time/In time* you decide which phone to buy, there'll be new models to choose from.
4 The scientists didn't say anything *at the time/by the time* but it was clear they were pleased with their robot.
5 Mobile phones are great. If somebody doesn't arrive *on time/in time*, you can just call them and find out where they are.

4 Complete the text with these words.

> develop   research   results   solution   test

It must be great being an inventor. You wake up with an exciting new idea and your job is first to 1) .....research....... it and then 2) .... it. You spend hours thinking about it and finally 3) .... it to make sure that your new product works well. If there are any problems you have all the time in the world to find the right 4) .... but if the 5) .... are good you might become famous.

5 Match the words with the parts of the body.

> audible   feel   hear   listen   scent   see   smell
> sonic   speak   speech   taste   tongue   touch
> visible   vision   visual

ears   ....audible..
eyes   ....
nose   ....
mouth   ....
hands   ....

6 Write the people nouns. Use these endings.

> -er   -or   -eer   -ian   -ist

1 art   ...artist......   6 mathematics   ....
2 create   .... 7 mountain   ....
3 engine   .... 8 music   ....
4 explore   .... 9 research   ....
5 invent   .... 10 write   ....

7 Complete the sentences with the correct preposition.

1 Can somebody switch *on/off* the light? It's so dark in here.
2 During the test the robot broke *up/down* and the scientists had to repair it.
3 If you don't speak *up/down* nobody will hear you.
4 I can't use my mobile at home. I always get cut *off/out*.
5 It's a bad line and you're breaking *up/down*. Can you try again in a few minutes?
6 I can't hear a word you're saying. Turn that music *down/up*!

8 Complete the sentences with the correct form of the verbs.

> break   cut   speak   switch   turn

1 She can't hear well and has to ......turn.......... up the TV to hear it.
2 If a machine .... down an engineer can usually repair it.
3 The audience asked the scientist to .... up because they couldn't hear him.
4 If we are .... off I'll leave a message on your answerphone.
5 I didn't want to .... off the DVD because the film was so exciting.

Grammar

9 Decide if the action underlined happens first or second in the sentence.

1 The battle took place on a site where <u>families had been living</u>. ......first......
2 She didn't know that <u>her grandmother had written a book</u> about her life. ....
3 <u>They discovered an island</u> where prisoners and criminals had lived. ....
4 <u>He had been working as a farmer</u> when the Captain invited him on his ship. ....
5 <u>The people left the village</u> where their families had died. ....
6 He had been looking for his uncle's diary when <u>he found the treasure.</u> ....

10 Complete the sentences with the correct form (past perfect simple or past perfect continuous) of the verb in brackets.

1 The pirates came home with stories about the adventures they .....had had........ (have) at sea.
2 When the invaders arrived early in the morning the villagers .... (leave).
3 The prisoners didn't know the guards .... (listen) to them while they were talking.
4 She ran to the museum but it .... (close) ten minutes previously.
5 By the time they solved the problem, scientists .... (work) on it for ten years.
6 They began the test after they .... (gave) the robot a name.

11 Complete the sentences with the correct form of can, could, be able to.

1 My grandfather .....could........ play the piano when he was three years old.
2 The prisoners .... to escape because there were too many guards.
3 Do you think you .... come to the exhibition with us next week?
4 I'd like to .... understand robotics.
5 .... you understand the scientist when he spoke to you?
6 At first the robots ....walk but they .... talk. Now they can do both.
7 I don't know if I .... to finish this exercise, it's taking me ages.

12 Complete with the correct passive form of the verb in brackets. Use the tense given.

1 The robot is .....tested....... (test) by the scientists. (present simple)
2 The science students .... (show) the results. (present continuous)

3 At the time the research.................. (do) by a young student from Japan. (past continuous)
4 The results .... (publish). (present perfect)
5 The idea .... (tested) to see if there are any problems. (future simple)

13 Complete the second sentence so that it has a similar meaning to the first sentence.

1 The engineers are examining the results.
The results .are being examined.. by the engineers.
2 Scientists were researching the theory for more than twenty years.
The theory .... for more than twenty years.
3 The explorers have discovered a new island in the middle of the Pacific Ocean.
A new island .... in the middle of the Pacific Ocean.
4 People send and receive hundreds of email messages every day.
Hundreds of email messages .... every day.
5 Creators of robotic toys will test them so that they are safe.
Robotic toys .... so that they are safe.

14 Choose the correct question tag.

1 You saw the test, *didn't you/don't you*?
2 The signal has been lost, *hasn't it/has it*?
3 A robot can't cry, *can it/does it*?
4 She didn't detect any change, *did she/does she*?
5 You didn't touch it, *did you/didn't you*?
6 She was pleased with the results, *was she/wasn't she*?
7 It's not going to break down again, *is it/isn't it*?

15 Complete the text with one word which best fits each gap.

No more robots!

I can't understand all this fuss about robots, 1) .....can....... you? Every time I switch 2) .... the TV there's something about robots. In China a robot tour guide is 3) .... tested and I've just seen a football match that 4) .... played between robot footballers. That was quite interesting but often the demonstrations go 5) .... For example, when a robot talks it isn't easy to understand it, 6) .... it? When the sound is turned 7) .... all you can hear is a strange noise that is nothing like a human voice. I think it will be a long time before the perfect robot 8) .... invented.

Did you remember all the vocabulary and grammar points?

→ Vocabulary File, pages 158 and 159
→ Grammar File, pages 170 and 171

9 Getting on .....

Get ideas

1 Is it sometimes difficult to make new friends? Why/Why not? Which activities can help you make friends?

doing homework   doing sport   going shopping
playing computer games   texting   watching TV
other activities

2 Describe the people in the photos. How do you think they feel? Use these words to help you.

friendly   happy   nervous   relaxed
sociable   uncomfortable   worried

Time to read

3 Read the review on page 97. How did the contestants feel when they first met each other?

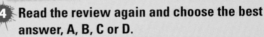

SKILLZONE

Are you reading for details? Read the questions first. Then, read the text and make a note of the paragraph or line numbers where you find information about each question. Finally, choose the best option.

4 Read the review again and choose the best answer, A, B, C or D.

1 How were the contestants in *Teen Big Brother* similar?
   A They had the same culture.
   B They were all about the same age.
   C They were from a similar background.
   D They were all boys.

2 Why did Hasan like Caroline?
   A Because she was attractive.
   B Because she was the first to arrive.
   C Because she laughed a lot.
   D Because she was positive.

3 What did they learn in the *Big Brother* house?
   A They learned to do things together.
   B They learned how to be different.
   C They knew all about each other's personalities.
   D They decided to get on with each other.

4 Why is it difficult for teenagers to do without their personal possessions?
   A They can't phone their friends.
   B Their possessions are everything to them.
   C They can't show others what they are really like.
   D They can't wear clothes.

5 Why was James angry?
   A He wanted to hold his possessions.
   B He wanted to be alone.
   C He wanted to be himself.
   D He didn't like *Big Brother*.

6 What happened after *Big Brother*?
   A They tried to be themselves again.
   B They tried to remain like each other.
   C They all gave themselves new names.
   D *Big Brother* became a house of individuals.

Home   **News**   **Watch**   **Gallery**   **Housemates**

Contact

Search

Watch

Teen Big Brother is here!

1 Imagine living with people you don't know – it could be fun or it could be a nightmare! Eight British teenagers recently had the chance of a lifetime – to be Big Brother housemates in the most famous house in the UK. With the world watching them, they had just ten days to get to know each other – how would they get on?

2 The final eight contestants were among thousands of British teenagers who had applied to take part in *Teen Big Brother*. They came from different backgrounds and cultures and had just one thing in common – their age.

3 Caroline and Hasan were the first to arrive in the house. Caroline was very confident and positive about their new home and this immediately attracted Hasan to her. They got on very well and laughed a lot together. However, when Jade, the third housemate, arrived she was nervous and couldn't make eye contact. James, on the other hand, was very friendly and made a good first impression. He introduced himself and said, 'Nice to meet you'. He was polite but it was also a good way to start making friends.

4 Paul, Shaneen and Tracey were all very likeable from the start because they were honest. When Caroline asked how they were feeling, they admitted they were scared and this is often a way to win friends. When Tommy finally burst into the house he appeared confident and arrogant. It was difficult for the quieter housemates to approach him.

5 Over the course of ten days, the group got to know each other, like each other, and sometimes dislike each other! They had to put up with each other's habits, attitudes and personalities. They learned to live as a group and make decisions together.

6 The programme showed how they got on with each other in different situations. The housemates had to do various tasks together. These varied from unblocking the loo and planning shopping lists to controlling a simulated aeroplane.

7 So how was the *Big Brother* house different from home? The main difference was that these housemates were on TV every day. However Big Brother told them there would be no communication with the outside world except in emergencies. The show's organisers also told them to leave mobile phones at home as well as other personal possessions such as make-up.

8 Ten days without mobiles and make-up is probably difficult for most teenagers. Dr Smith, a psychologist who was watching the show, explained why. He said that image was everything to a teenager and personal possessions reflected their personalities to the outside world. He said that Big Brother had stripped the housemates of their identities and that all of them had found that difficult.

9 The housemates reacted in different ways to these house rules. Dr Smith said that Jade had had the strongest reaction to them. He added that she was usually quite a confident girl but without her make-up she became very insecure.

10 James also had difficulty. He was quite laid-back and funny, but he didn't like the rules. Inside the house he had tried to hold on to his individuality and had got angry when Big Brother had taken that away. Dr Smith said that Big Brother was a house of individuals and whatever Big Brother tried to do, the housemates would always want to remain themselves. When the programme was over the housemates tried again to show their individuality and some of them even changed their names.

---

5 **Find words and phrases in the review that match these meanings.**

1 have a friendly relationship (para 1)
2 someone's education, family and experiences (para 2)
3 look directly at somebody (para 3)
4 moved into the house quickly and suddenly (para 4)
5 people you live with who aren't family (para 4)
6 accept something without complaining (para 5)
7 work you must do (para 6)
8 powder, creams and lipstick you put on your face to make yourself look attractive (para 7)
9 taken away (para 8)
10 keep (para 10)

Summarise

In your own words, describe:
• the programme *The programme was about ...*
• the housemates *James was friendly ...*
• the house rules *They couldn't ...*

Time to talk

6 **What do you think the housemates liked/disliked about the house? What would you like/dislike about living with your friends?**

 Coming up ... *Friends united* on DVD. See page 105.

Describing personalities

1 **Match the words in bold in the sentences with the meanings (A–D).**

Jade was usually quite a **confident** girl but without her make-up she became very **insecure**.

James was usually quite **laid-back** and **funny** but he didn't like rules.

A relaxed
B not sure about yourself
C tells jokes
D sure about yourself

2 **Read the sentences and find the adjectives used to describe each person.**

1 Caroline enjoys being the leader. She is ambitious and competitive but can also be bossy.
2 Paul is an extrovert and loves to show off. He is cheeky and humorous but can be sensitive, too.
3 Skater-boy Tommy is very imaginative. He writes his own songs and is into graffiti art. He is shy and at times not very assertive.
4 Tracey is very talkative! At times, however, she can seem immature.

3 **Match the adjectives in Exercise 2 with the descriptions.**

1 She drives me mad because she never stops talking. ....
2 I like playing tennis but I get angry when I lose. ....
3 Our teacher makes us laugh in class. ....
4 He is able to understand other people's feelings. ....
5 She acts like a five-year-old not a fifteen-year-old! ....
6 He likes to tell other people what to do. ....

4 **Complete the sentences with a suitable adjective. Then compare your answers with a partner.**

1 Jim is very .... to his teachers but sometimes they can't help laughing.
2 Sometimes I'm too .... and get upset if people say things about me.
3 Lucy is really .... She's always thinking up new and interesting ideas!
4 Olivia's really .... and plans to be rich one day!
5 Tyler should be more .... He's often afraid of saying what he thinks.

Here's a good way to increase your vocabulary. Learn new **words** and their **opposites** (**antonyms**) together.

sensitive – insensitive
mature – immature
humorous – serious
talkative – quiet
bossy – timid

→ Vocabulary File, page 160

5 **Write the opposites.**

hard-working   laid-back

1 imaginative   ....
2 loud   ....
3 unattractive   ....
4 hard-working   ....
5 serious   ....
6 assertive   ....
7 sensitive   ....
8 confident   ....

6 **Complete the sentences with these words.**

big-head   extrovert   gossip   snob

1 Don't ever tell Yvonne a secret. Everybody knows she's a/an .... and the whole school will know about it by tomorrow.
2 He's such a/an .... He keeps telling everybody how good he is at Maths.
3 Daniel has loads of friends at school. I wish I were a/an .... like him.
4 Ruby's such a/an .... She always thinks she's better than others.

7 **Describe somebody you know well and say why you get on/don't get on with that person.**

Memorise

Play the game.
Student 1. *She's shy.*
Student 2. *She's shy and funny.*
Student 3, *She's shy, funny and ... (add another adjective).*

Go round the class. Who can make the longest sentence?

Reported speech

> ### GRAMMARZONE
>
> #### Reported statements
>
> **A** the main verb usually moves one tense into the past
> *'Image is everything to a teenager,' he said.*
> *He said that image was everything to a teenager.*
>
> **B** other verbs: *will > would; may > might; can > could; must > had to*
> *'The housemates will always want to remain themselves,' said Dr Smith.*
> *Dr Smith said that ... the housemates would always want to remain themselves.*
>
> #### Reported questions
>
> **C** the word order changes
> *'How are you feeling?' Caroline asked.*
> *Caroline asked how they were feeling ...*
>
> #### Reported commands/requests
>
> **D** *ask/tell* + person + *to*-infinitive
> *'Leave your mobile phones at home!' the show's organisers told them.*
> *The show's organisers told them to leave their mobile phones at home.*
>
> → Grammar File, page 172

1 **Find all the examples of reported speech in the review on page 97.**

2 **Write what these people said earlier.**

1 Big Brother told them there would be no communication with the outside world.
'There will be no communication with the outside world,' Big Brother told them.
2 He said that Big Brother had stripped the housemates of their identities.
3 He said that personal possessions reflected their personalities to the outside world.
4 Dr Smith said that Jade had had the strongest reaction to them.
5 He added that she was usually quite a confident girl but without her make-up she became very insecure.
6 Dr Smith said that Big Brother was a house of individuals.

3 **Choose the correct form to complete the sentences.**

1 Sam said that Paul *is going out/was going out* with Julia.
2 Joe asked if I *can help/could help* him with his homework.
3 She said that she *will phone/would phone* him the next day.
4 James said that he *has got on/had got on* well with the housemates.
5 The man said that he *must leave/had to leave* immediately.
6 She said she *will help/would help* if she had more time.
7 Joel said he *doesn't like/didn't like* living with friends because they were noisy.
8 I told you *not to be/don't be* so bossy.

4 **Rewrite the sentences using reported speech. Use the correct tenses and pronouns.**

1 'I don't like being with competitive people,' Jim said.
Jim said he .....didn't like being..... with competitive people.
2 'How many people live in your house?' Jade asked Patricia.
Jade asked Patricia how many people .... house.
3 'Stop interrupting me,' Nina told Sam.
Nina told Sam ....
4 'I haven't watched any TV in ages,' said Sophie.
Sophie said .... any TV in ages.
5 'I've been trying to fix the DVD player,' said Jack.
Jack said .... to fix the DVD player.
6 'I'm going to watch *Teen Big Brother* tonight!' Ben said to Adam as he left.
As he left Ben told Adam ....

5 **Complete the text with the correct form of the verbs in brackets.**

Last week I was having a chat with my mum. I told her I
1) .....was going..... (go) to live with friends when I
2) .... (grow up). She laughed and said first I
3) .... (have) learn how to cook and clean for myself. 'Fine,' I said. 'Teach me.' So the next day, she told me 4) .... (tidy) my room. After that she said I 5) .... (can) wash up the breakfast things, prepare some lunch then finish the ironing. Next day, when the teacher asked me why I
6) .... (not do) my homework, I told him I
7) .... (be) exhausted!

Time to talk

6 **Describe a housemate from *Teen Big Brother*. Would you get on with this person? Why/Why not?**

'I can't stand ...'

Get ideas

1 Do you argue more with family or friends? Why? What do brothers and sisters argue about?

Time to listen

 2 Listen and answer the questions.

1 What's the relationship between David and Jennie?
2 Why are David and Jennie arguing?
3 Where are David and Jennie going?

Do you need to match speakers with what they said? It's easy!

Try to understand
• their **relationship**
• the **situation** they are in

SKILLZONE

3 Listen again and match the statements with the speakers, David (D), Jennie (J) or Mum (M).

1 It's not your computer.
2 I'm going to get Mum.
3 What's going on?
4 How many times have I told you?
5 Oh no, not that hat, it looks really stupid.
6 He's horrible!
7 Now I think you should say sorry.
8 She's laughing.

4 What can you remember about the conversation?

1 Where does the conversation take place?
2 What is Jennie doing?
3 What does David want to do?
4 What does Mum decide?
5 How does Jennie feel about Mum's decision?
6 What is Mum planning for the evening?

5 Listen and repeat.

1 fair   far
2 hair   her

6 Listen and underline the word you hear.

1 fair/far
2 hair/her
3 care/car
4 wear/were

Time to talk

7 Is arguing a good or a bad thing? Why?

Get ideas

1 **Have any of these situations ever happened to you? Say what happened.**

- Somebody laughed at your clothes or hairstyle.
- Somebody was being noisy and you couldn't sleep.
- Two of your best friends went to the cinema without telling you.
- You helped a friend with his/her homework and he/she got a better mark.

Time to speak

2 **Look at the photos. What do you think is the relationship between the people? How do they feel?**

3 **Complete the conversation with phrases from Useful phrases. Then practise it with a partner.**

Mum: And what time do you call this?

Joel: Sorry, Mum. I walked home with Mark – he's such a laugh. He said I could go and play his new computer game.

Mum: 1) .... eleven o'clock is too late when you've got school tomorrow!

Joel: Oh, I 2) .... having to come home so early. Everybody else stays out later than me.

Mum: 3) .... during the week you come home at ten and at the weekend at eleven. Is that clear?

Joel: I suppose so, but 4) .... it's fair.

Mum: Pardon, Joel?

Joel: Nothing, Mum.

4 **Do you agree with Joel or his mum? Why?**

Useful phrases

Giving opinions

I think/I don't think … In my opinion, …
Personally, … As far as I'm concerned, ….
What I think is that … I prefer …
I don't mind …

Expressing strong feelings

I really think/feel that …. Because …
I hate … I can't stand …

5 **Choose one of the situations in the photographs and act out a conversation with a partner.**

'I really think it's time you tidied up your room!'

'You promised not to tell anyone!'

a/an, the or zero article

Don't forget! Use *a/an* to talk about someone/something for the first time or about things in general.
*He is **an** Art student.*

Use *the* to talk about something specific, or someone/something that you know about.
***The** new housemate is very friendly.*

Use zero article (no article) to talk about people and things in general.
Friends are important.

➔ Vocabulary File, page 160

1 Choose the correct article to complete the sentences.

1 They have *the/an* unusual relationship.
2 She's *a/an* very imaginative girl at times.
3 *The/–* teenagers today are more independent.
4 Could you shut *a/the* door?
5 She's *a/the* most laid-back person in *a/the* house.
6 Would you like *a/–* biscuit?

2 Complete the sentences with *a/an, the* or no article.

1 I wouldn't like to have ..*a*.. TV programme made about my family.
2 She said that everybody at school had liked ..... colour of her hair.
3 ..... Soap operas are always about family problems.
4 Mum said she wanted you to use ..... money to buy some new shoes not a skateboard!
5 I've got ..... older sister and ..... younger brother and we all get on really well.
6 When ..... teenagers argue with their parents they're usually trying to show their independence.

3 Write the opposites. Use the correct article.

1 a sensitive girl   *an insensitive girl*
2 an hard-working man   ....
3 a serious person   ....
4 a mature housemate   ....
5 an insecure student   ....
6 an attractive boy   ....

 4 Complete the text with one word which best fits each gap.

my **big** family

Living in 1) ..*a*... big family can be fun but it isn't always easy to get on with everybody. I'm 2) ..... youngest in our house and I enjoy being on my own. I prefer staying in my room and listening to music. 3) ..... problem is that when my brother is in 4) ..... house I never get 5) ..... moment's peace. He's completely different from me and he and his friends are very loud. He's really good at playing football and wants to play professionally but he's such 6) ..... big-head! He drives me mad sometimes.

"it isn't always easy to get on with everybody"

Then there are my twin sisters who are 7) ..... good laugh. Everybody calls them 8) ..... terrible twins. I don't mind being at home with them because they're cheeky and make me laugh. Then there's Mum. I think she's 9) ..... unusual mum because she puts up with four children and she's quite laid-back about things. We get on well although she can be a bit of 10) ..... gossip and likes to know what everybody's up to. On the whole I'd say we're just 11) ..... average family.

-ing form and *to*-infinitive

GRAMMAR ZONE

-ing form

A after certain verbs, e.g. *imagine, enjoy, finish*
I enjoy being on my own.

B after prepositions, e.g. *interested in, good at, bad at*
He's really good at painting.

C after certain expressions, e.g. *look forward to, mind, can't stand*
I don't mind being at home with them.

to-infinitive

D after certain verbs, e.g. *want, hope, decide*
... he wants to play professionally.

E after certain adjectives, e.g. *easy, happy, possible*
...it's not always easy to get on with everybody.

-ing form and/or *to*-infinitive

F after certain verbs, e.g. *like, love, hate* and *prefer* when there is no change in meaning
I prefer staying/to stay in my room.

→ Grammar File, page 173

1 **Match the beginnings (1–6) with the endings (a–f).**

1 We are good at
2 Can you imagine
3 He's decided
4 When you finish
5 Do you think it's possible
6 I'm sure she wants

a to live on his own.
b making decisions together.
c to live with your friends and not argue?
d you to spend more time with her.
e living with your best friends?
f using the computer can I check my email?

2 **Complete the sentences with the correct form (*-ing* or *to*-infinitive) of the verbs in brackets.**

1 Do you want ....to help........ (help) me with the meal?
2 I'm looking forward to .... (get) my own flat one day.
3 My dad's really bad at .... (tell) jokes and it's so embarrassing!
4 John says he's decided .... (live) with his grandparents.
5 I like .... (watch) how other families get on at home.
6 It's important .... (get on) with the people you live with.

3 **Complete the sentences so that they are true for you.**

1 I'm good/bad at ...
2 I like ...
3 I've decided ...
4 It's easy for me ...

4 **Complete the second sentence so that it has a similar meaning to the first sentence using the word given.**

1 'We've been studying their behaviour for two weeks,' the producer explained.   HAD
The producer explained that .... their behaviour for two weeks.

2 You mustn't argue with your parents any more.   STOP
You must .... with your parents.

3 'Where do you live?' the interviewer asked Hasan.   HE
The interviewer asked Hasan ....

4 'Clean your room before your friends come round,' said Mum to Lucy.   TO
Mum told Lucy .... before her friends came round.

5 They don't work very well as a group.   GOOD
They aren't .... as a group.

6 'Why do you want purple hair?' Paul asked Jade.   SHE
Paul asked Jade .... purple hair.

Time to talk

5 **What are the advantages/disadvantages of big families? Is it better to have a big family or a big group of friends? Why?**

Get ideas

1 Who do you get on best with in your family? Why? If you could be somebody else for one day who would you be? Why?

Find the right words

2 Look at the photo and read the text. Choose adjectives to describe each person.

angry confident happy immature old smart
well-dressed creative young

3 Read text A. Then choose the correct adjective to complete the sentences.

1 Tess is *understanding/ambitious*.
2 Tess has a *busy/organised* life.
3 Tess shouts at Anna because she is *confident/stressed*.
4 Anna and Tess get on better now, because Tess is more *mature/relaxed*.

4 Complete text B with these words and phrases.

can't stand funny get on with good at
hard-working sensitive and mature

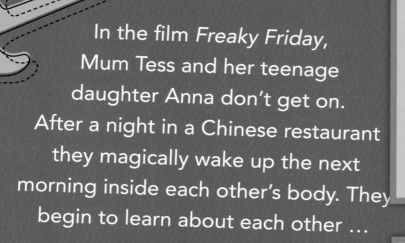

In the film *Freaky Friday*, Mum Tess and her teenage daughter Anna don't get on. After a night in a Chinese restaurant they magically wake up the next morning inside each other's body. They begin to learn about each other …

A
Anna describes Tess …

My mum is in her forties and is quite attractive and slim for her age. She has short, red hair and always wears sensible, smart clothes. She is good at helping people with problems. She is always talking but never finishes a conversation. She often ends up shouting.

We argue a lot, but things are getting better. She's got a new boyfriend, and she's getting married. She's much more laid-back and we get on like a house on fire.

B
B Tess describes Anna …

Anna is a typical teenager. She 1) …*can't stand*… getting up for school in the morning. She's very pretty and has long, red hair. Most of the time Anna wears baggy jeans and trendy T-shirts.

She can be 2) ……………… and gets good marks at school when she tries. Anna doesn't 3) ……………… some of the other students or her teachers. She is outspoken and has lots of arguments. In her free time Anna is very creative and she loves playing the guitar and is in a band. She's really 4) ……………… writing her own songs.

Anna and I haven't always got on. Once she told me I was ruining her life. I told her I just wanted her to do well at school.

The best thing about Anna is that she can be 5) ……………… and makes people laugh. We're now more like friends than mother and daughter. Anna has become very 6) ……………… .

Plan ahead

SKILL ZONE

Are you **writing a description**?

Choose your special person and make notes about what they look like and what kind of personality they have.

Add one 'special' feature about that person.

Separate your notes. First write about their appearance.

Then add information about their personality.

Then describe what is special about the person.

Finish with a sentence about why you get on so well.

5 **Which of this information would you include in a description of a person?**

1 What he/she looks like
2 When he/she was born
3 His/her hobbies/interests
4 His/her best/worst feature
5 What he/she likes to eat
6 What he/she is like as a person
7 Where he/she lives

6 **Read text B on page 104 and find some of the information about Anna in Exercise 5.**

1 Anna is pretty and she has long, red hair.

7 **Find examples of -ing and to-infinitive forms in text B. Which verbs do they come after?**

8 **Complete the sentences in your own words.**

1 My sister/brother/cousin is really funny/is good at telling jokes.
2 My mum/dad likes …
3 My best friend is …
4 My teacher is …
5 I think I am …

9 **Answer the questions in Exercise 5 about a person who is special to you.**

Time to write *a description*

10 **Read the announcement and write your entry for the competition. Write 120–180 words.**

Competition announcement

Send us an email describing a special person in your life. Is it a parent, your brother or sister or even a friend? Write a description of that person and tell us why you get on so well. The winning entry will appear in next month's magazine.

Time to watch *Friends united*

11 **Watch the DVD and do the activities on page 160.**

10 Planet Earth

Get ideas

1 Have you ever been away from home with a group of friends? Which weather conditions would you find it hardest to cope with?

Time to read

2 Look at the photo below, and read the articles on page 107. Which trip did these people go on?

3 Read the articles again and choose the best answers, A, B, C or D.

1 Which expedition involved helping more than one endangered animal?
   A 1   **B** 2   **C** 3   **D** 4

2 Which expedition involved travelling by water?
   A 1   **B** 2   **C** 3   **D** 4

3 Which two destinations had low temperatures?
   A 1 and 2 **B** 2 and 4 **C** 2 and 3 **D** 1 and 4

4 On which trip did team members ride on the back of animals?
   A 4   **B** 3   **C** 2   **D** 1

5 Which two groups saw small dangerous animals?
   A 1 and 3 **B** 2 and 4 **C** 2 and 3 **D** 1 and 2

6 Which two texts mention that the teams built an enclosure?
   A 2 and 3 **B** 1 and 2 **C** 3 and 4 **D** 2 and 4

4 Match these words with their meanings.

deadly (2)   glacier (1)
enclosure (2)   habitat (4)
endangered (3)   global warming (1)
frostbite (1)   survival (1)

1 This is a safe area which is surrounded by a wall or fence.
2 If a species of animal is this, it is now very rare.
3 This is a large sheet of ice in a mountainous area.
4 If you can find food and shelter in any environment, you have good skills in this.
5 If your fingers and toes become frozen, you may suffer from this.
6 Very dangerous, likely to cause death.
7 A general increase in world temperature.
8 The local environment in which an animal lives.

SKILL ZONE
Do you need to answer questions about multiple texts? Read all the questions first. Then read each text quickly to find the information you need. Remember, the answers may not be in the same order as the questions.

Summarise

Describe each expedition in your own words.
• What was the weather like?
• What animals did they see?
• How did they travel?

Time to talk

5 Would you like to go on one of these trips? Which one?

Extreme environments!

1 Serious Arctic

Name of programme? 'Serious Arctic'
Accommodation? tents
Weather conditions? -20°c, snow and ice, blizzard
Reasons for going? 1 to protect the polar bear 2 to visit a glacier and measure the effects of global warming on the ice
Highlight of trip? riding on sledges pulled by husky dogs

It was like a roller coaster. It was amazing!

The temperature outside was -20°c, we were in a blizzard, and we had to spend the night in a tent! Snow and ice are only fun when you can return to a warm home. Our team wouldn't have survived the extreme conditions if we hadn't learnt survival techniques before we went and worn special clothing to protect us from frostbite. Our best experience was travelling on sledges pulled by teams of huskies when we went to visit a glacier. Our job was to measure the changes caused by global warming and our work will help to protect polar bears.

2 Serious Amazon

Name of programme? 'Serious Amazon'
Means of transport? canoe along the river
Weather conditions? hot and humid
Reasons for going? 1 to save pink river dolphins 2 to protect red uakari monkeys
Highlight of trip? a fantastic evening celebration at a tribal village in the rainforest

The Amazon team travelled by canoe because there aren't many roads in the rainforest. We went to destroy the illegal fishing nets that catch pink river dolphins. Cutting the nets is dangerous. If we had touched one of the deadly piranha fish in the river, it might have attacked us.
The baby red uakari monkeys needed a safe home. If they had been born in the wild, they would have been in danger from hunters. Building their enclosure was very hard work because it's very hot and wet in the rainforest. When we finished, the team had a great celebration with the local people. It made me feel really proud … It's a brilliant feeling!

3 Serious Desert

Name of programme? 'Serious Desert'
Accommodation? huts made of cow dung
Means of transport? on foot
Weather conditions? extreme heat!
Reason for going? tracking endangered rhinos
Worst parts of trip? heat, insects and snakes

Our huts are made of cow dung!

The Namibian village certainly didn't offer luxury accommodation! We were very surprised to discover that cow dung is used for building. It was boiling hot and there were bugs and insects everywhere! If we hadn't been careful, poisonous snakes might have bitten us. We found out that crossing the desert is very difficult, because the sand moves under your feet. It was worth it to see the black rhinos, though, as they're so rare. Working with camels was another unusual experience. They're smelly and they make funny noises, but if we hadn't had camels to carry our luggage, the trip would have been impossible.

4 Serious Andes

Name of programme? 'Serious Andes'
Place visited? Andes Mountains in Ecuador
Means of transport? riding on horseback
Reason for going? to build a home for spectacled bears
Highlight of trip? climbing Mount Cotopaxi

Spectacled bears are really rare. They get their name from funny markings on their faces that look like glasses. They live high in the Andes mountains.
Beto and Leo, two spectacled bears, had been living in small cages. They needed a large enclosure so they could explore their natural habitat safely. If our team hadn't made them an enclosure, they'd still be in their cages. When the bears learn what they can eat and where they can sleep safely, they can go free. It was a long climb to reach the bears' new home, so we rode on horseback part of the way. Some of the team were nervous about that! Our final challenge was climbing over 6,000 metres up a snow-covered volcano. It was freezing cold, and we climbed through clouds and mist to reach the top of Mount Cotopaxi. It was tough, but we made it!

Coming up … *Serious Amazon* on DVD. See page 115.

Weather and environment

1 Write **E** next to environment words and **W** next to weather words.

Arctic (n) .E.   blizzard (n) .....   cloud (n) .....   mist (n) .....
desert (n) .....   glacier (n) .....   humid (adj) .....
jungle (n) .....   rainforest (n) .....   volcano (n) .....

2 Match these weather words with the correct definitions.

drought   flood   heatwave   hurricane
lightning   thunderstorm

1 a long period of dry weather
2 a large amount of water that covers an area that is usually dry
3 a powerful flash of light in the sky caused by electricity
4 a storm that moves over water and has very strong winds
5 a period of unusually hot weather
6 storm with thunder and lightning

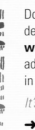

WORDZONE

Do you want to describe **extreme weather**? Add an adjective ending in -ing.

*It's **boiling** hot.*

→ Vocabulary File, page 161

3 Match the beginnings (1–4) with the endings (a–d).

1 It's boiling …   a … with rain.
2 It's pouring…   b … cold.
3 It's freezing …   c … wet.
4 I'm soaking …   d … hot.

4 Complete the text with these words. There are three extra words that you do not need.

blizzard   boiling   heatwave   lightning   rain   humid
snow   soaking   thunderstorm   weather   wind

DURING a 1) ......heatwave....... in Denver, USA, seventeen-year-old Jason Bunch was in the garden. It was a 2) .... hot day. The air felt sticky and 3) .... Jason was mowing the lawn and listening to his iPod. Suddenly the 4) .... changed. There was a strong 5) .... and it began to pour with 6) .... Before Jason realised what was happening, he was struck by 7) .... and knocked to the ground. His iPod melted and he suffered severe damage to his ear. Fortunately, Jason recovered. Doctors advise people never to use an iPod or a mobile phone during a 8) .... !

Memorise

In groups: write as many words as you can in each category. Score one point for each word.

weather   environment

Third conditional; wishes

GRAMMARZONE

Third conditional

for something that was possible in the past, but did not happen

A *If* + *had* + past participle + *would have* + past participle
Our team wouldn't have survived … if we hadn't learnt survival techniques.
If they had been born in the wild, they would have been in danger.

B *If* + *had* + past participle + *may/might/could have* + past participle
If we had touched one of the deadly piranha fish in the river, it might have attacked us.

Wishes

C present: *wish* + *could/was/were*
I wish we could get out of the rain.
I wish it was/were warmer.

D past: *wish* + *had* + past participle
I wish I had gone on the expedition.

➜ Grammar File, page 173

1 Find more conditional sentences in the articles on page 107. Are they all third conditionals?

2 Complete the sentences with the correct form of the verbs in brackets.
1 If we .... (go) to the Arctic it .... (be) much colder!
2 If I .... (not/enjoy) the trip I .... (not/stay) there.
3 You .... (go) on the expedition, if you .... (want) to.
4 If he .... (hear) the thunder, he .... (switch off) his iPod.

3 Complete the sentences in your own words.
1 It's too cold.
   I wish ....
2 You've got too much homework.
   I wish ....
3 You didn't watch your favourite programme yesterday.
   I wish ....
4 You argued with your friend and you feel bad.
   I wish ....

4 Complete the web article below with the correct form of the verbs in brackets.

Time to talk

5 Is there anything you wish you had/hadn't done yesterday or today?

Jungle diary ✖ Close

12 July

Today is humid and we've worked hard. I wish it 1) ......was...... (be) a bit cooler here! After we had built the enclosure, we introduced the monkeys to their new home. I wish you 2) .... (see) them, they were really excited! If we 3) .... (not/finish) the enclosure, we 4) .... (not go) on the trip to the tribal village.

I was so tired that I wanted to stay at the camp, but if I 5) .... (have) a rest I 6) .... (not/meet) the Ashual tribe. If I 7) .... (not/go), I 8) .... (miss) the best evening of my life! Sometimes I wish I 9) .... (can) stay in the jungle forever. But if I didn't go home I 10) .... (not/see) my family, and I really miss them!

Eat me!

ants

cockroach

worm

frog

porridge

Get ideas

1 **What's the worst food you've ever eaten? If you had to eat one of the things in the photos which one would you choose?**

Time to listen

 2 **You are going to hear some teenagers talk about their experiences of food and drink on their trip. Listen and answer the questions.**

1 Which food in the photos is NOT mentioned?
2 What other food and drink is mentioned?

 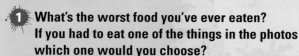

Do you need to decide who says something? You may find that some people say similar things, and they may even use the same words. Listen very carefully for the differences.

3 **Listen again. Match the statements (A–F) with the speakers (1–5). There is one extra statement.**

1 Tony 2 Natasha 3 Michael 4 Nicola 5 Simon

A The local environment provides all the necessary food.
B If we hadn't finished the work, we wouldn't have had a meal.
C I'm not enjoying my favourite food and drink!
D I'm glad my food made me ill!
E They make sure we have enough liquid so we don't get ill.
F If I hadn't eaten it, I would have regretted it.

4 **Two pairs of speakers had very similar experiences. Can you match the statements to the names?**

1 We wish we hadn't eaten or drunk so much of one thing.
2 We would never have eaten these things if we weren't on survival training.

A Tony and Natasha
B Natasha and Michael
C Simon and Tony
D Nicola and Simon

Harry in the Andes

Get ideas

1 What food would you miss most on a trip like this? What people and things would you miss?

Time to speak

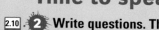

2 Write questions. Then listen and check. Repeat the interviewer's questions.

1 miss / family?
Did you miss your family while you were away?
2 often / have showers?
3 wear / clean clothes / every day?
4 be / mosquitoes, spiders or snakes?
5 sleep / in bed?
6 what / accommodation / like?
7 how / cope / temperature?

3 Listen again. Make a note of the extra words the interviewer used.

SKILLZONE

Are you asking for information? Remember to use the correct question words.

Think about which tense you need, and whether you need the auxiliary verb *do/did*.

Add names and extra bits of information to make your questions more personal.

4 Listen and repeat Harry's answers.

1 Of course. I missed them a lot.
2 We had showers every few days, but the water was very cold.
3 No, of course not! It was too cold to change clothes!
4 Well, ... not really. There were some wild panthers, though!
5 No way! We usually slept in sleeping bags.
6 Well, I wish we'd stayed in a five-star hotel! Actually, we slept in tents. We had to put them up ourselves first!
7 We all had the right clothes for the conditions. There was snow and ice, and some heavy rain, but sometimes the weather was quite nice!

5 Work with a partner.
Student A: You are the interviewer. Ask Harry the questions in Exercise 2.
Student B: You are Harry. Answer the questions.

6 Ask and answer the questionnaire with a partner. Make a note of your partner's answers. Report back to the class on any different answers for C.

Could you have coped in the

Amazon
Jungle?

1 If you had found a tarantula in your tent, would you have ...
A screamed? B been excited? C something else?

2 If you had walked miles through the jungle in high temperatures, would you have ...
A complained? B sung songs? C something else?

3 If you had to spend the night in a small shelter in the middle of the jungle, would you have ...
A been scared?
B gone straight to sleep?
C something else?

4 If you couldn't wash yourself or your clothes, would you ...
A get upset? B be happy? C something else?

5 If one of your team members had annoyed you, would you have ...
A had a big argument?
B stayed quiet?
C something else?

7 You have been on a trip to the Amazon or the Arctic. Ask and answer questions with a partner. Use the Useful phrases to help you and add two more of your own.

miss?   dangerous animals?   best/worst thing?
temperature?   friends/family?   clean clothes and showers?
other team members?   accommodation?   do it again?

Useful phrases

What/When/Why/Where did you …?
How (often) did you …?
What was … like?
How/What about …?
Would you …?

111

-less, -free; re-

WORDZONE

You want to change the meaning of a word? Add a new beginning or ending!

re- means again
-less and *-free* mean without

reuse, use**less**, care**free**

→ Vocabulary File, page 161

1 Match these words with their meanings.

careful   careless   chlorine-free   harmful
harmless   recharge   recycle   replace   reuse

1 to use something again
2 causing harm
3 trying hard to avoid damaging something
4 to put a new thing in place of an old one
5 to put a new supply of energy into something
6 not paying enough attention to what you are doing
7 to start using something new instead of what you use now
8 not likely to cause any harm
9 without chlorine

2 Complete the sentences with a word from Exercise 1.

1 Don't throw glass bottles away, ... them.
2 People who leave litter behind are really ....
3 When you need to .... your light bulbs, buy energy-saving ones.
4 Buy these special batteries which you can .... again and again.

3 Read the article and choose the best answer, A, B, C or D.

1 A revise   B recycle
  C replay   D remove

2 A recyclable   B reusable
  C battery-free D non-battery

3 A recharge   B return
  C replace   D recycle

4 A environmental   B ecological
  C economical   D environmentally-friendly

5 A careful   B carefree
  C uncaring   D careless

6 A reuse   B reduce
  C replace   D renew

7 A careless   B carefree
  C harmful   D unharming

8 A Return   B Replace
  C Rethink   D Revise

9 A chlorine-free   B non-chlorine
  C chlorine   D chlorine-less

10 A lead-less   B non-lead
   C leaded   D lead-free

Environmentally-friendly ideas!

If you want to save the environment, start with three simple steps: reduce, reuse and 1) ..B.. If you are not sure how to do this, you can have your house checked by an eco-company.

GADGETS!

Here are some of the latest inventions to help. How about this radio? Normal radios use batteries which contain dangerous metals such as mercury. A wind-up radio solves the problem. What about a 2) ..... torch? To switch it on, you simply shake it! Have you ever wished you could 3) ..... your phone when you were out and about? Try a solar-powered mobile phone charger.

ELECTRICITY

Other 4) ..... things you can do include: Don't leave your TV on stand-by. Don't be 5) ..... – switch off lights where possible as lighting uses 10–15 percent of home electricity. You could use energy-saving light bulbs and get solar panels installed, too.

OTHER STUFF

Remember to 6) ..... plastic bags and bottles. Chlorine, which is used to bleach paper, is very 7) ..... to the environment. 8) ..... your tissues and toilet paper with harmless 9) ..... versions. Most cars use 10) ..... petrol these days, but buses, bikes or walking are better!

have/get something done

1 Read Luke's notes and complete the sentences.

'We're having some work done on our house, to make it more eco-friendly.'

Things we have had done:
1 solar panels / install / roof
   We've had solar panels installed on our roof.
2 water butt / deliver / to collect rainwater
3 walls insulate / to stop heat escaping

Things we're going to get done:
4 wildlife-friendly garden / design
5 walls / paint with eco-friendly paint
6 tap / mend / to stop wasting water

2 Rewrite the sentences to say what these people have had done.

Lord Toffee is going on a business trip.

1 Lord Toffee's secretary has booked his tickets for him.
He's had his tickets booked for him.
2 His wife has packed his case.
3 His photo has been taken.

Stephan and Monica are going on holiday.

4 Their tent has been mended.
5 Stephan's bike has been checked by an expert.
6 Monica's mobile phone has been stolen.
7 Stephan's hair has been cut.

3 Write questions with *Have you ever ...?/ Would you ever ...?* Use the prompts to help you.

1 hair / dyed
2 hair / cut very short
3 nails / painted
4 photo / taken by a professional photographer
5 portrait / painted

Time to talk

4 Ask and answer the questions from Exercise 3 with a friend. Add some more questions of your own.

Get ideas

1 **How can you protect the environment? Which of these projects would you prefer to be involved in?**

2 **Your school council wants to raise money for an environmental project. Read the two web pages, and make notes of the main points in the table below.**

PROTECT A DOLPHIN

>> INFORMATION
>> OBJECTIVES
>> DOWNLOADS

Our charity now has thousands of supporters across the world. We work to educate fishermen to use different nets so that dolphins don't get caught in them. This is the main danger to several species of dolphin. We support a sanctuary for injured dolphins which are later released back into the wild. We also provide free posters, brochures and education packs which encourage everyone to be more aware of where their food actually comes from.

Plant a tree

We are a new charity, and still quite small. We use your donations to plant trees in villages in some of the driest areas of Africa which are badly affected by drought. Our trees improve the lives of local African people as they provide fruit, and wood for building and making things. These trees also improve the quality of the soil so that villagers can grow their own food crops and raise animals which they were unable to do before. We provide free yearly newsletters with information about all our projects.

3 **Read the report below and match the headings (A–D) with the paragraphs (1–4).**

A Plant a tree   B Protect a dolphin
C Conclusion   D Introduction

	A	B
Size of project?		
Who/What does it help?		
Improvements to environment?		
Free information?		

« Back to Inbox

Environmental project: dolphins or trees?   Inbox

To: **School Council** From: **Matt Baker**   More options   Date: 10th April 2008

1 The purpose of this report is to recommend which charity we should support this year.

2 If we gave money to this charity, it would benefit the environment in two main ways:
First, it would help to educate fishermen to use different nets so that dolphins don't get caught in them. Secondly, it would make everyone think more about where their food actually comes from. As a result, we might make better choices about the food we eat.

3 The advantages of this charity are:
First, it would benefit the local African people. If they had more trees they could eat fruit from the trees and use wood for building and making things.
Secondly, the trees should improve the quality of the soil. This would make a better environment for animals and food crops, too.

4 Although I wish we could support both charities, it's necessary to choose one. While dolphin conservation is very attractive, I think it is already a popular charity. The Plant a tree charity, however, is quite a new charity and needs more support. In addition, it benefits people in need and it would also help to improve the environment more. For these reasons, I suggest we support this charity.

Find the right words

4 Read the report again and answer the questions.

1 Which words and phrases does Matt use to organise his argument?
2 Which tense does Matt use for many of the verbs? Why?
3 What is the purpose of the conclusion? Do you agree with Matt's choice?

Plan ahead

5 Your head teacher has asked you and some friends to decide where you will go on a five-day school trip. Read the two web pages and complete the notes below.

Skiing trip

Stay in a beautiful wooden chalet high in the mountains

Share a room with four or five of your friends
Have ski lessons every morning with a professional ski instructor
Have loads of fresh air and exercise
Enjoy the sunshine and snow
Bring warm clothes and snow boots

Cost: 1000 euros, including travel, accommodation and food
NB ski hire and ski pass not included

English Language trip

Stay with an English family
Have your own room
Have English lessons every morning with a native speaker
Go on trips to Madame Tussaud's and the London Eye
Enjoy the cool English climate!
Bring warm clothes, trainers and an umbrella or waterproof coat

Cost: 800 euros, including travel, accommodation and food

Accommodation: ....
Lessons: ....
Weather: ....
Cost: ....
Other points: ....
My preference: ....

6 Choose one of the trips and give reasons for your choice. Discuss your reasons with a partner.

Holiday: ....
Reasons: ....

Time to write *a report*

7 Write your report (150–180 words). Use Matt's report and your notes from Exercise 5 to help you.

SKILLZONE

Are you **writing a report**? Make sure you order the information logically.

Be clear about your opinion/choice and give good reasons for it.

Use organising phrases so your reader can easily find all the information.

First/Firstly, …
Second/Secondly, …
One advantage/benefit is …
Another advantage/benefit is …
In addition …
For these reasons …
In conclusion …

Time to watch *Serious Amazon*

8 Watch the DVD and do the activities on page 161.

Vocabulary

1 Match the adjectives with the descriptions.

| assertive | competitive | extrovert | humorous |
| imaginative | immature | insecure | laid-back |

1 Laura's very confident and people
take notice of her. .....assertive.....
2 Adam is a very relaxed person,
he doesn't worry about anything. ....
3 Vicky has always been very creative
as she has loads of great ideas. ....
4 Do you ever feel unsure of yourself? ....
5 Michael is quite funny, he always
makes us laugh. ....
6 Sara and Monica are ambitious and
they really want to be successful. ....
7 People with a really sociable
personality like to be in a crowd. ....
8 Justin often seems young for his age. ....

2 Put these words into the correct category in the word maps.

blizzard	boiling	desert	flood	freezing	drought
glacier	heat wave	humid	jungle	mountain
rain	rainforest	soaking	volcano

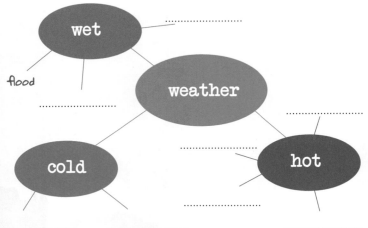

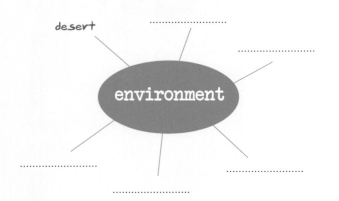

3 Complete the sentences with *a, an* or *the*. Leave a blank where necessary.

Personal profile
Max is off to the Arctic

1 I'm Max and I'm from ..a.. small town in .....
Scotland.
2 I go to ..... school in Edinburgh which is ..... great
place.
3 I think I'm ..... adventurous person and I'm .....
sociable, too.
4 I've always wanted to visit ..... other countries so
I'm really looking forward to going to ..... Arctic.
5 I don't mind ..... cold and I think it will be ..... fun!
6 I'm quite laid-back about ..... trip because .....
people I'm going with are ..... great group.
7 We can't wait to build ..... igloo and see loads of
..... polar bears!

4 Complete each sentence with the correct form of the words in capitals. Use *-less, -free, re-*.

Some people say it is 1) .....useless......
to try and stop climate change.   USE
However, I disagree. Here are five simple
ways you can protect the environment!
One, check that you 2) ....
paper and glass.   CYCLE
Two, try to use 3) .... forms of
transport, such as bikes.   HARM
Three, buy batteries which you can
4) ....   CHARGE
Four, make sure you and your family
5) .... plastic bags.   USE
Five, 6) .... normal lightbulbs
with low-energy ones.   PLACE
Don't be 7) .... be responsible! CARE

5 Match these phrasal verbs with the meanings 1–7.

| burst into | get on (with) | go out with | wash up |
| put up with (something) | stay out | take (something) away |

1 enter a room suddenly .....burst into.....
2 clean dishes in water ....
3 remove ....
4 have a friendly relationship ....
5 remain away from home late at night ....
6 accept a bad situation without
complaining ....
7 be boyfriend and girlfriend ....

Grammar

6 **Complete the second sentence so that it has a similar meaning to the first sentence, using the word given.**

1 'Climbing a volcano is really hard work,' explained Simon.
Simon explained that climbing a volcano
was really hard work. **THAT**

2 'What was the highlight of your trip?'
Nina asked Megan. **HER**
Nina asked Megan what the highlight ....

3 'Bring your warmest clothes,' the
organisers told them. **TO**
The organisers told them ....

4 Mike said 'I haven't seen my family
for two weeks!' **HIS**
Mike said .... for two weeks!

5 'I'll miss living in a tent!' laughed James. **HE**
James said .... in a tent.

6 'How are you managing in the freezing cold?'
the interviewer asked them. **THEY**
The interviewer asked them .... in
the freezing cold.

7 **Underline the correct form of the verb, or both if both are possible.**

1 Carla hopes _to be_/_being_ an explorer when she's older.
2 They were interested in _to help_/_helping_ endangered animals.
3 I hate _to eat_/_eating_ the same food every day.
4 We've finished _to put_/_putting_ up our tent.
5 We loved _to ride_/_riding_ on the sledges with the huskies.
6 It wasn't always possible _to get_/_getting_ on well with the whole group.
7 _To build_/_Building_ an enclosure took several days.
8 I can't stand _to have_/_having_ a wash in the river!

8 **Choose the best answer to complete each sentence.**

1 If you had taken part in _Big Brother_, you .... !
  A might win **B** might have won
  C had won **D** won

2 If the teenagers .... their mobiles at home, they would have been happier.
  A don't leave **B** didn't leave
  C wouldn't leave **D** hadn't left

3 We wish the _Big Brother_ rules .... so strict!
  A weren't **B** could be
  C might be **D** wouldn't be

4 A few of the girls wish they .... more fashionable clothes on _Big Brother_.
  A wore **B** may wear
  C didn't wear **D** had worn

5 If Tommy had been less arrogant, he .... more friends.
  A might make **B** might have made
  C hadn't made **D** will make

9 **Write affirmative or negative sentences or questions about the _Big Brother_ house. Use _have/get_ and the verb provided.**

1 The floors – clean?
  Have they had the floors cleaned?
2 the bedrooms – decorate?
3 the beds – make
4 living room – tidy
5 a swimming pool – install?
6 the front door – paint / gold
7 the cameras – check

10 **Complete the text with one word which best fits each gap.**

Do you enjoy 1) ......_watching_....... reality TV programmes like _Big Brother_? Or do you think they're a waste of time? A lot of us are happy to see real people on TV. Where do they come 2) .... ? Will they get 3) .... ? Or will they end up hating each other? Questions like these give us a reason to keep watching.

I interviewed 4) .... group of young people who gave their opinions. Lina from Greece told me that she loves 5) .... hear all the latest news from BB. However, Jorge from Brazil said that he thought reality shows 6) .... a cheap form of entertainment. They're annoying, too. 'If I hadn't watched BB last summer, I 7) .... have had a lot more free time!' he added. Flora from Australia agreed. 'My mum told me 8) .... stop watching, but I couldn't!'

Kate from Ireland decided 9) .... take part in _Big Brother_. She filled in an application form and 10) .... her photo taken but then she changed her mind. 'If I'd gone on 11) .... show I wouldn't 12) .... enjoyed it, she explained.' Kate said 13) .... the people who took part were all extroverts who were only interested in fame.

Did you remember all the vocabulary and grammar points?

→ Vocabulary File, pages 160 and 161
→ Grammar File, pages 172 and 173

Get ideas

1 Would you like to do sport every day at school? Why/Why not?

2 Look at the photos and answer the questions.

1 Do you do any of these sports? Which ones?
2 Which three sports are part of the triathlon?
3 What is the order of the sports in the triathlon?

Time to read

3 Read the article on page 119 and check your answers to Exercise 2.

4 Read the article again. Choose from the sentences (A–F) the one which best fits each gap (1–5) in the article. There is one extra sentence.

A So what are you waiting for?

B Professional triathletes can also have the best clothes for their sport.

C There may be hundreds of people in the race and you can't waste time looking for it.

D Second, you mustn't forget to eat well, and avoid unhealthy snacks.

E Part of the fun of the triathlon is that it combines three very different activities.

F It's important you don't run too fast at this stage of the race.

SKILL ZONE Do you need to understand difficult words or phrases? Continue reading the text. The situation will give you an idea of what the words mean.

5 Find words in the article that match these meanings.

1 for young people below a certain age (line 3)
2 very tiring (line 8)
3 ready to try it (lines 13–14)
4 use all of something and not have any more left (line 19)
5 frightening (line 23)
6 difficult (line 29)
7 special glasses for swimming (line 32)
8 made you not want to do something (line 40)
9 see the good points of things (line 41)
10 so enjoyable you don't want to stop (line 51)

Summarise

Answer the questions in your own words:
• What is a triathlon? *A triathlon is three sports, …*
• How do you train for a triathlon? *You have to …*
• Why is the triathlon sometimes dangerous? *It can be dangerous because …*
• What are the benefits for professional triathletes? *Triathletes get … they don't have to …*

We train hard for ... the Triathlon

The event

Can you swim four hundred metres, cycle eight kilometres and then run three kilometres? That's the junior triathlon. The triathlon became an Olympic event in 2000, and it's popular with both
5 sexes and all ages. 1) .... . Competitors usually swim in open water, that's in a river, a lake or the sea, and then cycle and run on the roads.

We get fit

It's an exhausting race, so if you don't want to be out of breath in the first five minutes, now is the
10 time to start getting fit. Firstly, champion triathletes have to train really hard every day. That means no parties on Saturdays and no lying in bed on Sunday mornings. Are you still up for it? First, you must decide to make exercise a part
15 of your daily routine and turn the gym into your second home. As well as swimming, cycling and running, you need a regular workout to build up muscle strength and stamina. 2) .... . If you don't eat the right food you'll run out of energy and
20 you won't finish the race.

What is the Triathlon?

	Junior	Classic
Swimming:	400m	1.5km
Cycling:	8km	40km
Running:	3km	10km
First Olympics:	Australia 2004	

Triathlon: an instant hit

Q Who does the Triathlon?
A It's popular with men and women, boys and girls.
Q Who are the champions?
A Olympic Gold medallists in 2004 were
Men: Hamish Carter from New Zealand
Women: Kate Allen from Austria

We get tips from ... Stuart Hayes

Training for the race isn't just hard work; it can be dangerous as well. Professional triathlete Stuart Hayes tells some scary tales, including: 'sharks in the sea when I've been swimming in Australia',
25 and 'dogs jumping out at me and attacking me'. In addition, 'I've seen people just step out and walk across the road, smack into a load of cyclists,' Stuart says. 'The first part of a race – the swim – is tough,' Stuart told us. He explained that because
30 everybody starts at the same time you have to try and get away fast. 'You'll have people swimming over the top of you, elbows flying. Goggles get pulled off. People come out with black eyes and split lips.' After the swim you mustn't forget
35 where you left your bike. 3) .... When you've finished the cycling, put on your running shoes as fast as you can and start the run – slowly. The final part is the most difficult and you will have to save your energy.

We get the equipment

40 Have these horror stories put you off? Let's look on the bright side: professional triathletes get free bikes, and they don't have to repair them because the triathlon company takes care of the technical maintenance. 4) .... . Years
45 ago they had to wear swimsuits but now a tight Lycra suit is much better. 'It has to be tight or it would slow us down on the swim and bike,' says Stuart.

We get up and go

Are you still wondering why people want to go
50 running and cycling in their swimsuits when it's cold and wet? Triathletes say it's addictive, once you start you're hooked. Or in the words of one of Britain's top triathletes, '(5) .... . Get out and give triathlon a go!'

Time to talk

6 Which part of the triathlon would be most difficult for you? Why? What new sport would you like to try and why?

Coming up ... *Tough triathlon* on DVD. See page 127

Health and fitness, sport

1 Complete the text with these words and phrases.

get fit   a healthy diet   out of breath   race
regular exercise   sporting event   stamina   training
triathlon   unhealthy

I never thought I was particularly
1) ....
until a few months ago.
I was late for the school
bus and had to run to
catch it. I was soon
2) .... and
decided that it was time to
3) ....
I now try to eat
4) .... and
take 5) ....
It's not easy when you get
lots of homework every
day! Then one day I saw
an advert in the local
paper for a new
6) .... called
the 7) ....
My friends and I have
started 8) ....

together for it. Every
Sunday we swim for
twenty minutes, then we
cycle for half an hour and

**Every Sunday we
swim for twenty
minutes, then we
cycle for half an hour**

then finish with a run.
That's the most difficult
part as you are tired and
have to have lots of
9) ....
It's a very exciting
10) ....
because you have to be
good at all three sports. I
don't think we'll win it this
year but we are much
healthier!

2 Match the sports categories (1–6) with the definitions (a–f).

1 Extreme sports
2 Water sports
3 Contact sports
4 Winter sports
5 Spectator sports
6 Team sports

a sports where players touch each other
b sports that are done on snow and ice
c dangerous or fast sports
d sports that you go and watch
e sports that you play or do in water
f sports where you play in a group

3 Think of two sports for each category.

Extreme sports   ....triathlon....   ....
Water sports   ....
Contact sports   ....
Winter sports   ....
Spectator sports   ....
Team sports   ....

WORDZONE

Do you want to talk about a **sportsperson**?
Add a new ending to the sport. Change **-ing**
to **-er** or **-ist**.
*running – runn**er**, cycling – cycl**ist***

Look! When the sport has a different
ending, the sportsperson is different:
*athletics – **athlete***
*gymnastics – **gymnast***
*hockey – **hockey player***

→ Vocabulary File, page 162

4 Write the name of the sportsperson.

Sport	Sportsperson
1 football	....
2 boxing	....
3 skiing	....
4 gymnastics	....
5 swimming	....
6 motor racing	....
7 basketball	....
8 tennis	....
9 snowboarding	....

5 Choose the correct word to complete the sentences.

1 What a disaster! The final *score/total* was 6–1.
2 Everybody knows Brazil is the best football *group/ team* in the world.
3 Poland are playing well and might *beat/win* Spain tonight.
4 If they lose at the weekend they will be at the bottom of the football *league/list*.
5 If you want to *play/do* tennis you must join a club.
6 Who *won/beat* the race on Saturday?
7 In football you *kick/catch* the ball but in basketball you *bounce/drop* it.
8 He *made/scored* a goal in the final minute of the match.

6 Complete the sentences with words from Exercise 5.

1 Do you think John will .... the triathlon?
2 I'd like to be good enough to be in the volleyball ....
3 Tom's a great football player! Watch him .... the ball.
4 John said he would like to .... hockey instead of tennis.
5 You always .... me when we're in a race because you're faster.

Memorise

Say a **sport** and ask your partner to say the name of the **sportsperson**.

Obligation (modal verbs)

GRAMMAR ZONE

must

A talk about something that is necessary and important
First, you must decide to make regular exercise a part of your daily routine.

have to

B say that something is necessary because it is the rule or the law
Triathletes have to train really hard every day. They had to wear swimsuits.

don't have to

C talk about something not necessary
Professional triathletes get free bikes, and they don't have to repair them.

must not (mustn't)

D to say it is necessary/important NOT to do something
After the swim you mustn't forget where you left your bike.

➜ Grammar File, page 174

1 **Find examples of obligation in the text on page 119.**

2 **Choose the correct form of the verb.**
1 She said she *must/had to* train last weekend.
2 Jim has decided he *mustn't/doesn't have to* eat so many crisps if he wants to get fit.
3 Cynthia said she *must/had to* get up really early when she was in the gym club.
4 You *mustn't/don't have to* buy any special clothes – you can just wear something comfortable.
5 You *don't have to/mustn't* eat too much before you go for a run or you'll get stomachache.
6 We *must/mustn't* use our bikes more instead of going on the bus.

3 **Complete the sentences with the correct form of** *must, mustn't, have to, don't/doesn't have to.* **Sometimes more than one option is possible.**
1 When you're training for a marathon you .... have good running shoes.
2 James .... swim thirty lengths every day but he just likes keeping fit.
3 Liz carried a bottle of water, because she knew she .... drink plenty of water during the race.
4 You aren't allowed to bring food with you. You .... eat in the gym.
5 We .... run every day – three or four times each week is enough.
6 The athletes .... understand the rules of the race.

4 **Complete the second sentence so that it has a similar meaning to the first sentence using the word given.**
1 Training every day is important if you want to win.   MUST
You .... every day if you want to win.

2 It isn't necessary to buy special equipment for running.   HAVE
You .... special equipment for running.

3 Shouting at the other players is not permitted.   MUST
You .... at the other players.

4 A bicycle helmet is necessary these days.   MUST
You .... these days.

5 The club makes the gymnasts practise for three hours every Saturday.   TO
The gymnasts .... for three hours every Saturday.

6 You mustn't eat such unhealthy food.   STOP
You .... such unhealthy food.

7 It isn't necessary to buy new goggles.   HAVE
You .... buy new goggles.

Time to talk

5 **Would you like your school to offer sport every day? Why/Why not? What could you do to become healthier/fitter?**

Have a go!

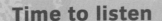

Time to listen

SKILL ZONE

Are you **completing** notes?
Before you listen, look at the notes and predict what information you need.

2.13 **3** Listen to journalist Ruby Smith talking about her first zorbing experience and complete her notes.

Location: 1 ....

Zorbing was invented in: 2 ....

Date of origin of zorbing: 3 ....

Size of zorb: 4 ....

Maximum number of people in

zorb: 5 ....

Time required to fill zorb with air: 6 ....

Maximum speed of zorb: 7 ....

Latest zorb experience: 8 ....

Get ideas

1 What sort of people like extreme sports? Have you tried or would you like to try an extreme sport? Why/Why not?

2 Look at the photos below and answer the questions.

1 Do you think zorbing is dangerous?
2 Where is the best place to zorb?
3 Do you think you zorb on your own or with people?

2.14 **4** Listen again and check your answers.

Get ideas

1 What do you think is the best way to keep fit? How much sport do you do?

2 Ask and answer the questions with a partner.

How SPORTY are you?

1 I like doing sport.
a Yes, every day b Yes, sometimes
c No, never

2 I like to go for a walk.
a Yes, every day b Yes, sometimes
c No, never

3 I enjoy swimming.
a Yes, every day b Yes, sometimes
c No, never

4 I love riding my bike.
a Yes, every day b Yes, sometimes
c No, never

5 I'd like to try/I have tried an extreme sport.
a Yes b Maybe c No

6 I go to the gym.
a Yes, every day b Yes, sometimes
c No, never

7 I enjoy being in the fresh air.
a Yes, every day b Yes, sometimes
c No, never

8 I enjoy the games we play in gym at school.
a Yes, all of them b Yes, some of them
c No, none of them

9 I think dancing is fun.
a Yes b Maybe c No

10 There should be more teenage sport on TV.
a Yes b Maybe c No

2.15 3 Listen to the conversations and underline the word or expression you hear.

1 Do you like sport?
Really/Well, most of the time it's good fun.

2 I'd love to go swimming but the pool is closed.
Oh no!/Oh, I see. When does it open?

3 Mum says I should do some sport every day.
OK, but/Oh, really have you got time?

2.16 4 Listen again and repeat the replies.

Time to speak

5 Complete the conversation with phrases from Useful phrases. Then practise it with a partner.

Tim: I'd love to learn yoga.
Rick: .... I know a great teacher.
Tim: .... Do you do yoga then?
Rick: .... I've joined a sports club. It's a great way to make friends.
Tim: .... but you have to buy expensive clothes to do sport.
Rick: .... You can wear anything.
Tim: .... Still, I'd like to do sport every day at school. What about you?
Rick: .... I think twice a week is enough for me.

SKILL ZONE Are you trying to keep the conversation going and to sound 'natural'? Use the Useful phrases. Say the phrases and practise them in a sentence. Remember, ask questions to keep the other person talking.

6 Now go round the class. One person starts with a sentence from Exercise 2. The next person must add something. How long can you keep the conversation going?

Useful phrases

Showing interest or surprise
Really!/Oh, really? Oh, I see …
Oh, right/good/no …

Reacting to somebody else's opinion
That's right. Well, yes/OK, but …
Yes/yeah, that's true/you're right, but …

Giving more information
Well … Actually … Anyway …

123

do, play or go

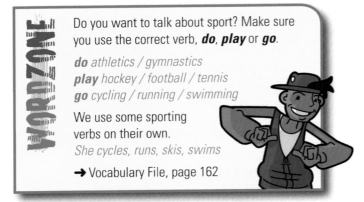

WORDZONE

Do you want to talk about sport? Make sure you use the correct verb, **do**, **play** or **go**.

do athletics / gymnastics
play hockey / football / tennis
go cycling / running / swimming

We use some sporting verbs on their own.
She cycles, runs, skis, swims

→ Vocabulary File, page 162

1 **Put the sports in the correct column.**

athletics   boxing   cycling   gymnastics
hockey   motor racing   rugby   running   skiing
snowboarding   swimming   tennis

do	go + verb + -ing	play
athletics	cycling	hockey

2 **Complete the sentences with the correct form of do, play or go. Be careful with tenses!**

1 We .... kayaking every day while we were on holiday.
2 She's been .... gymnastics for three years now and is getting really good.
3 This summer I really want to .... tennis.
4 We've just .... cycling along the new cycle path.
5 He's really sporty. He .... hockey, basketball and rugby.
6 I'd like to .... swimming this weekend at the outdoor pool.
7 He's not here at the moment. He's .... athletics at the local club.
8 If you want to .... boxing you'll have to buy some good gloves.

3 **Read the article and choose the best answer, A, B, C or D.**

1	**A** go	**B** play	**C** do	**D** try
2	**A** match	**B** game	**C** competition	**D** score
3	**A** scored	**B** won	**C** beat	**D** succeeded
4	**A** sport	**B** class	**C** league	**D** team
5	**A** practised	**B** played	**C** went	**D** did
6	**A** training	**B** train	**C** trainer	**D** trainers
7	**A** do	**B** go	**C** make	**D** win
8	**A** make	**B** do	**C** play	**D** go
9	**A** go	**B** do	**C** practise	**D** play
10	**A** visit	**B** train	**C** make	**D** go
11	**A** exercise	**B** fit	**C** training	**D** better

You should have seen me!

Every Saturday I 1) .A. kayaking. Last week my local club organised a 2) .... and I was very pleased because I 3) .... ! You see, I couldn't have done it two years ago but now I'm really fit and I love it.

I like being good at things and would be embarrassed at school if the other girls were better than me. I hated basketball and hockey because I was never picked to be in the school 4) ..... . When we 5) ..... running, I always came last. I must have been quite unfit!

Then two years ago somebody gave a talk at our school about kayaking. I had a go at it and really enjoyed it. For the first time in my life I liked 6) .... and I now 7) .... other sports with the kayaking group. Every week we 8) ..... cycling, 9) ..... athletics and I 10) ..... to the gym for regular workouts.

I could have tried these other sports before I started kayaking but I didn't have a reason. Now I'm more motivated because I want to get 11) ..... and be healthy.

People are always saying that we must get fit. I would say to all those who don't like sport: join a club and try something different. You might be surprised!

could/must/should + have + past participle

GRAMMAR ZONE

could have + past participle

A to talk about something that was possible in the past
*I **could have done** these other sports before I started kayaking but ...*

must have + past participle

B when we are certain that something happened in the past
*I **must have been** quite unfit.*

should have + past participle

C to talk about something that did not happen but we wish it had
*You **should have** seen me!*

➜ Grammar File, page 174

1 Choose the correct form to complete the sentences.

1 Jo ran a marathon. That *must/could/should* have been very tiring!
2 We didn't manage to finish the marathon; we *must/could/should* have trained harder.
3 I'm sorry you didn't bring your costume; we *must/could/should* have gone swimming.
4 It was a fantastic match. You *must/could/should* have come with us.
5 What a pity John wasn't able to run; he *must/could/should* have won the race.
6 The team is celebrating! They *must/could/should* have won the league.

2 Complete the text with the correct modal form of the verbs in brackets.

Joe: Hi Pete, you 1) .... (come) to the match with us last night. We had a great time!

Peter: Well, somebody 2) .... (tell) me about it! I didn't know there was a match on.

Joe: That's strange. I asked Jake to phone you. He 3) .... (forget). Didn't you get a message?

Peter: Oh, I think I 4) .... (be) in the shower when he called. I heard my phone but couldn't answer it.

Joe: Well, next weekend make sure we can contact you. It was a great match.

3 Complete the second sentence so that it has a similar meaning to the first.

1 It was wrong to cycle at night without lights. CYCLED
We .... at night without lights.

2 It was impossible for him to run faster. HAVE
He .... run faster.

3 It was not a good idea to take his bike without asking. ASKED
You .... if you could take his bike.

4 It was possible for her to win the race. COULD
She .... the race.

5 She thought the music was too loud. HAVE
She thought the music .... quieter.

6 It was not a good idea to miss training last week. HAVE
You .... training last week.

Time to talk

4 Who's your favourite sportsperson? What are the most popular sports in your country?

Get ideas

1 When did you last try a new sport? What was it? Would you like to have more time for sports? Why/Why not?

Find the right words

2 Complete the texts with these words and phrases.

On the one hand   on the other hand

Firstly   secondly   finally

To conclude,   Many people say that   Because of that

> **1** I don't think I want to try horse-riding for various reasons. .... none of my friends do it, ... I haven't got the right clothes and .... I'm quite scared of horses!

> **2** .... cycling is fun because you can go quite fast but .... it's very hard work if you live in the mountains like I do!

> **3** .... I think everybody can find a sport they like if they keep looking.
> **4** .... yoga is really good if you're stressed. .... I always go to yoga classes when I've got lots of exams at school.

3 Put the words and phrases from Exercise 2 in the correct place in the table.

Introducing a topic or idea	Firstly,
	....
Adding more information	....
Contrasting ideas	On the one hand
	....
Talking about the result of an action	....
Giving an example	such as
Finishing	....
	....

4 Describe a sport you like doing. Write three sentences.

1 Give three reasons why you like the sport.
> I like football because it's fun to play, it's good exercise and I play it with my friends.

2 Write a good thing about the sport.
> Football is fun, because you're in a team.

3 Write one problem about the sport.
> Football is dangerous and you can get injured.

5 Use phrases from Exercises 2 and 3 to link your sentences.

> I like playing team sports such as football. On the one hand it's good exercise and it's fun to play it with friends but on the other hand it is dangerous and you can get injured.

Plan ahead

6 Read the essay *Sport can be fun!* and choose the correct function of each paragraph, a or b.

Paragraph 1
a gives the writer's opinion
b introduces the topic

Paragraph 2
a agrees with the title
b disagrees with the title

Paragraph 3
a offers more information
b offers contrasting information

Paragraph 4
a finishes with an opinion
b finishes with an opinion and a suggestion

7 Find words and phrases in the essay that:

1 introduce a topic or ideas ....
2 contrast ideas ....
3 add information ....
4 talk about the result of an action ....
5 give examples ....
6 finish the composition ....

8 Read the essay again and answer the questions.

1 Why does the writer think sport is important?
2 What reasons does he give for *not* doing sport?

Sport can be fun!

1 Many people say that sport can be fun. However some people don't take regular exercise because they can't find a sport that they really like.

2 To begin with I think that there are good reasons for doing sport and that it can be fun. On the one hand, regular exercise helps you stay fit and helps you concentrate at school. Sport also helps you to relax. I might have had a stressful day at school and I know that a nice bike ride is the perfect way to forget about things. As well as that, sport is very sociable. Joining a gym or a sports club could be a great way to make new friends.

3 On the other hand sometimes it's difficult to find a sport that you like and do well. I have to play football and basketball at school. I quite like them but I'm not very good at them. Lots of people like me never get picked to be in a team. Because of that we stop doing sport.

4 To conclude I think that we must find ways of trying different sports. There are lots of new sports such as rock-climbing and skateboarding that look energetic and good fun.

Time to write *an essay*

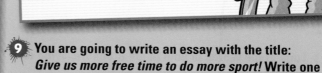

SKILLZONE

Are you **writing an essay**? Make sure you put your information in a logical order. Give each paragraph a clear function:

Paragraph 1: introduce the topic

Paragraph 2: explain why you agree or disagree with the title

Paragraph 3: give information that contrasts with paragraph 2

Paragraph 4: finish with your opinion and a suggestion.

Use phrases to introduce each paragraph.

9 You are going to write an essay with the title: *Give us more free time to do more sport!* Write one sentence for each of these.

1 introduce the topic
2 agree or disagree with the title
3 contrast with your sentence in 2
4 conclude your composition

10 Now write your essay in 100–150 words. Use the Skillzone to help you.

Time to watch *Tough triathlon*

11 Watch the DVD and do the activities on page 162.

12 Thrills and chills

Get ideas

1 What theme parks do you know? Why are they popular?

Time to read

2 Look at the photos of the Europa-Park brochure and answer the questions.

   1 What type of activities do you think offer thrills and chills in Europa-Park?

   2 Which photos do you think show the newer attractions?

3 Read the brochure quickly and check your answers.

4 Look at the words in bold in the brochure. What do they refer to?

   1 It (line 6)   **A** Europa-Park
                       B Germany

   2 Their (line 8)   **A** the gardens
                       B your family

   3 that (line 20)   **A** the football experience
                       B England

   4 they (line 26)   **A** younger visitors
                       B the latest sports shoes

   5 It (line 28)   **A** the harbour
                       B the ship

5 Find words in the *Little tips for great adventures* section in the brochure that match these meanings.

   1 things you give someone as a present

   2 experienced and qualified

   3 the group of people who work for an organisation

   4 food that is prepared and eaten quickly

Are you reading for facts? First read for the general idea, so that you know what the text is about. Then find the parts that answer the questions.

SKILL ZONE

6 Read the questions and choose the best answer, A, B, C or D.

   1 How would you describe the accommodation at Europa-Park?

      A There's a good choice.

      B It's adventurous.

      C It's near the main entrance to the park.

      D You have to sleep in a tent.

   2 A father takes his son to Europa-Park for his fifteenth birthday. How much will it cost?

      A €56,50

      B €60,00

      C €34,00

      D €53,00

   3 What happens if you buy presents in the morning?

      A You can leave them at the shop until 3p.m.

      B You can pay extra and your hotel will keep them for you.

      C You don't have to pay for them.

      D They can be taken to the main entrance or your hotel.

   4 Which attraction is also educational?

      A Italy's Ghost Castle.

      B The Pegasus roller coaster in Greece.

      C The Atlantica SuperSplash in Portugal.

      D The Magic Cinema.

   5 Paul is six years old and 125 cm tall. Which attraction(s) can he go on?

      A The Eurosat and Swiss racing track.

      B All of them except the Silver Star.

      C The Arena of Football and Pegasus roller coaster.

      D All of them.

Summarise

Describe the theme park in your own words.
There are a lot of …
For safety, some rides have …
Visitors can learn about …
Visitors can stay …

Time to talk

7 Which attraction seems most exciting to you? Why? What would you do first if you went to Europa-Park with friends?

EUROPA PARK

Looking for ideas for a great day trip? Trying to find the perfect family holiday? You'll find thrills and chills for all the family at Europa-Park! It's the biggest and most thrilling theme park in Germany!
5 Located in the beautiful gardens of the historic Balthasar Castle, **it** has over 100 attractions and fascinating shows.

This year give your family **their** best holiday ever at Europa-Park! The rides are better than ever, we've never had as much fun as
10 we had at Europa-Park!

Thrills

No other tourist destination in Germany is as thrilling as Europa-Park. See thirteen exciting European destinations in one day! Visitors can stroll around the various attractions or ride on the Europa-Park train. The tour begins at the train station in
5 Germany and takes you through thirteen exciting European destinations. First stop, Italy, where there's spine-chilling fun in our scariest attraction, the Ghost Castle of the Medici. Then it's off to France for a ride on Silver Star – Europe's highest and biggest roller coaster. Next, we go to England for a
10 fantastic Football experience **that** offers sport and entertainment for the whole family. Have fun in the Football Scooters – cars designed in the shape of the latest sports shoes – or watch exciting games on large screens in the futuristic 'Arena of Football'.
Younger visitors will enjoy an archaeological excavation in Greece where **they** can experience their first roller coaster ride in Pegasus. After that, the tour visits Portugal, where a

massive new sailing ship waits in the harbour. **It**'s the impressive entrance to the Atlantica SuperSplash water-coaster. Visitors of all ages can learn about shipbuilding and see the captain's cabin 30 on this model of a sixteenth-century ship. If you would rather have a more comfortable experience check out the sights, sounds and smells of the Magic Cinema with more than 440 interactive seats. Our newest attraction is Atlantis Adventure, an interactive indoor ride for the whole family. 35

Chills

Europa-Park has accommodation to suit everybody. More adventurous guests can stay in a tent in the Tipi Village and enjoy the typical Wild West scenery. Camping fans can use Europa-Park's large caravan site, just five minutes from the main entrance. Or perhaps you prefer a little more comfort? Then 40 choose from a Spanish country house, a medieval castle or a luxury hotel with the charming atmosphere of Italy or a Portuguese monastery.

Little tips for great adventures

Shopping: Buy your souvenirs and gifts before 3p.m. and they can be taken to the main entrance or your hotel free of charge.

Cash Dispensers: These are located at the main entrance and near the Information Office. Inside the park you can pay in many places with credit cards.

First Aid: The First-Aid Station is located next to the roller coaster in Russia. Trained staff are available during opening hours. In an emergency please contact a member of staff.

Restaurants: 30 different restaurants and fast food places.

Opening times: 1st March – 31st October
9a.m. to 6p.m. Open later during peak season.

Admission prices

Children under 4	free	Children (4–11)	€30,00
Adults	€34,00	Senior Citizens (60 +)	€30,00
Children on their birthday	free (up to 12th birthday)		

Annual tickets and group tickets are cheaper than individual tickets.

Height and age restrictions for rides.
Arena of Football and Pegasus roller coaster: from 4 years and minimum 100cm

Silver Star: from 11 years and min 140cm

Coming up … *Europa-Park* on DVD. See page 137.

Holidays and travel

1 **Find words in the brochure on page 129 that match these meanings.**

1 a short journey to visit a place (line 1)
2 interesting or enjoyable to see or do (line 6)
3 a journey for pleasure where you visit different places (line 14)
4 the place that you are travelling to (line 16)
5 a place to live, stay or work (line 36)
6 a vehicle that is pulled by a car, and you can live or sleep in (line 39)
7 comfortable, beautiful and expensive (line 42)

2 **Complete the sentences with these words.**

cruise   journey   tour   travel   trip   voyage

1 Marco Polo went on his first ......*voyage*........ at the age of seventeen.
2 My parents are going to do a .... of four Italian cities.
3 We had a terrible .... We didn't get home until midnight.
4 There's a school .... next month to the new theme park.
5 I prefer to .... when there isn't much traffic.
6 It would be fun to go on a .... around the Bahamas.
7 Did you have a good .... to Germany?
8 It was a very interesting .... and we visited lots of places.
9 I don't mind the .... to school because the bus is always warm and comfortable.
10 Japanese tourists like to do a European .... and see as many cities as possible.
11 I try not to .... during the busiest hours of the day.

Remember! We can make **compound nouns** by putting two nouns together. The first noun describes the second noun.

A **ticket** for a **plane** is a *plane ticket*.
A **trip** that lasts one **day** is a *day trip*.

→ Vocabulary File, page 163

3 **Match the nouns (1–5) with the nouns (a–e) to make compound nouns.**

1 boat   a journey
2 adventure   b guide
3 luxury   c trip
4 plane   d hotel
5 tour   e holiday

4 **Match these words and phrases with the correct verbs. Some words can go with more than one verb.**

a holiday   a rest   a ride   a ticket   a trip
accommodation   holiday   photos   sightseeing
souvenirs   the bus

1 have
2 go
3 go on
4 catch
5 buy
6 plan
7 book
8 take

5 **Complete the sentences with the correct form of the phrases from Exercise 4.**

1 Don't forget your camera so that you can .... of the castle.
2 I .... for my family in the museum gift shop.
3 If you are in Greece you must .... There are so many fascinating old buildings.
4 You'd better hurry if you want to .... It's about to leave.
5 It's easy to .... because the hotels are on the internet.
6 We're .... for next year but can't decide if we should go skiing or cycling.
7 When I go to the theme park I want to .... that is really fast and frightening.
8 I really want to .... this year. I didn't have one last year and I need one.

6 **Say two things about your last holiday or day trip using the phrases in Exercise 4.**

My dad booked the tickets. We had a ride on a roller coaster.

Memorise

How many holiday words can you remember? Write a list and compare with your partner. Score one point for each holiday word and an extra point for each compound noun.

Adjectives: comparatives and superlatives

GRAMMARZONE

Comparatives

To compare two things/people that are not equal, use the comparative + *than*.

A adjectives with one syllable end in *-er*
… group tickets are cheaper than individual tickets.

B adjectives ending in *-y* change to *-ier*
The park opens earlier in summer.

C two or more syllables use *more* + the adjective
More adventurous guests can stay …

D some adjectives are irregular: *good – better, bad – worse*, etc.
The rides are better than ever.

E To compare two things that are equal, use *as* + adjective + *as*
No other tourist destination in Germany is as thrilling as Europa-Park.

Superlatives

To compare three or more things, use the superlative. Don't forget to use *the* + the superlative

F adjectives with one syllable add *-est; the biggest, the highest*
The biggest … theme park in Germany.

G adjectives ending in *-y* change to *the -iest*
… in our scariest attraction

H two or more syllables use *most* + adjective
… and most thrilling theme park in Germany.

I some adjectives are irregular: *good – best, bad – worst,* etc.
Find the best place to stay.

➜ Grammar File, page 175

1 Read the information about the rides in Europa-Park and choose the correct information to complete the sentences.

Attraction	Date built	Min age	Min height	Max speed	Height
Eurosat	1989	6	1.20 m	60 km/h	45 m
Silver Star	2002	11	1.40 m	130 km/h	73 m
Pegasus	2005	4	1.00 m	65 km/h	15 m
SuperSplash	2005	6	1.20 m	80 km/h	30 m

1 The Pegasus is the *lowest/highest* ride in the park.
2 The Silver Star goes *faster/slower* than the SuperSplash.
3 The Silver Star is the *slowest/highest* ride in the park.
4 The Eurosat is *older/newer* than the Pegasus.
5 The Pegasus is *slower/faster* than the Eurosat.

2 Complete the text with the correct form (comparative or superlative) of these adjectives.

fast   high   old   slow   tall   young

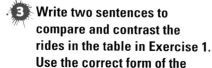

OUR RIDES

Eurosat is one of the 1) ....highest.... rides at Europa-Park. It was built in 1989 and can reach a maximum speed of 60 km/h. It is 2) .... than the Pegasus but at 45m it is one of the 3) .... rides in the park. The Silver Star is for 4) .... children only because it is the 5) .... and 6) .... ride of them all. The Pegasus on the other hand is ideal for 7) .... visitors as it only goes up to 15 m. However it is quite fast and is only 15 km/h 8) .... than the SuperSplash. Like the Eurosat, the SuperSplash is suitable for children who are 9) .... than 1.20 m. At 80 km/h it is 10) .... than the Silver Star.

3 Write two sentences to compare and contrast the rides in the table in Exercise 1. Use the correct form of the adjectives *exciting* and *scary*.

Time to talk

4 Talk about these things with a partner.
- Best or worst holiday.
- A scary dream.
- A frightening experience.
- An exciting day.

Fear or fun?

Get ideas

1 Do any of these things make you feel: scared? sick? excited? What other situations give you these feelings?

Time to listen

2.17 **2** Listen and match the feelings (A–F) with the speakers (1–5). There is one extra feeling.

Feelings	Speaker
A scared of heights	
B surprised how much he/she enjoyed it	
C sick and dizzy	
D thrilled with all the different things to do	
E exhausted by all the exercise	
F worried about safety	

SKILL ZONE

Do you need to match feelings to speakers? Don't choose your answer too soon! Make notes about each speaker the first time you listen. Check your notes the second time, then complete your answers. Do the ones you are sure of first.

2.18 **3** Listen again and match four of the photos with four of the speakers.

4 Read the statements. Do you agree or disagree with the speakers? Compare your answers with a partner.

1 I would scream on a roller coaster.
2 I would love to go on a massive water slide.
3 It would be great to get coaching tips from a famous sports person.
4 I wouldn't feel confident in a river.
5 I couldn't stand walking all day.

QUIZ

how adventurous are you?

1. Look at the day trips in the photos. Is your favourite:
a. a day at the beach or in the woods?
b. any of the sporting activities?
c. none of them – you'd prefer something more exciting, like bungee-jumping!

2. If you were going to a theme park, you would:
a. check the safety record before you go.
b. have fun with your friends, but avoid the really big rides.
c. head straight for the highest/fastest/most dangerous ride.

3. You're spending a day at the beach. Would you:
a. sunbathe, chat, read a book, have a little swim?
b. play racket ball/volleyball/football, swim a few times?
c. go windsurfing, sailing, diving, swim as far as you can?

Get ideas

1 Complete the quiz with a partner. Compare your answers with the rest of the class.

Time to speak

2 Listen and put the conversation in the correct order. Then practise the conversation with a partner.

A: Would you prefer to go walking or have a day at the beach? ..!..

A: I know, what about the theme park? .....

A: Me too! It's better than a theme park on a hot day! .....

B: Well, I'd rather go to the beach than go walking, but I'd prefer something more exciting. .....

B: That sounds good … Actually, I think I'd prefer to go to a water park. .....

3 Look at the photos on page 132. Which place would you prefer to go to? Why? Have a class vote for the most popular day out.

I would rather go to …   = I'd rather …
I would prefer to go to…   = I'd prefer …

4 Work with someone who has chosen a different place to go to. Compare the two trips. Giving reasons, decide which you think is:

- more exciting.
- more dangerous.
- more boring.
- more educational.
- more expensive.
- better for the whole family.

Useful phrases

not as bad as …
more fun than …
the most dangerous thing …
the best bit …

Are you **comparing different things?** Think about: what is similar, what is different, which you prefer. Use comparative and superlative adjectives.

Strong adjectives and descriptive verbs

1 Match these strong adjectives with their synonyms (1–12) below.

astonished dull exhausted fascinated hilarious mind-blowing* risky terrible terrified hectic thrilling wicked*

1 cool ......wicked......
2 scared ....
3 exciting ....
4 bad ....
5 surprised ....
6 interested ....
7 boring ....
8 dangerous ....
9 funny ....
10 busy ....
11 amazing ....mind-blowing..
12 tired ....

*very informal – used in speech with friends!

2 Can you think of any other strong words with similar meanings?

scared – petrified, alarmed

3 Replace the underlined words with a suitable strong adjective from Exercise 1.

1 I think skiing fast down a mountain is <u>amazing</u>! ....
2 I love *The Simpsons*, they're <u>funny</u>! ....
3 After a day at the theme park, I was <u>very tired</u>. ....
4 Our teacher was <u>surprised</u> that we all got 100 percent in the test. ....
5 My mum is <u>scared</u> of spiders. ....

4 Choose the correct meaning, A or B, for the verb or phrase.

1 talk quietly   A whisper
                 B moan
2 shout loudly   A chat
                 B yell
3 speak unclearly A mumble
                 B gossip
4 scream   A call
                 B shriek
5 cry   A sob
                 B speak
6 speak crossly   A grumble
                 B talk

5 Read the text and choose the best answer, A, B, or C.

1 A finally   B certainly   C recently
2 A visitors   B clients   C patients
3 A dangerous   B terrifying   C hectic
4 A whispering   B yelling   C sobbing
5 A Later   B After   C Further
6 A talking   B telling   C sobbing
7 A grumbling   B chatting   C calling
8 A fascinating B terrible   C risky
9 A away   B out   C over
10 A mumbling   B gossiping   C speaking
11 A dull   B dim   C pale
12 A scared   B bored   C exhausted

The weather is perfect so the theme park where I work has been really busy 1) ..C.. . Hundreds of 2) ..... pour in through the gates each day. Today was another 3) ..... day. As usual, several noisy and excited groups of schoolchildren were shrieking and 4) ..... to each other all the time. 5) ..... , I spotted a small child who was 6) ..... because he had lost his mother. When we found his mother she was 7) ..... because she was cross with him for running off. She said she'd prefer to go home rather than chase him around!

I was working on the roller coaster this afternoon. One grandfather had a 8) ..... ride. First his grandson was sick over him, then he realised that his false teeth had fallen 9) ..... at the top of the roller coaster. It was hard to understand what he was saying because he was 10) ..... . Luckily we found his teeth for him but they were really dirty. Yuck! Life is never 11) ..... at the theme park!

My friends asked me to go to the cinema at 9p.m. but I will have gone to bed by then because I'm 12) ..... ! Sometimes I'd rather have a quieter job, but I'll be working on the water splash tomorrow morning. It might be fun! By the end of next week I will have earned enough money to buy an amazing new bike!

Future continuous and future perfect simple

GRAMMAR ZONE

Future continuous

A an action that will be in progress at a certain time in the future
I'll be working on the water splash tomorrow morning.

Future perfect simple

B an action/situation that will be finished before a certain time in the future
I will have gone to bed by then!

→ Grammar File, page 175

1 Read Luke's work timetable and complete the sentences with the correct form (future perfect or future continuous) of the verbs in brackets.

Timetable

9.00 – 10.00	tickets
10.00 – 12.00	roller coaster
12.00 – 1.00	restaurant
1.00 – 2.00	lunch break
2.00 – 6.00	water splash

1 By 9.00 Luke will have arrived (arrive) at Europa-Park.
2 At 9.30 Luke .... (sell) tickets.
3 At 11.00 Luke .... (help) on the roller coaster.
4 By 12.01 .... (finish) helping on the roller coaster.
5 At 12.30 Luke .... (serve) in the restaurant.
6 By 2.10 Luke .... (eat) his lunch.
7 At 3.00 Luke .... (work) on the water splash.
8 By 7.00 Luke .... (go) home.

2 Complete the text with one word which best fits each gap.

---

mailbox Today | Mail | Calendar | Contacts

Reply | Reply All | Forward | Delete

To: **Alex**   From: **Theo**
Subject: **Holiday**

Hi Alex,

I'm going on holiday in the morning. We'll be 1) ....staying...... in a big hotel in Crete for a week. It will take a few hours to get there as we'll 2) .... travelling by car and by ferry. Dad says it's as fast 3) .... going by plane, but I don't believe him! Still, by this time tomorrow afternoon we'll 4) .... arrived and I'll be swimming in the hotel pool. Generally, I 5) .... rather have an active holiday, but Mum and Dad prefer 6) .... relax. I expect they 7) .... be sitting by the pool while I'm swimming!

Luckily for me there are some watersports on the beach. I think windsurfing will be more fun 8) .... sailing, don't you? Hopefully by the end of the week I 9) .... have learnt how to windsurf really well. That would be great! It will be 10) .... best holiday I've ever had. I'll send you a postcard!

Bye for now,

Theo

3 Complete the sentences in your own words.

1 This summer we ....
2 In a week's time ....
3 In the middle of August ....
4 In two weeks' time I ....
5 By the end of July I ....
6 .... by 15th September.

Time to talk

4 What will you be doing next month? What will you have done by the time you're twenty?

Get ideas

1 Think of a recent holiday or trip. What were the best or worst moments?

2 Read the letters and choose A, B or C to show how good or bad each story is.

> **A** Eek! Horrible!
> **B** Hmm. Not very dramatic!
> **C** Sounds like fun!

3 Find any 'strong' words in the letters.

Find the right words

4 Look at the letters again. What adverbs do the writers use? Where do the adverbs go in the sentences?

5 Match the adverbs and phrases that have similar meanings.

1	suddenly	**a**	fortunately
2	especially	**b**	finally
3	eventually	**c**	all of a sudden
4	luckily	**d**	at once
5	immediately	**e**	generally
6	usually	**f**	particularly

6 Complete the sentences with a suitable adverb or phrase. Then write two sentences of your own.

1 The teacher shouted at them to be quiet. .... , they stopped chatting.

2 I missed the bus home. .... , I had my mobile so I phoned Dad.

3 Leo was reading a book by the pool. .... , his sister shrieked loudly.

4 Anna loves camping. She .... enjoys sleeping in a tent.

5 We walked to the beach, swam all afternoon and had a picnic. .... , it was time to go home.

LETTERS

Readers' holiday experiences

1 We were on a camping holiday in France last year. One night, we were sleeping in our tent as usual. Suddenly, my mum woke up in the middle of the night. The floor of the tent was moving. She shrieked in horror – something was under the ground beneath us. She thinks it was a rat! Ugh! Fortunately, it didn't happen again, but we'll be staying in a caravan next year!
Erik, Germany

2 We were staying in a brilliant apartment in the Canary Islands last summer. One day we were swimming in the fantastic pool which was on a hill covered in olive trees. All of a sudden, we heard the sound of goat bells ringing. We looked up just as three goats jumped over the wall. They ignored us and started drinking water from the swimming pool! Luckily, my dad grabbed our camera and took a photo before they ran away.
Carla, Spain

3 The best moment of our holiday in Mar Del Plata was when we met up with some friends who were staying near us. We swam in their pool, played ball games and had a meal in the evening. At midnight it was my brother's birthday and he jumped up and dived into the pool with a big yell! He looked hilarious.
Luis, Argentina

Plan ahead

7 Read the story about a school trip and match the headings (A–C) with the paragraphs (1–3).

A Describing the place
B The main event
C Setting the scene

1
When I was fourteen, we had a school trip to a huge theme park. I was thrilled. We left early in the morning and everyone was really excited. During the long coach journey we chatted and laughed so much that time flew by. All of a sudden, we'd arrived.

2
The theme park was next to the beach and luckily the weather was fantastic. I felt dizzy after the journey. I would have preferred to stay on the beach, but we went straight to the theme park. My friends particularly wanted to ride on the new roller coaster – one of the fastest in Europe. It looked as high as our block of flats, maybe higher. I was terrified!

3
We queued for ages and I was feeling more and more uncomfortable. Eventually, we got into a roller coaster car and suddenly I realised I was going to be sick. Just then a kind man in uniform helped me out of the car. Unfortunately, I was sick all over his shoes! Everybody was staring at me. I felt terrible. It's something I'd rather forget about now!

Magda, Poland

8 Read Magda's story again and answer the questions.

1 Which words in the first paragraph tell you that Magda was having a good time?
2 Which words in the second paragraph tell you that Magda's feelings are changing?
3 What words and phrases does she use in the final paragraph to make the events seem more dramatic?
4 What two preferences does Magda tell us about in her description?

Time to write *a story*

9 You see this advert in an English-language magazine. Write your story in 120–180 words. Use Magda's story and the Skillzone box to help you.

My amazing trip!

Tell us about a recent trip or holiday experience. Was it good or bad? We will publish the best descriptions next month.

SKILLZONE

Are you **writing a story?** It's often a good idea to keep the main event until near the end. This makes the reader curious to find out what happened.

- Use strong adjectives and verbs to bring your writing alive.
- Use adverbs or adverbial phrases for dramatic effect.
- Check your tenses. Use mainly the past simple and continuous.

Time to watch *Europa-Park*

10 Watch the DVD and do the activities on page 163.

Vocabulary

1 **Match the sentences (1–7) with the definitions (a–g).**

1 eat the right foods   **a** get fit
2 do exercise to become healthy   **b** unhealthy
3 physical or mental strength that helps you do sport   **c** training
4 have difficulty breathing after exercise   **d** stamina
5 physical exercise to prepare you for a sports event   **e** healthy diet
6 not healthy   **f** out of breath
7 physical exercise that you do every day/week/month   **g** regular exercise

2 **Complete the sentences with the correct sportsperson for these sports.**

basketball   boxing   cycling   motor racing   running
skiing   swimming

1 A ...cyclist... must wear a helmet.
2 A .... must have good trainers.
3 A .... trains in cold weather.
4 A .... knows how to bounce the ball.
5 A .... can control a car well.
6 A .... has to wear special gloves.
7 A .... trains in water.

3 **Complete the sentences with the correct form of do, play or go and these sports.**

athletics   football   motor racing   running
snowboarding   swimming

1 Let's .go swimming... this afternoon at the beach. The water will be nice and warm.
2 As soon as the snow comes they .... in the mountains.
3 Daniel wants to........................ because he likes being in a team and can kick the ball.
4 Last year I .... and won a medal for the long jump.
5 If you want to .... you have to learn about cars first.
6 Anna usually .... in the park every day because she's training for a marathon.

4 **Complete the text with the correct word(s).**

accommodation   attractions   destination   gifts
travel   trip   tour

If I could have a free ticket to any 1) ...destination... in the world, where would I go? I think I'd like to 2) .... to New York. I'd book the best 3) .... in the city and go to the theatre every night. During the day I'd go on a 4) .... of the city to see the most important tourist 5) .... Then I'd relax on a boat 6) .... around the lake in Central Park. Before leaving I'd buy nice 7) .... for my family on the most famous shopping street, Fifth Avenue.

5 **Complete the sentences with the correct verb.**

book   go   have   take

1 You should always ....go........... sightseeing when you're in a new city.
2 I like to .... photos when I'm on holiday so that I can remember the places I've seen.
3 Luke wants to .... a rest in his room because he's tired after the journey.
4 Before I .... accommodation I always look at the hotel website to see if the rooms are big.
5 I'd like to .... on a ride that's fast and high.

6 **Use a word from each list (A and B) to make compound nouns to match the descriptions 1–6.**

A adventure   day   gift   luxury   theme   tour

B guide   holiday   hotel   park   shop   trip

1 You go here if you want to go on lots or exciting rides. theme park
2 A person who shows people around interesting places.
3 You buy things here to give to friends or family
4 You stay here if you want to be somewhere that is comfortable and expensive!
5 A visit to somewhere that takes less than twenty-four hours.
6 You go on one of these if you like being active.

7 **Complete the sentences with these strong adjectives.**

astonished   hilarious   terrible   terrified   thrilling

1 I was ...astonished... when I won the race because I didn't think I had trained enough.
2 Going on the highest ride at the theme park was .... and something I definitely want to do again!
3 We had a .... school trip. The bus broke down and it rained all day.
4 His jokes are .... and it's hard to stop laughing when you're with him.
5 Sam doesn't want to go on the boat trip because he's .... of water.

8 **Choose the phrasal verb that best matches the underlined words in sentences 1–6.**

build up   check out   head for   put (you) off   run out of
turn (something) into

1 Some runners eat the wrong things before a race and don't have enough energy. run out of
2 When people tell you that you are no good at sport it makes you not like it and not want to do it.
3 I saw her moving towards the gift shop to meet her friends.
4 Train every day for a long time, and you will begin to be an athlete.
5 I'm going to investigate the sports results on TV.
6 The roller coaster started to increase speed and suddenly I felt very nervous!

Grammar

9 Complete the sentences with *must, have to, had to, don't have to* or *mustn't*.

1 She ....._had to_...... buy new trainers when she started jogging.
2 I'm really tired, I'm glad I .... go to school today.
3 The sign says that small children .... stay with their parents at all times.
4 When we were at Europa-Park everybody .... wear a safety harness on the roller coaster.
5 You've only just arrived. .... you .... leave so soon?
6 Gymnasts .... eat too much before a competition.
7 My friends .... leave the park because it was closing.

10 Choose the correct alternative to complete the text.

Last Friday some friends organised a trip to the local water park to celebrate the end of the school year. It 1) *should have been/must have been* a good day out but it all went wrong for me. That morning I 2) *must have been/might have been* in a really deep sleep because I didn't hear my alarm at all. When Mum came into my room shouting, 'Get up lazybones!' she was so loud I think the whole street 3) *should have heard/could have heard* her. When I arrived at the bus stop, the bus had gone and nobody was there. Why hadn't my friends called me? Then I thought they 4) *might have sent/must have sent* me a text message. Then I looked at my mobile and saw three messages. They all said 'You 5) *should have come /must have come* with us ... it's great here!'

11 Choose the correct response.

1 I'm tired today.
   a You must have gone to bed earlier.
   b <u>You should have gone to bed earlier.</u>

2 Oh no! They've run out of tickets for the match.
   a They should have sold them yesterday.
   b They must have sold them all yesterday.

3 I haven't trained much for the race.
   a You could have trained with me.
   b You must have trained with me.

4 The roller coaster is empty at the moment.
   a It must have broken down.
   b It should have broken down.

5 They've won the league this year.
   a They should have trained hard this year.
   b They must have trained hard this year.

12 Complete the second sentence so that it has a similar meaning to the first sentence.

1 Wearing helmets was obligatory when we rode our bikes.   HAD
   We ._had to wear helmets_. when we were young.
2 It's important that children are not left on their own in the theme park.   LEAVE
   Parents .... on their own in the theme park.
3 It isn't necessary for you to wait for me.   HAVE
   You .... wait for me.
4 It was possible for her to try the roller coaster but she didn't want to.   COULD
   She .... but she didn't want to.
5 It was not a good idea to come without your money.   SHOULD
   You .... your money.
6 I'm sure he knew about the competition.   MUST
   He .... about the competition.

13 Complete the sentences with the correct (comparative or superlative) form of the adjective in brackets.

1 That's the ......_best_........ (good) theme park I've ever been to.
2 It's .... (easy) and .... (fast) to buy tickets online than by phone.
3 The rides were .... (exciting) than I thought they would be.
4 The .... (thrilling) ride for me was the Silver Star.
5 Some of the attractions are .... (dangerous) than others.
6 The food is .... (good) than you get at home.
7 It must be .... (big) theme park in Europe.
8 The .... (bad) thing about the whole day was the rain!

14 Choose the correct form to complete the sentences.

1 I won't see you later because *I'll be training in the park/I'll have trained* in the park.
2 After my holiday in Europa-Park this summer, *I'll be visiting/I'll have visited* all the best theme parks in Europe.
3 By the time Vanessa arrives *I'll be finishing/I'll have finished* my workout.
4 Don't call me tonight because *I'll be getting ready/I'll have got ready* for the trip.
5 Text me after 10p.m. when *we'll be finishing /we'll have finished* our dinner.
6 Be careful or *you'll be spending/you'll have spent* all your money on the first day of your holiday.
7 What do you think *you'll be doing/you'll have done* next year?

Did you remember all the vocabulary and grammar points?

→ Vocabulary File, pages 162 and 163
→ Grammar File, pages 174 and 175

Personal information Unit 1, p.13

Asking and answering questions

TIP! Use more than two or three words in your answers to sound interesting!

1 Ask your partner questions and complete the questionnaire.

Birthday: When is your birthday?

Hobbies:

Family:

Favourite school subject:

Favourite film:

Best friend:

Biggest fear:

Favourite dream:

Favourite singer:

Ambition:

Useful Phrases

Asking for information

What do you like doing….?
Can you describe your……(family, house, hometown)?
What's/who's your favourite/biggest…….?
Who's your best…..

Giving information

I love / like / enjoy / I'm (really) into …
I hate / I can't stand …

 2 Now tell the rest of the class two interesting facts about your partner.

(Name) can't stand …but he/she's really into….

Apologies and excuses Unit 2, p.23

Role play

TIP! Before you act out your conversation with your partner, work with another student taking the same role and plan what you can say.

1 Work with a partner. Choose a role and act out a conversation. Use the phrases to help you.

Student A

You arrive home from school and the computer isn't working. You need it for your homework NOW! You only have one hour then you have to go to a music class.

Student B

You are the parent. You are very busy and you don't have much time today. You have to prepare a meal, walk the dog, do the ironing and visit a friend who's sick.

Useful Phrases

I'm really sorry I didn't … but …
Sorry I … but …
I wasn't able to/I can't … because …
I'm very sorry, but you see….

Suggestions Unit 3, p.35

Agreeing and making decisions

1 Work in groups of three. Read the task. Then look at the pictures and suggest what you should take with you.

Task

You and your friends are going on a school trip. You're staying in a hotel in the city centre. In the mornings you will visit museums and galleries and the afternoons will be free. The weather will be hot.

TIP! When you suggest something, give a reason.

2 You don't have everything you need for the trip. Take turns to suggest what you need and decide a list of things you will have to buy.

Useful Phrases

Making suggestions

Why don't you/we … ?
Shall we …?
Do you want to … ?

Let's …
You/We could …
What about … -ing?

Replying

That's a good/great idea
I don't think so
I'd rather not …

Mm … I'm not sure
Yes, maybe we could….

Explanations and reasons Unit 4, p.45

Agreeing and making decisions

1 Work in groups of three. Read the task and make suggestions.

> ## Task
>
> Your Town Hall has decided to organise an International Youth Festival. It has asked local schools to suggest activities for the day. Discuss the following ideas and decide which three activities are best.

Useful Phrases

Giving explanations and reasons

because of ...
... in order to ...
The main reason ...

because ...
... that's why ...
That means ...

TIP! Listen to the other people and respond to their ideas.

2 Think of two more activities for a Youth Festival. Give reasons for your choice.

Opinions Unit 5, p.57
Agreeing and disagreeing

1 Read these comments and decide if you agree (A) or disagree (D).

1 If a student is bullying another student, it's the school's problem not the parents'.
2 Younger students often try to copy the behaviour of older students.
3 Most people smoke because their friends smoke.
4 You are never too old to have a tattoo!
5 Some people call other people horrible names because they're jealous of them.
6 If friends are ignoring you, you should ignore them.

2 Work in groups of three. Compare your answers and discuss your opinions.

> **TIP** Don't forget to say why you agree or disagree!

Useful Phrases

Giving your opinion

I'm not sure.   *I think …*
I prefer …   *If you ask me …*

more strongly..

I really think…   *I feel really strongly about this.*

Agreeing

Yes, you're right.   *Exactly!*
I agree completely.

Disagreeing

I don't agree.   *I don't think…*

Saying what you have done recently Unit 6, p.67
Asking and answering questions

> **TIP** Respond to your partner's answers with the correct response from Useful phrases.

Useful Phrases

Really?   *Oh!*   *Right!*
It sounds cool!   *Did/Didn't you?*

1 Work with a partner. Take turns to ask and answer questions.

Student A

1 What films have you seen recently?
2 Who have you spoken to today?
3 What have you learnt today?
4 Have you been to a party in the past month?
5 Which computer games have you played recently?

Student B

1 Which sports have you played in the past week?
2 Who have you phoned today?
3 What have you eaten today?
4 Who have you seen today?
5 What have you been talking about today?

2 Tell the rest of the class two facts about your partner.

Describing and comparing photos Units 7 and 8, pp.79, 89

TIP! When you're not sure about the correct word to describe an object or situation, describe it as well as you can.

When you compare two photos you need to decide what the connection is between the two.

Facts

1 Choose the words you need to describe each photo.

coins Colosseum historic objects illustrations library painting reference books soldier statue sword

2 Work with a partner. Use the questions below to help you describe the photos.

Student A: describe photo A.
Student B: describe photo B.

- Where? Is it inside or outside?
- What objects and people are there?
- What are the people doing?
- How are the objects helping the people ?

Useful Phrases

Well, this photo/the first/second photo shows …
It must be …
He/She/It/They seem(s) to be …
He/She/They look(s)….
I'm not really sure, perhaps …
It could be …
It's difficult to tell. Maybe …

Making guesses

3 The students in the photos are studying the same subject in different ways. Where are they? How are they studying?

4 What are the main differences? Which way would you prefer to study?

Useful Phrases

Similarites

Both photos show …
The people in both photos are …

Differences

There are several differences. For example, …
The first picture is … but the second one is …
In this picture I can see…. However, in the other one there's a …

Feelings Unit 9, p.101

Expressing strong feelings

 1 Describe the photos. Why do you think friends get on/don't get on?

We get on because ...

We don't get on because ...

 2 Read the lists. Which reasons do you think are most important?

Reasons we get on

We have the same interests.
We like the same clothes.
We live near each other.
We're in the same class.
We listen to the same music.
We are both sociable.

....

Reasons we don't get on

She/He copies what I wear!
She/He is too shy and never says anything!
She/He never wants to do what I want to do!
She/He never goes out!
She/He is really bossy!
She/He is insensitive!

....

 TIP! Remember! It's OK to express strong opinions, but be polite!

3 Work with a partner. Add one more reason to each list. Discuss why you think you get on and don't get on with your classmates.

Useful Phrases

Giving opinions

I think/I don't think ...   *In my opinion, ...*
Personally, ...   *As far as I'm concerned, ...*
What I think is that ...   *I prefer ...*
I don't mind ...

Expressing strong feelings

I really think/feel that...because
I hate...   *I can't stand ...*

Information Unit 10, p.111

Role play

> ## Useful Phrases
>
> **Asking for information**
>
> *What / When / Why / Where did you …?*
> *How (often) did you …?   What was … like?*
> *How/What about …?   Would you …?*
>
> **Giving information**
>
> *Yes, of course …   No, of course not!*
> *No way!*

 1 Work with a partner. Read the role cards and act out a conversation.

Student A

Your friend has just come back from a school trip camping in the mountains. You are thinking of going on the same trip next year. Prepare five questions to ask your friend about the trip.

Student B

You have just come back from a school trip camping in the mountains. Use the photos to help you answer the questions.

 Sound enthusiastic when you answer the questions and give lots of information.

2 Work with a partner. Do you think camping is a good or a bad idea for a school trip? Discuss your ideas.

Conversation strategies Unit 11, p.123

Keeping a conversation going

1 **Work with a partner. Do you agree or disagree with the following statements?**

1 There aren't enough sports facilities in our town.
2 Our school should offer new sports.
3 If there were more sports facilities, we would do more sports.
4 If you don't live near a sports centre, you can't keep fit.
5 People don't take physical education seriously.

2 **Work with a partner. Keep the conversation going as long as you can.**

> **Student A:** Did you know they're going to build a new sports centre?

Student B continue the conversation.

> **Student B:** We should do sport every day at school.

Student A continue the conversation.

TIP! Using the correct intonation when you reply makes you sound interested!

Useful Phrases

Showing interest or surprise

Really! /Oh, really?   *Oh, I see …*
Oh right/good/no …

Reacting to somebody else's opinion

That's right.   *Well, yes/OK, but …*
Yes, that's true/you're right, but …

Giving more information/explaining

Well …   *Actually …*
Anyway …

Preferences Unit 12, p.133

Expressing preferences and comparing

1 **Work with a partner. Look at the photos and compare the theme park rides.**

TIP! Use adjectives such as *scary, dangerous, fast, high, amazing, exciting...* to describe the rides.

Useful Phrases

not as good as …
more fun than …
the most dangerous thing …
the best bit …

2 **Work with a partner. Tell your partner which rides you would prefer to go on and why.**

An email or informal letter

Are you writing an email or an informal letter? Follow this plan.

1 An email or informal letter should be chatty and full of news.

2 Imagine you're talking to your reader – ask how they are.

3 Ask the reader to reply to you.

Plan

1 Begin your email or letter with a greeting.
Hi,
Dear (+ name)

Paragraph 1

2 Ask how your friend is.
How are you … ?
How are things?

3 Say something about their last email/letter.
It was good to hear from you.
Thanks for telling me about …

Paragraph 2

4 Say what your news is.
Did I tell you about … ?
I'm writing to let you know about …

Paragraph 3

5 Give more news.
By the way …
Actually …
In fact …

Paragraph 4

5 Tell your reader/friend to write back.
Write back soon.
Hope to hear from you soon.

6 End your letter.
Love,
Lots of love,
Bye for now (bfn)

Check your writing

Does your letter **begin** and **end** in a friendly way?

Is your language **friendly** and **informal**?

Remember to **ask questions** to get your reader's interest.

A story

Are you writing a story? Follow this plan.

1 Give your story a clear beginning, middle and end.

2 Think of key words to describe places/feelings, etc.

3 Write three paragraphs.

Plan

Paragraph 1 (30–40 words)

1 Set the scene. Say where you were and what you were doing.
When I was … (15/ on holiday in … / travelling to …)

2 Describe how you felt.
I was … (excited/sad/nervous)

Paragraph 2

3 Describe the place and give some background information.
The … was next to/near/in the middle of …
The weather was …
It looked … (high, dangerous, scary)
I decided to …

Paragraph 3

4 Describe the main event, and the outcome.
Eventually …
… suddenly I realised …
Unfortunately/Fortunately…
I felt …

Check your writing

Is the **sequence** of events clear?
I was … when …

Are your **tenses** correct?

• **past simple** for completed actions, and actions that interrupt actions in progress.

• **past continuous** for background actions and actions in progress in the past.

An article

Plan

Paragraph 1

1 Attract the attention of your reader.
Have you ever seen?/heard about/been to … ?
What was it like in…the 18th century/the 1960s …

2 Introduce the topic of your article.
(say what it is) … is the best/biggest festival/event/ …
(say who it is) … is a famous/talented/special musician/
rock star/politician/footballer/person because …
Life in the 18th century/the 1960's was …

Paragraph 2

3 Give the main information.
The event takes place in (place/time) on (day) at (time/place) …
(This person) has been a musician/rock star/politician
since… and has played/worked/travelled …
People were didn't have any money/TV/cars …
It wasn't possible to go to school/travel/find a good job …

Paragraph 3

4 Add extra information.
There's a great atmosphere.
He/She's especially nice to … /He/She always has time for …
Life was particularly dangerous/dirty/difficult because …

Paragraph 4

5 Summarise and give your opinion.
I've really enjoyed this event/show/celebration.
(Name) is important/interesting because …
I wouldn't have liked to live in the 18th century/ I'd have
enjoyed the music in the 1960s.
This has been the best/funniest/most interesting … I've
been to/seen.

Check your writing

Does your article sound **lively** and **informative**? Does it:
• begin with a question?
• use the correct punctuation?
• include interesting adjectives and facts?

Have you **organised** your article well?
• Is there a clear **beginning** and **end**?
• Is the **main information** in paragraphs 2 and 3?

A review

Plan

Paragraph 1

1 Say what you are reviewing.
[Title] is a [type] … book/film/game.
Stormbreaker is an action-adventure game.

2 Explain why you chose to review it.
It's a really exciting/interesting/ … book/film/game.

Paragraph 2

3 Describe the main characters of the book/film or the object
of the game.
The main character is [name] who …
The object of the game is to … /In this game, players …

Paragraph 3

4 Describe the story/game.
The book/game is about …
At first … then … after that …

Paragraph 4

5 Give your personal opinion and recommendation.
This book/film/game is fun/easy/exciting/… so I would
recommend it to …

Check your writing

Do your **subjects** and **verbs** agree?
• **singular** subject + **singular** verb
• **plural** subject + **plural** verb

Have you used the correct adjectives?
• **feelings**: adjectives ending in **-ed**
• **people or things**: adjectives ending in **-ing**

A letter of complaint

Are you writing letter of complaint? Follow this plan.

1 Use formal, polite language.
2 Be polite, but clear and firm.
3 Write three or four paragraphs.

Plan

1 Begin your letter with a greeting.
Dear Sir/Madam,

Paragraph 1
2 Explain why you are writing.
I'm writing about … which I booked/bought …

Paragraph 2
3 Say what the problem is.
Even though the advert stated …
I was disappointed because/that/to find …

Paragraph 3
4 Give more information about the problem if necessary.
In addition … /Another problem is that …

Paragraph 4
5 Say what you would like the person/company to do for you.
I would like …

6 End your letter.
I look forward to hearing from you.
Yours faithfully,
[your name]

Check your writing

Does your letter **begin** and **end** correctly?

Are the **relative pronouns** correct?
• *who* for people
• *which/that* for things

Is your language **formal** and **polite**?

A report

Are you writing a report? Follow this plan.

1 Think about your reader. Who is your report for? Reports are usually for teachers/parents/somebody official
2 Use formal language and a clear structure.
3 Write four paragraphs.

Plan

Paragraph 1
1 Say what the report is about.
The purpose/aim of this report is to … recommend/examine/look at …

Paragraph 2
2 Explain the advantages of the first idea.
Firstly …
Secondly …
The advantages of … are … and ….
One benefit is … Another advantage is …

3 Explain the consequences/results of the first idea.
As a result …

Paragraph 3
4 Introduce an alternative idea and explain the advantages.
Alternatively, … but …

5 Explain the consequences/results of an alternative idea.
This would make … better/easier …

Paragraph 4
6 Summarise your arguments, give extra information.
To sum up …
In conclusion …
In addition …

7 Make your personal recommendation.
For these reasons, I recommend …

Check your writing

Does your report **follow the plan**?

Does it use **organising words** and phrases?

Does it use the correct **linking words**?
• giving more information: *and … in addition …*
• contrasting points: *although … but …*
• different ideas: *on the one hand … on the other hand …*
• giving reasons: *because … so …*

A description

Are you writing a description?
Follow this plan.

1 Imagine who will read your description and what information will interest them.

2 Think of at least three key words or phrases to describe the person.

3 Describe one feature in each paragraph and add extra information.

Plan

Paragraph 1
1 Introduce the person you are going to describe.
My mum/sister is in her forties/is 15...
Anne is a typical teenager/rock singer/famous writer.
(Name) is a famous/important ...
(Name) is well known as ...
(Name) was a doctor/scientist who ...

Paragraph 2
2 Describe one key feature.
He's/she's attractive and slim.
He/she has long, black hair/blue eyes.
He/she wears sensible, smart clothes/baggy jeans and trendy T-shirts.

3 Add extra information.
He's/She's sociable, confident, shy, bossy, outspoken, creative.
He's/she's good at talking to people/listening to people/singing/writing stories ...
He/she can be hard-working/lazy/bossy.
He/she enjoys ...

Paragraph 3
4 Describe what is special about that person.
The best thing about (Name) is...
What I really like about (Name) is that he/she's...

Paragraph 4
5 Finish with a personal opinion.
I think that (Name) is a special person because he/she ...
(Name) is important because...

Check your writing

Have you used interesting **adjectives** to describe your person?

Have you included a special or important **fact**?

Do you have three or four clear **paragraphs**?

An essay

Are you writing an essay?
Follow this plan.

1 Decide if you agree or disagree strongly with the statement, or if you have no strong opinion.

2 Make your position clear in the first and last paragraphs.

3 Think about any examples you can use to illustrate your argument.

Plan

Paragraph 1
1 Introduce the topic with a general statement.
I completely agree/disagree with this statement for several reasons.
Many people say that / It's true to say that ...
Clearly there are two sides to this argument.

2 Explain the main problem in a few words.
However, other people disagree because ...
Of course, things are not that simple because ...

Paragraph 2
3 Give reasons to agree OR disagree. Add extra reasons.
To begin with, ... On the one hand, ...
Also, ... / As well as that, ...

Paragraph 3
4 Give reasons to agree OR disagree (the opposite of Paragraph 2). Add extra reasons.
On the other hand, ...
Because of that/In addition, ...

Paragraph 4
5 Summarise and give your opinion.
In conclusion/To conclude, ...
To summarise the situation/argument, ...
I think that.../Personally, .../In my opinion, ...

Check your writing

Is your essay **balanced** and **reasonable**? Does it:
• include suitable linking words or phrases?
• present information in a logical order?

Have you **organised** your essay?
• Is there a clear **introduction** and **conclusion**?
• Are the **main arguments for or against** in paragraphs 2 and 3?

1 A new you

Jobs

chef (n)
classical musician (n)
DJ (n)
farmer (n)
football manager (n)
hairdresser (n)
rock singer (n)
surfer (n)
web designer (n)

Skills (phrases)

be   a success
      under pressure
      good at
      talented

make   decisions
      money
      people laugh/happy

work   in a team
      on (my/your/his/her) own
      with animals
      with (his/her) hands

learn   fast

talk   to people

solve   problems

look   right

like   a challenge

Phrasal verbs

come from *page 9*
find out *page 14*
grow up *page 16*
look after *page 16*
look for *page 16*
look forward to *page 16*
pick up *page 14*
stay up *page 9*

Wordzones

Expressions with *do, get* and *find* page 10

do (+ work or tasks, activities, actions)
      (someone) a favour
      (something) like a professional
      badly
      nothing
      something
      something wrong
      the shopping
      well
      your best
      your homework

find (+ adjective = to experience something in a particular way)
      (something)
      boring
      difficult
      easy
      frightening
      hard
      impossible
      interesting
      relaxing

get (= to receive)
      a chance
      a letter
      a shock
      an email
      get (something)
      right
      wrong

get (= to become)
      bored
      dressed
      lost
      worried
      annoyed
      fed up

Adjectives *page 14*

Feelings: *I'm* + adjectives ending in *-ed*
bor**ed**
excit**ed**
frighten**ed**
interest**ed**

People or objects: *It's* + adjectives ending in *-ing*
bor**ing**
excit**ing**
frighten**ing**
interest**ing**

Adjective + preposition
annoyed **with**
bad **at**
bored **with**
fed up **with**
frightened **of**
good **at**
honest **about**
interested **in**
keen **on**
surprised **by**
worried **about**

DVD Activities

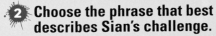

Faking it

Words you might need

decks the equipment for playing records

headphones wear these over your ears to hear music

records a round flat piece of plastic with a hole in the middle that music is stored on

speakers where the sound comes out

1 Predict! Then watch and check.

Sian wants to buy her own decks.   Yes / No

2 Choose the phrase that best describes Sian's challenge.

   A Pure hard work and no fun at all!

   B Difficult but surprisingly enjoyable.

Time to talk

3 Do you think Sian was the right person for the TV challenge? Why/Why not?

2 Rule the school

Education

assembly (n)
assembly hall (n)
canteen (n)
caretaker (n)
classroom (n)
cleaner (n)
corridor (n)
curriculum (n)
dance (n)
detention (n)
educational (adj)
essay (n)
examination (n)
film club (n)
football (n)
head teacher's office (n)
History (n)
homework (n)
language (n)
library (n)
orchestra (n)
project (n)
punishment (n)
revise (v)
revision (n)
rule (n) (v)
Science (n)
Science lab (n)
secretary (n)
skill (n)
staff room (n)
teacher (n)
uniform (n)

Wordzones

Changing verbs into nouns *page 20*

verb	noun + *-ment*
advertise	advertise**ment**
disappoint	disappoint**ment**
embarrass	embarrass**ment**
entertain	entertain**ment**
improve	improve**ment**
punish	punish**ment**

verb	noun + *-(at)ion*
concentrate	concentr**ation**
discuss	discuss**ion**
educate	educ**ation**
examine	examin**ation**
explain	explan**ation**
imagine	imagin**ation**
organise	organis**ation**
revise	revis**ion**

verb	noun + *-iour*
behave	behav**iour**

Verbs and phrases vs phrasal verbs *page 24*

Verbs and phrases

keep	a record of
	an eye on
make	friends with
	sure
put	pressure on
	your heart into
take	care of
	part in

Phrasal verbs with *keep, make, put, take*

keep on
keep up with
make for
make up
put on (clothes)
put up with
take off (clothes)
take up

Phrasal verbs

carry on *page 19*
burst out (laughing) *page 27*
deal with *page 19*
fall asleep *page 23, 26*
fall down *page 26*
look after *page 22*
make up *page 19*
take (somebody) around *page 27*
turn off *page 19*
wake up *page 23*
wash up *page 22*

DVD Activities

Rule the school

1 **Predict! Then watch and check.**
  a What lesson will you watch?
  b The adults think the headmistress looks really frightening.   Yes / No

2 **Choose the phrase that best describes the lesson you see.**
  A The students were not good at the lesson.
  B The students learned fast.

Time to talk

3 **Do you think the teenagers were good teachers? Why/ Why not?**

3 Room for improvement

Money and shopping

afford (v)
cash (n)
change (n)
cheque (UK) (n) / check (US)
cost (v)
credit card (n)
earn (v)
lend (v)
owe (v)
pay / paid (v)
pocket money (n)
price (n)
save / save up (v)
sell (v)
spend (v)
waste (v)

Wordzones

Changing nouns and verbs into adjectives *page 32*

noun/verb	adjective +-*able*
afford	afford**able**
comfort	comfort**able**
enjoy	enjoy**able**
notice	notice**able**

noun/verb	adjective -*ible*
horror	horr**ible**
possibility	poss**ible**
rely	reli**able**
sense	sens**ible**
terror	terr**ible**

noun/verb	adjective -*ous*
danger	danger**ous**
fame	fam**ous**
ambition	ambiti**ous**

noun/verb	adjective -*ful*
care	care**ful**
harm	harm**ful**
hope	hope**ful**
success	success**ful**
use	use**ful**

noun/verb	adjective -*y*
mess	mess**y**
mood	mood**y**
scare	scar**y**
sleep	sleep**y**

Making adjectives negative
page 36

im- immature
impatient
impossible
impractical

in- inappropriate
independent
inexpensive
informal
invisible

un- unable
unacceptable
uncomfortable
unfit
unreliable
untidy
unusual

Phrasal verbs

catch up *page 37*
chill out *page 31*
clear out *page 31*
clear up *page 31, 33*
come round *page 31*
end up *page 30*
find out *page 30*
get out (of bed) *page 36*
give back *page 33*
go out (with) *page 33*
grow up *page 36*
save up *page 33*
sort out *page 31*
stay up *page 37*
switch off *page 37*
take up *page 31*
throw out *page 31*
tidy up *page 31*
turn up *page 33*

DVD Activities

Teens know how

1 Watch part 1 and decide if the statements are true (T) or false (F).
  1 Natalie's father thinks he needs a mobile phone.
  2 Natalie got her mobile phone for her birthday.

2 Now watch part 2 and decide if the statements are true (T) or false (F).
  1 MC Heroik is a Hip Hop DJ.
  2 His mum doesn't like music.
  3 MC Heroik's computer is his musical instrument.

Time to talk

3 Would you prefer to spend money on mobiles or music? Explain why.

4 Festival fever

Outdoor entertainment

acrobat (n)
act (n)
actor (n)
amazing (adj)
artist (n)
atmosphere (n)
audience (n)
band (n)
cabaret (n)
carnival (n)
circus (n)
costume (n)
crowd (n)
entertainer (n)
entertainment (n)
event (n)
festival (n)
fireworks (n)
lights (n)
musician (n)
neon (n)
organiser (n)
parade (n)
park (n)
participant (n)
perform (v)
performer (n)
performance (n)
play (n)
raise (money) (v)
religious (adj)
show (n)
spectator (n)
stage (n)
stall (n)
tent (n)
theme (n)
tour (n)
tradition (n)
water (n)
workshop (n)

Wordzones

Compound nouns *page 42*

arts programme
audience participation
ballet fan
body painting
break dancing workshop
cabaret show
carnival atmosphere
carnival costume
carnival parade
chocolate factory
chocolate festival
chocolate fountain
chocolate party

circus act
craft workshop
dance festival
dance parade
factory tour
festival organiser
festival runner
fire festival
music festival
neon lights
stage lights
stage show
theme park
water park

Adverbs *page 46*

Regular

adjective	adverb
bad	bad**ly**
eas**y**	eas**ily**
energetic	energetic**ally**
happ**y**	happ**ily**
impressive	impressive**ly**
international	international**ly**
loud	loud**ly**
patient	patient**ly**
obvious	obvious**ly**
nervous	nervous**ly**
quick	quick**ly**
quiet	quiet**ly**
sad	sad**ly**
successful	successful**ly**
tid**y**	tid**ily**

Irregular

adjective	adverb
early	early
fast	fast
good	well
hard	hard

Phrasal verbs

build up *page 41*
join in *page 42*
look forward to *page 41*
put on (clothes) *page 41*
put up (my tent) *page 41*
set off *page 41*
try out *page 48*
tune up *page 41*
turn into *page 41*

DVD Activities

Scotland's fire festival

Words you might need:

longship a long, narrow boat with oars and sail, that the Vikings used

procession a line of people taking part in a ceremony

torch a burning stick

Vikings Scandinavian people who attacked the coasts of northern and western Europe from the eighth to the eleventh century.

1 **Predict! Then watch and check.**

The highlight of the festival is when people burn:
   a torches
   b the longship

2 **Watch the festival and match the information.**

   1 The capital of the Shetland Islands where the festival takes place.
   2 The name of the festival.
   3 The type of people who celebrated this festival.

   a Up Helly-Aa
   b Lerwick
   c Vikings

Time to talk

3 **Do you think this festival is more exciting than the ones in the reading text? Give reasons.**

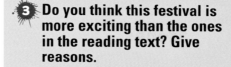

5 Extreme behaviour!

Right and wrong

against the law
agree (v)
approve (v)
bank account (n)
birth certificate (n)
body piercing (n)
bully (n / v)
by law
court (n)
disagree (v)
disapprove (v)
dishonest (adj)
disobey (v)
driving licence (UK) /
  driver's licence (US) (n)
fine (n)
get married (v)
honest (adj)
ID card (n)
illegal (adj)
irresponsible (adj)
judge (n)
law (n)
leave (someone) alone (v)
legal (adj)
obey (v)
permission (n)
prison (n)
proof (n)
responsible (adj)
right (n)
tattoo (n)
tease (v)
violence (n)
vote (v)

Wordzones

Making adjectives or verbs negative *page 54*

Remember! You can also make adjectives negative by adding *un-*, *im-* or *in-* (see Unit 3).

Adjectives

dis- dishonest

il- **il**legal
       illogical

im- **im**mature
       impatient
       impossible

in- **in**dependent
       insecure

ir- **ir**regular
       irresponsible

un- unfair
     unfastened
     unfortunate

verbs

dis- disagree
       disapprove
       disobey

un- unfasten

Verb + preposition *page 58*

at   point at, shout at,
        look at, stare at,
        laugh at

by   judge (somebody) by

for ask for, look for,
        blame (somebody) for

of   think of

to   talk to, point to

with agree with, argue with

Phrasal verbs

believe in *page 53*
bring back *page 60*
carry on (with) *page 53*
deal with *page 53*
give up *page 53*
hand over *page 53*
join in *page 60*
laugh at *page 53*
sort out *page 52*
tidy up *page 60*

DVD Activities

Solving a problem

Words you might need

Lunchbox a box in which food is carried to school

Trendy Wendy someone who always wants to be fashionable

1 **Predict! Then watch and check.**

The girl with the lunchbox is:

A upset
B embarrassed

2 **Answer the questions.**
1 What is the problem with the lunchbox?
2 How does Stacey think she can help the girl?
3 What happens in the end?

Time to talk

3 **Do you think Stacey gave the girl the right advice?**

6 Stay in or go out?

Computers and the internet

artificial (adj)
best-selling (adj)
console (n)
disk (n)
game-tester (n)
graphics (n, pl)
input (n) (v)
keyboard (n)
memory stick (n)
mouse (n)
online (adj)
portable (adj)
screen (n)

Wordzones

Compound nouns and adjectives *page 64*

Nouns one word:
bookworm
input
keyboard
laptop
microchip

Two words:
artificial intelligence
computer game
CD player
mobile phone

Hyphen:
game-tester

Adjectives one word:
online
widespread
worldwide

Hyphen:
action-packed
best-selling
built-in
hand-held
hi-tech
old-fashioned
touch-sensitive
user-friendly
well-known

Order of adjectives *page 68*

opinion - size - shape - age - colour - nationality - material - + noun

A powerful, new, Japanese motorbike.
A lovely, French leather jacket.
A fast, modern computer.
A huge, old American machine.

Phrasal verbs

bring up *page 70*
dress up *page 67*
find out *page 69*
wake up *page 63*

DVD Activities

Computer games

Words you might need:
Genre type

Soundtrack the recorded music from a film

Types of games

Adventure exciting games in which dangerous or unusual things happen

Film-based a game that uses the characters and plot from a film

God a game where the player is in charge of organising the game 'world'

Horror a frightening game

Knowledge an educational game with 'real world' subjects. These can include, e.g. Sports, Maths, Science, Business, etc.

Mystery a complicated game where you have to solve problems and discover secrets

Role play a game where you play the part of one of the characters

1 Answer the questions.
1 What types of games for children seem to be the most popular?
2 The soundtrack to a game can do two different things. What are they?

Time to talk

2 Do you think the children analysed the games in an interesting way?

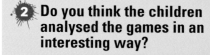

157

7 Horrible history

Dates and times

century (n)
date (n/v)
decade (n)
fortnight (n)
millennium (n)
the 1600s
the twenty-first century

Abbreviations after dates

AD (Anno Domini = in the year of our Lord)
BC (before Christ) /
BCE (Before the Common Era)

Wordzones

Writing and saying dates *page 76*

Write
1st January, 2nd February, 3rd March, 4th April, 5th May, etc.
1930s, 1600s

Say
The *first, second, third, fourth, fifth,* etc. *of January, February,* etc.

Up to 2000 e.g. 1998: 19-98 = *nineteen ninety-eight*

after 2000 e.g. 2010: *two thousand and ten* OR 20-10 = *twenty ten*
The *two-thousand and eight* Olympics in Beijing.
The *twenty-twelve* Olympics in London.

The 1930s/the 1980s = *the nineteen-thirties, the nineteen-eighties,* etc.

1600s = *sixteen hundreds*

17th century = *seventeenth century*

Expressions using time *page 80*

The train is **on time**.

By the time we arrived, the party was over.

At the time she couldn't speak English very well.

We visit our grandparents **from time to time**.

I enjoy my English lessons **most of the time**.

I didn't get to the bus stop **in time** to catch the school bus.

Remember!

after + time or event: *after five o'clock, after we moved to the city*

at the end of + period of time: *at the end of the day/week/month*

at + time: *three o'clock/the weekend*

before + time or event: *before six o'clock, before the birth of Christ,*

between … and …: *between Monday and Thursday; between 1984 and 1986*

during + period of time: *during the twentieth century, during the night*

for + period of time, *for three hours; for 15 years; for decades*

from … to … *from Sunday to Tuesday; from 1790 to 1810.*

in the end: *in the end, they had to leave*

in *the morning/afternoon/ evening; in May; in the nineteen-nineties; in 1802*

on + day/date: *on Thursday/17 May*

since + point in time: *since 1963*

until + up to and before + time or event: *until 2000, until we left*

Phrasal verbs

get into *page 75*
look for *page 75*
sit around *page 75*
wake up *page 77*

Pirate legends

Words you might need

buccaneer another word for pirate

booty valuable things

despised hated

galleon a type of ship

power the ability to control people or events

wealth a large amount of money or property someone has

legend someone who is famous for being good at something

1 **Predict! Then watch and check.**

The pirates will be
A sewing their clothes
B cleaning the ship
C preparing their weapons

2 **True or false?**
1 Pirates attacked Spanish ships because they wanted food.
2 The pirate Edward Teach or 'Blackbeard' wanted to be famous more than he wanted to be rich.

Time to talk

3 **Do you think Johnny Depp would make a good 'Blackbeard' in a film? Why/Why not?**

8 Communication breakdown

Science and communication

audible (adj)
design (n / v)
designer (n)
detect (v)
develop (v)
ear (n)
engineer (n)
equip (v)
eye (n)
feel (v)
hear (v)
hearing (n)
hold (v)
inventor (n)
listen (v)
look (v)
mathematician (n)
mouth (n)
nose (n)
program (n)
radar (n)
research (n) (v)
research tool (n)
researcher (n)
result (n)
scent (n)
scientist (n)
see (v)
sight (n)
smell (n)
solution (n)
sonic (adj)
sound (n)
speech (n)
taste (n)
test (n) (v)
tongue (n)
tool (n)
touch (n)
visible (adj)
vision (n)
visual (adj)

Wordzones

Making people nouns from verbs and nouns *page 86*

art	art**ist**
compet**ition**	compet**itor**
creat**e**	creat**or**
design	design**er**
engin**e**	engin**eer**
explore	explore**r**
invent	invent**or**
manufactur**e**	manufactur**er**
mathematic**s**	mathematic**ian**
mountain	mountain**eer**
music	music**ian**
own	own**er**
research	research**er**
scien**ce**	scien**tist**
writ**e**	writ**er**

Phrasal verbs *page 90*

break down
break up
cut off
depend on
fall apart
fall over
speak up
switch (something) off
switch (something) on
turn (something) up/down

in a phrasal verb, the prepositions often have these meanings:
down = decrease or stop
off = stop
on = start or continue
up = increase

Phrasal verbs

set up *page 92*
work out *page 92*

DVD Activities

Robot challenges

Words you might need:

sumo a Japanese form of wrestling, here a game to test how strong the robots are

1 Predict! Then watch and check.

The robots on the DVD will be playing football.   Yes / No

2 Decide if the statements are true (T) or false (F).

1 The Sugar Plum Fairy's team was unlucky.
2 Sprocket beats Bruiser in the sumo wrestling competition.

Time to talk

3 Were the robots as clever as the ones in the reading text?

9 Getting on ...

Describing personalities

ambitious (adj)
assertive (adj)
attractive (adj)
big-head (n)
bossy (adj)
cheeky (adj)
competitive (adj)
confident (adj)
extrovert (adj)
funny (adj)
gossip (n)
hard-working (adj)
housemate (n)
humorous (adj)
identity (adj)
imaginative (adj)
immature (adj)
individuality (adj)
insecure (adj)
insensitive (adj)
laid-back (adj)
laugh (n)
lazy (adj)
loud (adj)
mature (adj)
outspoken (adj)
quiet (adj)
sensitive (adj)
serious (adj)
show off (v)
shy (adj)
snob (n)
talkative (adj)
timid (adj)
unattractive (adj)
unimaginative (adj)

Phrases
get angry/upset
get on like a house on fire
get on with
get to know
have (something) in common
put up with

Wordzones

Words and their opposites *page 98*

attractive	unattractive
bossy	timid
confident	shy/insecure
friendly	unfriendly
hard-working	lazy
humorous	serious
imaginative	unimaginative
laid-back	nervous
loud	quiet
mature	immature
outspoken	quiet/shy
polite	rude/impolite
positive	negative
sensitive	insensitive
talkative	quiet

Articles *page 102*

a/an + singular countable noun – for things in general, and the first time you talk about something.
*Image is everything to **a** teenager.*

Remember! Use *an* before a word that begins with a vowel sound: ***an** hour, **an** orange*

the for something particular or when it's clear what you're talking about.
***The** most famous house in the UK. **The** final eight contestants … **The** (main) difference …*

zero article – for things in general: *I like music.* (= music in general) *I like **the** music* (= that is playing now).

Phrasal verbs

burst into *page 97*
come from *page 97*
end up *page 104*
get on (with) *page 97*
get up *page 104*
grow up *page 99*
hold on to (something) *page 97*
put up with (something) *page 97*
stay out *page 101*
strip (somebody) of *page 97*
take (something) away *page 97*
wake up *page 104*
wash up *page 99*

DVD Activities

Friends united

Words you might need

date an arrangement to meet someone, especially in a romantic sense.

gathering a party or meeting when people spend time together

argue shout and say angry things to someone because you disagree with them

1 **Predict! Then watch and check.**
The boys you see are from the same country.   Yes / No

2 **Which of these things *don't* they talk about together?**
A girls
B football
C school work
D what to wear

Time to talk

3 **The boys say they are good friends because they have lots in common. Do you agree this is important?**

4 **Do you agree that the things they mention are important in a friendship?**

10 Planet Earth

Weather and environment

Arctic (n)
blizzard (n)
boiling (adj)
cloud (n)
cold (adj)
desert (n)
drought (n)
flood (n)
freezing (adj)
glacier (n)
heatwave (n)
hot (adj)
humid (adj)
hurricane (n)
ice (n)
jungle (n)
lightning (n)
mist (n)
mountain (n)
pour (v)
rain (n)
rainforest (n)
river (n)
sand (n)
snow (n)
soaking (adj)
thunderstorm (n)
volcano (n)
weather (n)
wet (adj)
wind (n)

Wordzones

Describing extreme weather
page 108

boiling hot
freezing cold
pouring with rain
soaking wet
(be) struck by lightning
snow-covered
a sheet of ice

Changing the meaning of a word *page 112*

-less care**less**
       harm**less**
       use**less**

-free battery-**free**
       care**free**
       chlorine-**free**
       lead-**free**
       pollution-**free**

non- **non-**polluting
       non-smoker

re- **re**charge
      recycle
      replace
      replay
      reuse

DVD Activities

Serious Amazon

Words you might need:

achievement something important that you succeed in doing by your own efforts

adapt gradually change your behaviour and attitudes in order to be successful in a new situation

resident someone who lives or stays in a particular place

1 Predict! Then watch and check.

Which animals will you see?
A red uakari monkeys
B pink river dolphins

2 Answer the questions.

1 How did the children feel after their experience?
2 What effect has the trip had on them?

Time to talk

3 Would you ever think of going on a trip like this?

161

11 Get fit, have fun

Health and fitness; sport

addictive (adj)
basketball (n)
basketball player (n)
beat (v)
bounce (v)
box (v)
boxer (n)
boxing (n)
catch (v)
competitor (n)
contact sport (n)
cycle (v)
drop (v)
exercise (n)
exhausting (adj)
extreme sport (n)
football (n)
football player (n)
goggles (n, pl)
gymnast (n)
gymnastics (n)
healthy diet (n)
junior (adj)
kick (v)
league (n)
motor racing (n)
muscle strength (n)
out of breath (adj)
race (n)
racing driver (n)
regular (adj)
run (v)
score (n) (v)
ski (v)
skier (n)
skiing (n)
snowboarder (n)
snowboarding (n)
spectator sport (n)
sporting event (n)
stamina (n)
swim (v)
swimmer (n)
swimming (n)
team (n)
team sport (n)
tennis (n)
tennis player (n)
train (v)
training (n)
triathlon (n)
unhealthy (adj)
water sport (n)
win (v)
winter sport (n)
workout (n)

zorb (n / v)
zorbing (n)

Wordzones

Sportspeople *page 120*

sport	person
athletics	athlete
basketball	basketball player
boxing	boxer
cycling	cyclist
football	football player
gymnastics	gymnast
hockey	hockey player
motor racing	racing driver
running	runner
skiing	skier
snowboarding	snowboarder
swimming	swimmer
tennis	tennis player

do*, *play* or *go *page 124*

do   athletics
      boxing
      gymnastics

play football
      hockey
      tennis

go   cycling
      motor racing
      running
      skiing
      snowboarding
      swimming

Phrasal verbs

build up *page 119*
get fit *page 119*
get up *page 119*
pull off *page 119*
put (somebody) off *page 119*
put on *page 119*
run out of *page 119*
slow down *page 119*
step out *page 119*
turn into *page 119*

DVD Activities

Tough triathlon

Words you might need

lap one journey around a race track or swimming pool

pace the speed at which someone moves

transition/changeover a change from one activity to another

1 **Decide if the statements are true (T) or false (F).**

  1 The TV presenter will do a full triathlon.

  2 Triathlons can be won or lost at the changeovers between the three sports.

Time to talk

2 **Does the DVD make you want to try triathlon? Why/ Why not?**

12 Thrills and chills

Holidays and travel

accommodation (n)
adventure (n)
boat (n)
book (v)
cruise (n)
funny (adj)
guide (n)
hilarious (adj)
holiday (n)
hotel (n)
journey (n)
luxury (n)
plane (n)
rest (n)
ride (n)
sightseeing (n)
souvenir (n)
ticket (n)
tour (n)
travel (v)
trip (n)
voyage (n)

luxury hotel
plane ticket
roller coaster ride
sports shoes
theme park
tourist destination
train station

Phrases

book   accommodation
a hotel
tickets

buy   some souvenirs

catch the/a bus

go   on holiday
sightseeing

have a holiday
a rest
a ride

plan a holiday
a trip

take photos
a trip

Wordzones

Compound nouns *page 130*

In compound nouns, the first noun
describes the second noun:
admission price
beach holiday
bus ride
captain's cabin
caravan site
country house
credit card
day trip
family holiday
identity card
information office

**Strong adjectives and
descriptive verbs** *page 134*
amazing (adj)
astonished (adj)
bad (adj)
boring (adj)
busy (adj)
call (v)
chat (v)
cool (adj)
cry (v)
dangerous (adj)
dull (adj)
excited (adj)
exhausted (adj)
fascinated (adj)
gossip (v)
grumble (v)
hectic (adj)
interested (adj)
mind-blowing (adj)
moan (v)
mumble (v)
risky (adj)
scream (v)
shout (v)
shriek (v)
sob (v)
surprised (adj)
talk (v)
terrible (adj)
terrified (adj)
thrilling (adj)
tired (adj)
whisper (v)
wicked (adj)
yell (v)

Phrasal verbs

check out
head for

DVD Activities

Europa-Park

**1 Predict! Then watch and
check.**

There are more than 100
attractions at Europa-Park.
Yes / No

2 Answer the questions.
1 Which of the following rides
do we see on the DVD?
A Silverstar
B Pegasus
C Atlantica Supersplash
D Euromir
2 How high is the roller coaster?
A 130 feet
B 230 feet
C 330 feet

Time to talk

**3 Would you prefer to go to
Europa-Park or another
theme park you know?**

Unit 1

Present simple

Positive

I/We/You/They	work.
He/She/It	work**s**.

Negative

I/We/You/They	**don't** work.
He/She/It	**doesn't** work.

Questions

Do	I/we/you/they	work?
Does	he/she/it	work?

Short answers

Yes,	I/we/you/they	**do**.
	he/she/it	**does**.
No,	I/we/you/they	**don't**.
	he/she/it	**doesn't**.

We use the present simple to talk about:

- a fact, situation that is permanently true, or true now
  Classical musicians work very hard.
- a habit or repeated action or event.
  She starts school at 9a.m. every day.

We also use the present simple for fixed timetables.
The bus leaves at 10.30.

Present continuous

Positive

I	**am ('m)**	
He/She/It	**is ('s)**	wait**ing**.
We/You/They	**are ('re)**	

Negative

I	**am ('m) not**	
He/She/It	**is not (isn't)**	wait**ing**.
We/You/They	**are not (aren't)**	

Questions

Am	I	
Is	he/she/it	wait**ing**?
Are	we/you/they	

Short answers

Yes,	I	**am**.
	he/she/it	**is**.
	we/you/they	**are**.
No,	I	**'m not**.
	he/she/it	**isn't**.
	we/you/they	**aren't**.

Notice the spelling changes:
*sit > si**tt**ing; mak**e** > making*

We use the present continuous to talk about:

- an action that is happening at the moment of speaking.
  Who are you waiting for?
- for situations/states that are true for a limited period (temporary)
  She's training to be a dancer.

→ Present continuous for future see Unit 3.

State verbs

There are some verbs which describe states we don't use in the present continuous. Common state verbs include:

- verbs of thinking: e.g. *agree, believe, know, remember, think, understand*
- verbs describing attitudes: e.g. *hate, like, love, need, prefer, want, wish*
- verbs of perception: e.g. *hear, see, smell, taste*
- verbs describing appearance, qualities: e.g. *appear, look* (=seem), *seem, sound*
- verbs of being and possession: e.g. *be, belong, contain, have, own*
- other verbs: e.g. *cost, fit, mean, owe*

We use some state verbs in the continuous when we describe actions. These include: *be, have, see, smell, taste* and *think*.
I think (= believe) *you're right. I'm thinking about* (= considering) *it.*
I see (= understand) *what you mean. I'm seeing* (= meeting) *him tomorrow.*

We can use *feel* and *look* in the continuous with no change in meaning.
I feel/am feeling ill. You look/are looking tired.

We often use *can* with sense/perception verbs.
I can't hear you. I can see something.

See and *hear* are stative verbs but *look* and *listen* describe actions.
Can you see it? I'm looking at the photos.
I can hear voices next door. I'm listening to the music.

Adverbs of frequency

We use adverbs of frequency to say **how often** something happens.

most often — always
usually
frequently/often
sometimes/occasionally
rarely/hardly ever
least often — never

Adverbs of frequency come:

- **before** main verbs
  *I **always** have English lessons on Monday.*
- **after** be
  *I'm **hardly ever** late for English lessons.*
- **after** auxiliary and modal verbs
  *I've **never** been to England.*
  *I can **usually** understand my English pen friend.*

Unit 2

Past simple

Positive

I/He/She/It/We/You/They	work**ed**.

Negative

I/He/She/It/We/You/They	**didn't work.**

Questions

Did	I/we/you/they he/she/it	**work**?

Short answers

Yes,	I/he/she/it/we/you/they	**did.**
No,		**didn't.**

Notice the spelling changes:
*try > tr**ied**, mov**e** > mov**ed**, cla**p** > cla**pped***

We use the past simple to talk about:

- completed past actions.
  *We all **worked** hard.*
- One completed action after another.
  *Everyone **sat** down and the lesson **began**.* (= everyone sat down, and then the lesson began)
- A past habit or regular past event.
  *We **went** to the cinema **every week**.*

Past continuous

Positive

I/He/She/It	**was**	wait**ing**.
We/You/They	**were**	

Negative

I/He/She/It	**was not (wasn't)**	wait**ing**.
We/You/They	**were not (weren't)**	

Questions

Was	I/he/she/it	wait**ing**?
Were	we/you/they	

Short answers

Yes,	I/he/she/it	**was.**
	we/you/they	**were.**
No,	I/he/she/it	**wasn't.**
	we/you/they	**weren't.**

We use the past continuous to talk about:

- something which was in progress at a time in the past.
  *We **were waiting** for the bus.*
- something that was going on in the background which 'set the scene' for a specific event or action.
  *We **were waiting** for the bus when we **saw** them.*

Defining relative clauses

The girl	**who**	loves me
The CD	**which/that**	I'm listening to is very good
The woman	**whose**	dog always follows her
The square	**where**	the best cafés are
That was the time	**when**	I got bad marks at school

We use defining relative clauses to say who or what we are talking about. We don't use commas in defining relative clauses.

We use these relative pronouns:

- *who* or *that* for people
- *which/that* for things/animals
- *whose* for possession
- *where* for a place
- *when* for a time

A relative pronoun can be the subject or object of a relative clause.
*The girl **who** loves me lives in this house.* (**The girl** loves me. = subject)
*The girl **who** I love lives in this house.* (I love **the girl**. = object)

We can omit the relative pronoun when it is the object.
The girl I love lives in this house.

Non-defining relative clauses

We use non-defining relative clauses to give extra information about something or somebody. We use commas to separate non-defining relative clauses from the rest of the sentence. We don't use *that* in non-defining relative clauses. We can't leave out the relative pronoun.
Paul, who doesn't like house music, never goes to clubs.

Grammar File

Unit 3

The future *will*

Positive

I/He/She/ It/We/You/They	will ('ll)	stay at home tomorrow.

Negative

I/He/She/ It/We/You/They	will not (won't)	stay at home tomorrow.

Questions

Will	I/he/she/it/we/you/they	stay at home tomorrow?

Short answers

Yes,	I/he/she/it/we/you/they	will.
No,		won't.

We use *will*:

- to make a prediction.
  Our team will win the league this year.
- to make a promise or an offer.
  I'll buy you the DVD for your birthday.
- for unplanned decisions that we make at the time we are speaking.
  We'll take it!

→ *will* in conditional forms see Unit 5.

Future forms, *be going to*

Positive

I	am ('m)	going to	watch TV.
He/She/It	is ('s)		
We/You/They	are ('re)		

Negative

I	am not ('m not)	going to	watch TV.
He/She/It	is not (isn't)		
We/You/They	are not (aren't)		

Question

Am	I	going to	watch TV?
Is	he/she/it		
Are	we/you/they		

Short answers

Yes,	I	am.
	he/she/it	is.
	we/you/they	are.
No,	I	'm not.
	he/she/it	isn't.
	we/you/they	aren't.

We use *be going to* to talk about:
- a future prediction based on evidence we know or can see now.
  It's going to fall down!
- intentions and plans when we have already decided to do something
  I'm going to watch a good programme on TV tonight.

Present continuous for future use

We use the present continuous to talk about future events:
- when an arrangement is certain and fixed for a set time in the future.

We often state the future time with the present continuous:
e.g. *this evening, next week, at the weekend, on Friday, in the summer.*

shall

We usually use *shall* to make a suggestion or an offer. In both cases we use the question form:
Shall we buy something to eat? Shall I help you clear up?

Certainty

must, can't

We use *must/can't* to say we are sure about something now.
This must be John's bike. (= I'm certain it's John's bike.)
It can't be Jessica's jacket, it's too small. (= I'm certain it isn't Jessica's jacket.)

We use *must/can't be + -ing* form to talk about actions happening now.
Toby must/can't be playing football.

→ *must have (been)* and *can't have (been)* see Unit 11.

Probability

should/ought to

We use *should* and *ought to* to say that we think something is likely now or in the future, but we aren't sure.
They should/ought to be at home by now. (= I think they are at home.)

Possibility

may/might/could

We use *may/might/could* to say that something is possible now or in the future.

We use *may/might/could* + infinitive to talk about the present or the future.
It may/might/could be hormone changes that make teenagers sleepy in the morning.

→ *may/might/could* + *have* + past participle see Unit 11.

Unit 4

Present perfect simple

Positive

I/We/You/They	have ('ve)	played.
He/She/It	has ('s)	

Negative

I/We/You/They	have not (haven't)	played.
He/She/It	has not (hasn't)	

Questions

Have	I/we/you/they	played?
Has	he/she/it	

Short answers

Yes,	I/we/you/they	have.
	he/she/it	has.
No,	I/we/you/they	haven't.
	he/she/it	hasn't.

We use the present perfect simple to talk about:

- a past action or experience up to the moment of speaking
  I've known my best friend for ten years.
- a past action or experience that is still true at the moment of speaking.
  We've been friends for ten years. (We're still friends now.)
- a past action or experience with results in the present.
  She's bought a new MP3 player. (She has it now.)

Past   Now

◄   We've been friends for ten years.   ▼
      I've known my friend for ten years.

→ Present perfect simple with adverbs (*just, yet, already, since, for, ever, never*) see Unit 6.

Present perfect continuous

Positive

I/We/You/They	have ('ve)	been	playing.
He/She/It	has ('s)		

Negative

I/We/You/They	have not (haven't)	been	playing.
He/She/It	has not (hasn't)		

Questions

Have	I/we/you/they	been	playing?
Has	he/she/it		

Short answers

Yes,	I/we/you/they	have.
	he/she/it	has.
No,	I/we/you/they	haven't.
	he/she/it	hasn't.

Past   Now

◄   She's been learning English since   ▼
      she was four years old.
      She's been working too hard.   (She looks tired)

We use the present perfect continuous to talk about:

- an action that started in the past and continues now.
  She's been learning English since she was four years old.
- An action that started in the past and finished recently but the results are evident in the present.
  She's been working too hard. (She looks tired.)

We use these expressions with the present perfect continuous:
since, for, how long?, all day/all night/all morning.

Unit 5

Conditionals zero, first, second

Zero conditional

If clause	main clause
present simple	present simple

We use zero conditional to talk about things that are always or generally true as a result of an action or situation.
*If my friend **has** a problem, I always listen.*
*I always **listen** if my friend **has** a problem.*

First conditional

If clause	main clause
present simple	*will*

We use the first conditional to talk about possible actions in the future.
*If I'm thirsty, I'**ll** buy a drink.*

Note:
We can use *can/could/may/might* in the main clause instead of *will*.
*If you **take** your phone to school, you might lose it.*

We can use an imperative in the main clause instead of *will*.
*If you're hungry, **have** a sandwich.*

Second conditional

If clause	main clause
past simple	*would*

We use the second conditional:

*   to talk about 'unreal' present or future situations, i.e. things that are not happening or will not happen.
    *If I **had** more pocket money, **I would spend** it on clothes.*
*   to talk about unlikely present or future situations, i.e. things that probably won't happen.
    *If I **won** the lottery, I'**d** buy a house.*
*   to give advice.
    *If I **were** you, I'**d** save my pocket money.*

We can use *could* or *might* in the main clause instead of *would*.
*If I **had** more money, I **could** buy some clothes.*

We can use *unless* instead of *if ... not* in any conditional sentence.
*I **can't help** my friend, **unless** I **listen** to her problems.*
***Unless** our team **wins** this match, we won't be happy.*
*I **wouldn't save** my pocket money **unless** I **wanted** something special.*

so, such a, too, not … enough

We use *so* and *such a* to emphasise adjectives, adverbs and quantities.

*   *so* + adjective/adverb
    *The film was **so boring**. It all happened **so quickly**.*
*   *so* + *many/much* + noun
    *There were **so many people**! I've got **so much** work.*
*   *such a* + noun
    *It was **such a surprise** to see her again.*
*   *such (a)* + adjective + noun
    *That was **such a good concert**.*
*   *such a lot of* emphasises the amount
    *The teachers give us **such a lot of** homework.*
*   *so…that/such …that* + clause
    *Our new teacher is **so** good **that** I'm sure I'll pass my exams this year.*
    *The party was **such** a disaster **that** I cried all the next day.*

Too means more than you need, or more than is acceptable or possible.

*   *too* + adjective/adverb
    *The tea was **too hot**. He drives **too fast**.*
*   *too* + adjective/adverb + infinitive
    *I'm **too tired to go** to the party.*
*   *too* + adjective/adverb + *for*
    *The shoes are **too small for** her.*
*   *too much/too many* + noun
    *There's **too much noise** in the classroom.*

not … enough means less than you need, or less than is acceptable or possible.

*   (*not*) adjective/adverb + *enough* + infinitive
    *They are**n't fast enough to** win the race.*
*   (*not*) adjective/adverb + *enough* + *for*
    *My bag is**n't big enough for** all the books.*
    *She is**n't good enough for** the team.*

not + adjective/adverb + *enough* and *too* + adjective/adverb mean the same thing.
*These trousers are**n't long enough** for me.*
*These trousers are **too short** for me.*

Unit 6

Past simple

➜ past simple forms, see Unit 2.

Present perfect simple

➜ present perfect forms, see Unit 4.

We use the **present perfect** to talk about an action that happened at some time in the recent past. We don't say when it happened, because we're more interested in the present result of the action. (*I've printed the document.*) We use the **past simple** to talk about an action completed at a specific time in the past. (*I printed the document this morning.*)

Present perfect with adverbs

We use *just* for very recent events.
We've just heard the news.

We use *yet* when we are expecting something to happen. *Yet* is normally used for questions and negatives and goes at the end of the clause.
***Have** you **seen** the new James Bond film **yet**?*

We use *already* when something has happened before now.
*I've **already sent** him an email.*

We use *since* when we refer to the starting point in time.
***since** I was twelve/2004/the beginning of term*

We use *for* when we refer to the period of time.
***for** about a year/a long time/three minutes*

We use *ever* in questions and statements to talk about whether an event or experience has/hasn't happened at some time in the past.

We use *never* for something that hasn't happened, and for a negative answer.
***Have** you **ever** played 'The Sims'? No, I**'ve never** played it.*

Countable nouns

Countable nouns are individual objects, people or ideas.

- They have singular and plural forms.
  *game, game**s**; child, child**ren**; foot, **feet***
- We normally use *a/an* before singular countable nouns.
  ***a** computer, **an** armchair*
- We can use numbers (two or more) or *some* before plural countable nouns.
  three** computer**s**, **some** gadget**s
- We use singular or plural verbs with countable nouns.
  *My phone **is** very hi-tech. Their computers **are** old-fashioned.*

Uncountable nouns

Uncountable nouns are things we can't count.

- They have no plural form.
  patience, concentration, food,
- We always use singular verbs with uncountable nouns.
  *The food **is** very good.*
- We use *some* before uncountable nouns.
  *There's **some** food on the table.*

Some nouns can be either countable or uncountable.
*There's **a hair** in my sandwich! Jack's **hair** is really long now.*

Quantifiers

	+ uncountable noun	+ plural countable noun	+ plural countable/ uncountable noun
Positive sentences	*a little, a bit of*	*a few (of), several, each (of), every*	*some, a lot/lots of, plenty of, no*
Negative sentences and questions	*much*	*many*	*any, a lot/lots of, enough*

We use *some* in positive sentences and in requests or offers.
*I've got **some** new games. Shall I bring **some** CDs?*

We use *any* in negative sentences and questions.
*They didn't give us **any** advice. Have they got **any** mobile phones?*

We use *much* with uncountable nouns and *many* with countable nouns in negative sentences and questions.
*There isn't **much** information on the website. How **many** computer games have you got?*

Unit 7

Past perfect simple

Positive

I/He/She/It/We/You/They	**had ('d)**	**finished**.

Negative

I/He/She/It/We/You/They	**had not (hadn't)**	**finished**.

Questions

Had	I/he/she/it/we/you/they	**finished**?

Short answers

Yes,	I/he/she/it/we/you/they	**had**.
No,		**hadn't**.

We use the past perfect simple to show that one action happened before another action in the past.
*The ship **had sailed** when they arrived at the port.* (= first the ship sailed, then they arrived at the port.)

Past ——————————————— Now
◄   The ship had sailed   ▼
        when they arrived at the port.

We use many of the same time expressions that we use with the present perfect with the past perfect: *when, after, by, by the time, before, as soon as, until, already, just, ever, never, the day/week/month before.*
*She didn't come to the cinema, because she **had already seen** Pirates of the Caribbean.*
*The ship **had just left** the port when the pirates attacked it.*
*Jim **had never been** on a ship before we went to America.*
***By the time** they got home, they **had spent** all their money.*

Past perfect continuous

Positive

I/He/She/It/We/You/They	**had ('d)**	**been**	danc**ing**.

Negative

I/He/She/It/We/You/They	**had not (hadn't)**	**been**	danc**ing**.

Questions

Had	I/he/she/it/we/you/they	been	danc**ing**?

Short answers

Yes,	I/he/she/it /we/you/they	**had**.
No,		**hadn't**.

We use the past perfect continuous for:

- a past action that continued over a period of time but stopped before another action happened or before a specific time.
  *We'**d been preparing** for the festival for weeks when the town hall cancelled it.*

- a past action that continued over a period of time until another action interrupted it.
  *She'**d been watching** TV for an hour when her mother called her for dinner.*

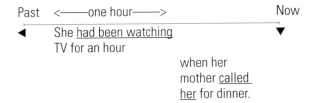

Past   ◄——one hour——►   Now
◄   She had been watching   ▼
        TV for an hour
                              when her
                              mother called
                              her for dinner.

We use these time expressions with the past perfect continuous: *for, since, all day/night/week/year*
*She'**d been reading for** two hours when she fell asleep.*
*He'**d been learning** the trumpet **since** he was five.*
*They'**d been cooking** for the party **all day**.*

When there are two actions in a sentence and one action has been completed before the second one, we use the past simple for the second action.
*They **had been listening** to their MP3s when the teacher **told** them to go back into class.*

Ability *can, could*

Positive

I/He/She/It/We/You/They	**can** **could**	**sing**.

Negative

I/He/She/It/We/You/They	**can't** **couldn't**	**sing**.

Questions

Can/Could **Can't/Couldn't**	I/he/she/it/we/you/they	**sing**?

Short answers

Yes,	I/he/she/it/we/you/they	**can**./**could**.
No,		**can't**./**couldn't**.

We use *can, could* and *be able to* to talk about ability and possibility.

We use *can* and *am/is/are able to* for a general ability to do something now, in the present.
*Historians **can** learn about ancient people from their buildings. They **are able to** say how the people lived.*

We use *could* and *was/were able to* for a general ability or possibility to do something in the past.
*The people **could** make metal arrows. They **were able to** make beautiful jewellery.*

We use *will be able to* for a general ability or possibility to do something in the future.
*When we visit the museum, we'**ll be able to** see the things they found.*

Unit 8

The passive

We form the passive with the correct tense of *be* + past participle. The object of an active sentence is the subject of a passive sentence.

Present simple passive

*Hundreds of mobile phones **are sold** every week.*
*The robot **isn't controlled** by a joypad.*
*How **is** the robot **controlled**?*

Present continuous passive

*The research **is being done** in the laboratory.*
*The designs **aren't being developed**.*
*Is the signal **being detected**?*

Past simple passive

*The first film **was shown** in Paris.*
*Film **isn't used** in a digital camera.*

Past continuous passive

*The robots **were being programmed** to play football.*
*New robots **weren't being developed**.*
*Were the robots **being produced**?*

Future passive

*One day, human footballers **will be beaten** by robots.*
*We **won't be met** by a human receptionist.*
***Will** robot receptionists **be used** in hotels?*

Present perfect simple passive

*The game **has been tested**.*
*The reports **haven't been read**.*
***Has** the message **been received**?*

We use the passive:

- In formal writing, especially in reports and newspapers.
  *The new shopping centre **will be opened** tomorrow.*
- When we don't know who does the action.
  *Two of the windows **are broken**.*
- To pay more attention to the action than the person doing it.
  *Our classroom **has been painted** blue.*
- When we want to emphasise the importance of the person doing the action, e.g. if someone has done a special or well-known job. In this case we use *by* + person.
  *Romeo and Juliet **was written by** Shakespeare.*

Some verbs only have a passive form:
*Bart Simpson **was born** in Springfield.*

Question tags

We form question tags with the same auxiliary or modal verb as the main clause + a personal pronoun.

- We use *do/does* for present simple tags.
- We use *did/didn't* for past simple tags.

We normally use a negative tag after a positive statement and a positive tag after a negative statement.

positive statement	negative question tag
*Paul**'s** good at football,*	***isn't** he?*
*You**'ve** got a brother,*	***haven't** you?*
*They **can** swim,*	***can't** they?*
*She **likes** karate,*	***doesn't** she?*

negative statement	positive question tag
*Paul **isn't** good at football,*	*is he?*
*You **haven't got** a brother,*	*have you?*
*They **can't swim**,*	*can they?*
*She **doesn't like** karate,*	*does she?*

We use question tags to check information.

- An affirmative statement + a negative tag expects an affirmative answer.
- A negative statement + an affirmative tag expects a negative answer.

Unit 9

Reported speech

We use **direct speech** to show the exact words that a person used.
Julia: 'I want to go home.'

We use **reported speech** to tell somebody else what a person said.
Julia said (that) she wanted to go home.

Reported statements

After a past tense reporting verb the original verbs usually shift back one tense into the past, and the pronouns and possessive adjectives change.

direct speech	reported speech
present simple *Anna said, 'I **am** happy.'*	past simple *Anna said (that) she **was** happy.*
present continuous *Luke said, 'They**'re listening** to music.'*	past continuous *Luke said (that) they **were listening** to music.*
past simple *Angela said, 'I **saw** Peter.'*	past perfect simple *Angela said (that) she **had seen** Peter.*
past continuous *Adam said, 'I **was working**.'*	past perfect continuous *Adam said (that) he **had been working**.*
present perfect simple *They said, 'We**'ve seen** Paul.'*	past perfect simple *They said (that) they **had seen** Paul.*
present perfect continuous *Zoe said, 'I**'ve been working**.'*	past perfect continuous *Zoe said (that) she **had been working**.*
past perfect simple / continuous *Paul said: 'I didn't go to the cinema because I **had** already **seen** the film.'* *Zoe said: 'I felt tired because I **had been working** all day.'*	no change *Paul said that he hadn't gone to the cinema because he **had** already **seen** the film.* *Zoe said that she had felt tired because she **had been working** all day.*
am/is going to *Sam said, 'I**'m going to** work harder.'*	was/were going to *Sam said (that) he **was going to** work harder.*
will *Elena said, 'I **will** do the washing-up.'*	would *Elena said (that) she **would** do the washing-up.*
can/could *Andrea said, 'I **can** do it.'*	could *Andrea said (that) she **could** do it.*
may *Peter said, 'I **may** come to the cinema with you.'*	might *Peter said he **might** come to the cinema with us.*
must/have to *He said, 'I **must** train every day.'*	had to *He said (that) he **had to** train every day.*
should/could/ might/ought to/would *Robert said, 'I **should** eat more fruit.'*	no change *Robert said (that) he **should** eat more fruit.*

We use the present simple for the reporting verb and don't change tenses when:

- the information is still true.
  *Emily: 'I**'m** hungry.'*
  *Emily says (that) she**'s** hungry.*
- an action was in progress in the past when something else was happening.
  *John: 'I **was studying** when the phone rang.'*
  *John says (that) he **was studying** when the phone rang.*

Expressions of time and place

We also change some expressions of time and place.

Direct speech	Reported speech
now	*then*
today, tonight	*that day, that night*
tomorrow	*the next day/the following day*
yesterday	*the day before/the previous day*
tonight	*that night*
next week/month/year	*the following week/month/year*
last week/month/year	*the previous week/month/year*
a month/week ago	*the previous month/week*
here	*there*
this	*that*
these	*those*

Reported questions

We change tenses and expressions of time and place in reported questions in the same way as reported statements.

When we report direct questions, we change the word order and use *if/whether*.
'Can I have a drink?' she asked.
*She asked **if/whether she could have** a drink.*
'Has he gone out?' asked Peter.
*Peter asked **if/whether he had gone** out.*

When we report *wh-* questions, we use the same question word and change the word order.
'Where does Sally live?' asked Michael.
*Michael asked **where Sally lived**.*
'When did he leave?' asked Jack.
*Jack asked **when he left**.*

Reported commands/requests

When we are telling somebody to do something, we use *to* + infinitive.
'Go away!' she said to him.
*She told him **to go** away.*
'Don't come home late', his mum said.
*His mum told him **not to come** home late.*

say or *tell*?

The most common reporting verbs for statements are *say* and *tell*.
*She **said** she was leaving.*
*Charles **said** they were going on holiday the next day.*

We can use *tell* when we know who somebody is talking to.
*She **told** him/her (that) …*
*Ben **told** Kate (that) …*

Personal pronouns and possessive adjectives

We change personal pronouns (*I, you, mine*) and possessive adjectives (*my, his, your,* etc.) so that it's clear who or what they refer to.
*Kate said, '**My** best friend comes from Argentina.'*
*Kate said (that) **her** best friend came from Argentina.*
*They said, '**We** don't like **our** new school.'*
*They said (that) **they** didn't like **their** new school.*

-ing form

We use *-ing* forms:

* when the verb is the subject or the object of the sentence.
  ***Learning** to be a DJ is hard work.*
  *Her favourite sport is **sailing**.*
* after certain verbs, e.g. *avoid, begin, continue, hate, imagine, keep, like, love, prefer, practise, remember, start, stop, suggest.*
  *I enjoy **cooking** for friends.*
* after phrases that end with prepositions, e.g. *interested in, good at, bad at, bored with, fed up with, fond of, tired of.*
  *He's really good at **making** decisions.*
* after certain expressions, e.g. *looking forward to, mind, can't stand, it's no use, it's not worth*
  *I don't mind **living** in the city.*

to-infinitives

We use infinitives:

* after certain verbs, e.g. *advise, agree, allow, appear, ask, begin, choose, continue, decide, expect, force, forget, hate, help, hope, learn, like, manage, offer, order, plan, prefer, prepare, promise, refuse, seem, start, stop, want, would like, would love.*
  *He's forgotten **to bring** his books.*
  *The waiter ordered them **to leave**.*
* after certain adjectives, e.g. *happy, possible, sorry, pleased.*
  *She was happy **to help**.*
  *I'm glad **to be** here.*

-ing form and/or *to*-infinitive

We use *-ing* forms or infinitives with the same meaning after some verbs, e.g. *begin, continue, hate, like, love, prefer, start.*
*I love **going** to parties/I love **to go** to parties.*

We use *-ing* forms or infinitives after some verbs, but the meaning changes, e.g. *forget, remember, stop, try.*
*I stopped **training** last month. (I don't train any more)*
*I stopped **to talk** to a friend. (I stopped what I was doing to talk to a friend)*

Unit 10

Third conditional

If clause	main clause
had + past participle	*would/could/might* + *have* + past participle

We use the third conditionals to talk about possible events in the past which did not happen.
*If I **had known** about the piranhas, I **wouldn't have swum** in the river.*
*If they **hadn't drunk** lots of water, they **could have died** in the desert.*

Wishes

We use *wish* + past simple or past continuous to talk about something in the present that we would like to be different.
*I wish I **could** dance well.*
*I wish we **had** a dog.*
*I wish I **was lying** on a beach!*

We use *wish* + past perfect to talk about something in the past that we would like to be different.
*I wish I **hadn't failed** my exam.*

have/get something done

We use *have/get* + object + past participle when someone else does something for us.
*They're **having/getting** their hair **cut** this afternoon.*
*Where do you **have/get** your bike **mended**?*
*He **had** his eyes **tested** yesterday.*
*She's just **had** her photo **taken**.*
*We're going to **have** solar panels installed.*

get something done has the same meaning as *have something done*, but it is less formal.

To say who did the action, we use *by*.
*I always have my hair cut **by** Gianni.*

Unit 11

Obligation, *must*, *have to*, *don't have to*, *mustn't*

Present/future (must)	You **must** go.	**Must** you **go**?
Present (have to)	You **have to** go now.	**Do** you **have to** go now?
Past	He **had to** go home.	**Did** he **have to** go home?
Future	He **will have to** go home.	**Will** he **have to** go home?
Present perfect	He **has had to** go home.	**Has** he **had to** go home?

We use *must* and *have to* for present obligation.

must

We use *must*

- when the obligation is personal.
  *I **must** finish my homework before I go out.*

have to

We use *have to*

- to talk about rules or obligation from someone else.
  *My parents say I **have to** finish my homework before I go out.*
  *We **have to** take our shoes off in the gym.*
- to talk about obligation in the past or future.
  *She **will have to** go to the dentist if she's got toothache.* (future)
  *I didn't go out last night because I **had to** look after my brother.* (past simple)
  *Paula **has had to** walk home because she missed the bus.* (present perfect)
- with adverbs of frequency *always*, *often*, *sometimes*, etc.
  *I **never have to** clean my own room.*
  *She **sometimes has to** work in the evenings.*

don't have to

We use *don't/doesn't have to*

- when there is <u>no</u> obligation.
  *You **don't have to** go if you don't want to.*

mustn't

We use *must not* (*mustn't*)

- when it is necessary NOT to do something or it's prohibited.
  *You **mustn't** forget to bring your gym kit tomorrow.*
  *You **mustn't** talk during the exam.*

could/must/should + *have* + past participle

could have

We use *could/might/may* for the possibility of an action in the past.
*I **could have danced** all night.*
(= I didn't dance all night but it was possible.)
*He **might have gone** to the cinema.*
(= It's possible he has gone to the cinema.)

must have

We use *must* or *can't/couldn't* for the certainty of an action in the past.
*He **must have had** a good time because he looks really happy.*
(= I'm sure he had a good time because he looks happy.)
*They **couldn't have gone** to the concert because they didn't have tickets.*
(= I'm sure they didn't go to the concert because they didn't have tickets.)

should have

We use *should/ought to* to give an opinion about an action in the past.
*Isaac **should have spoken** to his teacher about his exam result.*
(= I think it was wrong Isaac didn't speak to his teacher.)
*You **shouldn't have taken** the CD from her room without asking.*
(= It was wrong to take the CD without asking.)

We use *would* for third conditional/unreal situations.
*David **would have taken** you to the party if you'd asked.*
(= You didn't ask so David didn't take you.)

Unit 12

Adjectives, comparatives and superlatives

type	comparative	superlative
adjectives with one syllable, ending in -e *wide, nice*	Add -r *wider, nicer*	Add -st *the widest, nicest*
adjectives with one syllable *cheap, clean, tall, fast*	Add -er *cheaper, cleaner, taller, faster*	Add -est *the cheapest, cleanest, tallest, fastest*
adjectives with one syllable ending in one vowel and one consonant *big, fat, thin*	Double the consonant, add -er *bigger, fatter, thinner*	Double the consonant, add -est *the biggest, fattest*
adjectives with two syllables ending in -y *easy, happy*	Delete -y add -ier *easier, happier*	Delete -y add -iest *the easiest, happiest*
Other adjectives with two or more syllables *attractive, dangerous*	*more* + adjective **more** *attractive*, **more** *dangerous*	*the most* + adjective *the* **most** *attractive*, **most** *dangerous*

irregular adjectives	comparative	superlative
good	*better*	*the best*
bad	*worse*	*the worst*
far	*further*	*the furthest*
little	*less*	*the least*
much	*more*	*the most*
many	*more*	*the most*

We use comparative adjectives + *than* to compare two things that are not equal.
*Jasmine is **taller than** Julia.*

We use the superlative form to compare three or more things.
*Jasmine is taller than Julia but Sofia is **the tallest**.*

We use *as* + adjective + *as* to compare two things that are equal.
*John is **as tall as** his father.*

Future continuous

Positive

I/He/She/It/ We/You/They	**will ('ll)**	**be**	study**ing** at 10.00p.m.

Negative

I/He/She/It/ We/You/They	**will not (won't)**	**be**	study**ing** at 10.00pm.

Questions

Will	I/he/she/it/we/ you/they	**be**	study**ing** at 10.00pm?

Short answers

Yes,	I/he/she/it/we/you/they	**will.**
No,		**won't.**

We use the future continuous to talk about
- an action which will be in progress at a certain time in the future.
  *I'**ll be having lunch** at half past one.*
- future arrangements which are already planned.
  *I'**ll be going** into town tomorrow. Do you want me to get you anything?*

Future perfect simple

Positive

I/He/She/It/ We/You/They	**will ('ll)**	**have**	**finished** by 10.00pm.

Negative

I/He/She/It/ We/You/They	**will not (won't)**	**have**	**finished** by 10.00pm.

Questions

Will	I/he/she/it/ we/you/they	**have**	**finished** by 10.00pm?

Short answers

Yes,	I/he/she/it/we/you/they	**will.**
No,		**won't.**

We use the future perfect simple to talk about an action or situation which will be finished by a certain time in the future.
*The match **will have finished** by 5p.m.*

Pearson Education Limited,
Edinburgh Gate, Harlow
Essex, CM20 2JE, England
and Associated Companies throughout the world

www.pearsonELT.com/examsplace

First published 2010
Second Edition 2012
Fifth impression 2019

Set in Univers Condensed and Congress Sans
Printed in Slovakia by Neografia

ISBN: 978 1 2921 7896 7

Authors' Acknowledgements

We would like to thank Tessie Papadopoulou-Dalton and her team at Pearson Longman for unfailing energy and enthusiasm and in particular Jill Florent for her thorough and professional support.

And a very special thank you to our families who joined us on this odyssey providing thoughtful and helpful comments along the way.

Acknowledgements

We are grateful to the following for permission to reproduce copyright material:

The BBC for extracts from "Newsround's Rachel reports from Cannes" by Rachel Gibson published on www.news.bbc.co.uk 15th May 2004, "Argument over schoolgirl's tattoo" published on www.news.bbc.co.uk 23rd July 2004, "Insects on menu at food festival" published on www.news.bbc.co.uk 13th October 2004, "Press Pack Reports: Your Reports - Kayaking" published on www.news.bbc.co.uk 20th January 2005, "Late nights and laziness" published on www.bbc.co.uk 21st September 2006 and "Extreme Sports: Zorbing" by Eleanor Fell published on www.bbc.co.uk 24th October 2006 copyright © www.bbc.co.uk 2004, 2005, 2006; Europa Park for information adapted from www.europapark.de; Anthony Horowitz for an extract adapted from www.anthonyhorowitz.com; and mizz magazine for extracts adapted from "blush-o-meter" and "MC Plat'num" both published in mizz magazine.

In some instances we have been unable to trace the owners of copyright material and we would appreciate any information that would enable us to do so.

The publisher would like to thank the following for their kind permission to reproduce their photographs:
(Key: b-bottom; c-centre; l-left; r-right; t-top)

A1 PIX: Geopress 114r; akg-images Ltd: 78 (Sword); Archives CDA/St Genes 78 (Jewellery); Museum Kalkriese 78 (Coins); Alamy Images: A T WIllett 108; Ace Stock Ltd 53b; Adams Picture Library t/a apl 43; Adrian Sherratt 8cl; Alex Segre 18cr; Arco Images 32bl; Big Cheese Photo LLC 66bc; Coolangie 146c; D Hurst 30 (Computer); Danita Delimont 80t; David Cordner 142bc; David R Frazier Photolibrary Inc. 8br; David Sanger Photography 132tl; Dennis Macdonald 22r; Dick Makin 30 (CD player), 89l; Emilio Ereza 34c; Eric Nathan 118bc; Frances Roberts 63tl; Frankie Angel 141tl; Huw Jones 142cl; imagebroker 122tr; Imagesandstories 78 (Dig); Imagestate 132cl; Ingram Publishing (Superstock Ltd) 23t; Joe Tree 30 (Radio); Kim Karpeles 132b; Mark Boulton 44r; Melba Photo Agency 56tr; moodboard 127l; Photofusion Picture Library 31; PhotosIndia.com LIC 56c; Photow.com 40cr; Rob Lacey/vividstock.net 144r; Stan Kujawa 132tr; Stockdisc Classic 112r; Stockfolio 126; StockShot 122c; Tetra Images 32tl; William S Kuta 147b; Ancient Art & Architecture: 78 (Tools); Art Directors and TRIP photo Library: 41r; Bubbles Photolibrary: 36, 53t, 101t; Corbis: Bettmann 122bl; Bloomimage 22 (cooking); Brand X 8bl; Comstock Select 79l; David Pollack 22tl; Fabio Cardoso/zefa 66t; Gabe Palmer 16bl; image100 30r, 96b, 118tc; Julia Grossi/Zefa 18br; Michael Kevin Daly 122tc; Michael S Yamashita 75bc; Mike Powell 122tl; moodboard 112c; Piotr Redlinski 40br; Randy faris 23br, 118b; RF 41l; Rick Doyle 8tr; Rick Gomez 82t; Rune Hellestad 44bl; Taili Song Roth 16r; Wolfgang Deuter/Zefa 147c; zefa / Ajax 96c; DK Images: 110br, 110tl, 141bl; Frank Greenaway 34l, 110c; Howard Shooter 141cr; Jerry Young 110bl; Paul Bricknell 141br; Tim Ridley 110tr; Dragon News & Picture Agency: 33; ECTACO Inc: 89r; Education Photos: 142cr; Europa Park Germany: 129bl, 129br, 129tl, 129tr; Mary Evans Picture Library: 75bl; FLPA Images of Nature: Michael Durham/Minden Pictures 136tr; Werner Forman Archive Ltd: Moravian Museum, Brno 78 (Jug); Osaka-jp Tenshukaku, Osaka 78 (Arrows); FotoLibra: 21b; Fotostock-Mallorca: Ditta U Krebs 40tl; Freeplay: 112l; Getty Images: 49l, 56tl; AFP 84l; AllSport Concepts 118t; Aurora 114l;

Hulton Archive 82b; Iconica 111; Image Bank 118c, 122br; Photographer's Choice / Ty Allison 24; Photographers Choice 58; Photonica 66tc, 146b; Publicity 84cr; Purestock 122bc; Stone 32tr, 142br, 147tl; Tax 66c; Taxi 40bl; Uppercut Images 44tl; Haldun Komsuoglu: Dr Haldun Komsuoglu 84r; iStockphoto: Ayaaz Rattansi 141tr; Liga Lauzuma 141cl; Matjaz Boncina 35cr; Kobal Collection Ltd: Corona/Allied Artists 80b; Walt Disney Pictures 75br; Weinstein Company 68l; Masterfile: Bob Mitchell 125; Tim Kiusalaas 18bl; © National Maritime Museum, London: 75t; PA Photos: AP 87; Empics Entertainment/Doug Peters 70; Matt Faber 84cl; Paul Sakuma/AP 63tr; Pearson Education: 62; Photolibrary.com: Aflo RF 8cr; PhotoDisc 78 (Skull), 146t; PunchStock: 23tr; Bananastock 22b; Blend Images 40c, 142bl; Brand X 35cl; Comstock 35b; Corbis 8tl; Creatas 30 (DVD player); Designpics 16br; Designpics.com 101b; Digital Archive Japan 35t; Digital Vision 136b, 144l; Goodshoot 66b; Image Source 22 (playing football), 145b; PhotoAlto 96tl; PhotoDisc 22 (washing up), 23bl; Pixland 15; Purestock 18t; Radius 46; Stockbyte 30 (TV), 96tr; Thinkstock 145t; Rex Features: 32br, 34r, 56bl, 71t, 132cr, 147tr; Linda Rich - Dance Photography: 142tr; SuperStock: Age fotostock 137t; David Forbert 79r; TopFoto: Walt Disney Pictures 104; Weinstein Company: 68b; West Coast Chocolate Festival, British Columbia, Canada: 40cl

All other images © Pearson Education

Picture Research by: Hilary Luckcock

Every effort has been made to trace the copyright holders and we apologise in advance for any unintentional omissions. We would be pleased to insert the appropriate acknowledgement in any subsequent edition of this publication.

Designed by Matthew Dickin.

Activate characters designed by Philip Pepper.

Illustrated by: Andrew Painter (Lemonade Illustration) pages 11, 12, 45, 77, 98, 113, 132, 135; Neil Jeffery (Lemonade Illustration) page 100.